DIALECT IN USE

SOCIOLINGUISTIC VARIATION IN CARDIFF ENGLISH

THE INTERNATIONAL PHONETIC ALPHABET

(Revised to 1979)

	Bilabial	Labiodental	Dental, Alveolar, or Post-alveolar	Retroflex	Palato-alveolar	Palatal	Velar	Labial-Palatal	Labial-Velar	Uvular	Pharyngeal	Glottal
Nasal	m	ɱ	n	ɳ		ɲ	ŋ			ɴ		
Plosive	p b		t d	ʈ ɖ		c ɟ	k g		k͡p g͡b	q ɢ		ʔ
(Median) Fricative	ɸ β	f v	θ ð s z	ʂ ʐ	ʃ ʒ	ç ʝ	x ɣ		ʍ w	χ ʁ	ħ ʕ	h ɦ
(Median) Approximant		ʋ	ɹ	ɻ		j	ɰ	ɥ	w			
Lateral Fricative			ɬ ɮ									
Lateral (Approximant)			l	ɭ		ʎ						
Trill			r							ʀ		
Tap or Flap			ɾ	ɽ						ʁ		
Ejective	p'		t'				k'					
Implosive	ɓ		ɗ				g					
(Median) Click	ʘ		ʇ									
Lateral Click			ʖ									

S (pulmonic air-stream mechanism)
T
N
N
O
S
N (non-pulmonic air-stream)
O
C

DIACRITICS

˳ Voiceless n̥ d̥
˯ Voiced s̬ t̬
ʰ Aspirated tʰ
‿ Breathy-voiced b̤ a̤
. Dental t̪
˯ Labialized t̫
ʲ Palatalized t̡
˜ Velarized or Pharyn-
gealized ɫ, ɫ̣
. Syllabic n̩ l̩
˜ or ̴ Simultaneous ʃf (but see also under the heading Affricates)

ʹ or ˙ Raised e̍, e̝, e̩, w
ʻ or ˛ Lowered e̞, ɛ̞, e̞, ʁ
+ Advanced u̟+, i̟, t̟
- or ˍ Retracted i̠-, ḭ-, t̠
¨ Centralized ë
˜ Nasalized ã
ʴ, ˞ r-coloured a˞
: Long aː
ˑ Half-long aˑ
˘ Non-syllabic ŭ
ˎ More rounded ɔˎ
ˏ Less rounded yˏ

OTHER SYMBOLS

ɕ, ʑ Alveolo-palatal fricatives
ʃ, ʒ Palatalized ʃ, ʒ
ɺ Alveolar fricative trill
ɺ Alveolar lateral flap
ɧ Simultaneous ʃ and x
ʃ Variety of ʃ resembling s,
etc.
ɪ = ɪ
ʊ = ʊ
ɜ = Variety of ə
ɚ = r-coloured ə

VOWELS

	Front	Back		Front	Back
Close	i ɨ ɯ			y ʉ u	
Half-close	e ɘ ɤ			ø ɵ o	
Half-open	ɛ ɜ ʌ			œ ɞ ɔ	
Open	a ɐ ɑ			ɶ ɒ	
	Unrounded			Rounded	

STRESS, TONE (PITCH)

ˈ stress, placed at begin-
ning of stressed syllable:
ˌ secondary stress: ˉ high
level pitch, high tone: ˏ
low level: ˊ high rising:
ˎ low rising: ˆ high falling:
ˋ low falling: ˆ rise-fall:
ˇ fall-rise.

AFFRICATES can be
written as digraphs, as
ligatures, or with slur
marks; thus ts, tʃ, dʒ:
ʦ tʃ ʤ: t͡s t͡ʃ d͡ʒ.
c, ɟ may occasionally be
used for tʃ, dʒ.

DIALECT IN USE

Sociolinguistic Variation in Cardiff English

NIKOLAS COUPLAND

UNIVERSITY OF WALES PRESS
CARDIFF
1988

Published by the University of Wales Press, 6 Gwennyth Street, Cardiff
CF2 4YD.

British Library Cataloguing in Publication Data
Coupland, Nikolas
Dialect in use: sociolinguistic variation
in Cardiff English.
1. English Language—Dialects—Wales
—Cardiff (South Glamorgan)
I. Title
427'.942987   PE1904.C3

ISBN 0-7083-0958-5

Printed in Great Britain at the Bath Press, Avon

For B.E.
and B.Ll.
(young Cardiffians)

Contents

Acknowledgements

The publishers and author would like to thank the following for their kind permission to reproduce extracts which have already appeared in other publications:

Academic Press for a table first produced in H. Giles and P. F. Powesland's *Speech style and social evaluation* (1975); *Language in Society* for extracts taken from an article by Nikolas Coupland entitled 'Style—shifting in a Cardiff work-setting', and a figure from an article entitled 'Language style as audience design'; John Benjamins Publishing Co., for a table first produced in an article in the volume *Focus on England and Wales* (1985) edited by Wolfgang Viereck; and Basil Blackwell for a figure published in W. Labov's *Sociolinguistic Patterns* (1972). Acknowledgement is also given to the International Phonetic Association for kind permission to reproduce the International Phonetic Alphabet.

Preface

This volume centres on empirical sociolinguistic work I have done in Cardiff since 1978. In the early stages of that work, my aim was the relatively straightforward one of setting on record central aspects of English as spoken in the Welsh capital – a distinctive dialect-system that was at that time little investigated and given virtually no exposure on radio and television even in Wales. While representing a large block of the population of south-east Wales, Cardiff English seemed to be over-shadowed, both in academic research and often in the public consciousness, by the supposedly homogeneous concept of 'Welsh English', usually taken to be a form of English heavily influenced by the Welsh language.

However, in the course of the empirical work, a second and more ambitious aim developed. In trying to give an account of variation in Cardiff English, I felt it necessary to adopt a narrower focus than is possible through the wide-angled lens of sociolinguistic survey-techniques. To begin to understand why patterns of sociolinguistic variation exist, it seemed necessary to view dialect-variation not only as a correlate of social differentiation in the community but as a semiotic resource, offering communicators another dimension of meaning-potential to be manip-ulated in routine usage. And it was clear that these issues could not be adequately addressed within the traditional confines of dialectology or even sociolinguistics, since issues of human motivations, attitudes and sensitivities were at stake, making the study of dialect in use a thoroughly interdisciplinary enterprise. The book's most ambitious aim therefore became that of articulating a coherent approach to the study of dialect, drawing on the established paradigms of sociolinguistics, dialectology and social psychology, and exemplifying the sorts of analyses that such an orientation permits.

A number of the individual studies reported in the volume have previously appeared in other forms, although all have been extended and/ or extensively revised for inclusion here. The travel agency data were collected for my doctoral dissertation (referred to here as Coupland 1981). Aspects of variation in these data discussed in sections 3.4, 5.1.1 and 5.1.2 were reported in two published papers: Coupland (1980) 'Style-shifting in a Cardiff work-setting' *Language in Society* 9:1–12; Coupland (1984a)

'Accommodation at Work: some phonological data and their implications' *International Journal of the Sociology of Language* 46:49–70. The Welsh place-names study referred to in section 2.3 was the subject of a working paper (1984b) and is discussed in more detail in Coupland 1985a 'Sociolinguistic aspects of place-names: ethnic affiliation and the pronunciation of place-names in the Welsh capital' in W. Viereck (ed.) *Focus on: England and Wales. Varieties of English Around the World, G5* Amsterdam: Benjamins. Analysis of phonological variation in the radioshow data (section 5.2) also appears as a paper (Coupland 1985b): 'Hark, Hark the Lark: Social motivations for phonological style-shifting' *Language and Communication* 5,3: 153–171.

I am very grateful to Inger Mees and Sue Bates for allowing me to reproduce findings and observations from their postgraduate dissertations, albeit in very summary forms which do not adequately reflect the scope of their research. Richard Hudson and Peter Trudgill read and commented on the doctoral dissertation from which the travel agency studies in this volume derive. Jitendra Thakerar and, in particular, Howard Giles have pointed out errors in my understanding of social psychological processes, the grossest of which were thrown out with earlier drafts of the sections on interpersonal speech accommodation. Allan Bell, in published work, added interpretative depth to one of the book's central studies. Members of the Cardiff Linguistics Circle repeatedly sat through and constructively criticised several papers reporting empirical findings. Particular thanks are due to Gwen Awbery, Inger Mees, Penny Rowlands and Alan Thomas, all of whom read the whole manuscript in draft form and offered positive, detailed and informed help and criticism. As it is conventional but necessary to point out, they bear no responsibility for any remaining inaccuracies, naiveties and excesses. David Hollyman gave his time as well as his first-hand local knowledge to help with street-interviews. Frank Hennessy generously allowed me to treat his broadcast performances as 'data' at the same time as sources of entertainment. Not least, Jill Baily had the resilience to type large sections of the original, exotic-looking manuscript not once but twice. My greatest debt of gratitude is to Justine Coupland whose significant contributions to the production of this volume have been both quantifiable – in helping with data-collection and analysis and manuscript preparation – and unquantifiable – in providing constant encouragement and support. Without assistance from all these scholars and friends, the book would undoubtedly have been a less worthy effort (though it might have appeared in print at an earlier date).

NIKOLAS COUPLAND
Cardiff
June 1985

Transcription conventions

All analyses of the author's data are based on audio tape-recordings of speech, many extracts of which appear in the text of the volume. The following conventions have been followed:

1. Where practicable, English orthography has been used.

2. No upper-case letters are used, except in proper names, abbreviations and the pronoun I; strings of upper-case letters represent spelled words.

3. Most names have been deleted and replaced either by initials or, in part, by strings of underlined spaces (e.g. J___).

4. Fragments of speech-data in the text are italicized. Written forms and translation forms are in inverted commas. Phonemic transcriptions and items are enclosed in obliques; phonetic transcriptions and items are in square brackets; phonological variables are in round brackets.

5. Substantial pauses in transcribed extracts are marked by the word (pause); shorter pauses are impressionistically marked by the spacing of the transcribed words.

6. Underlining denotes heavy stressing of a segment.

7. No punctuation is included other than apostrophes and question marks (where an utterance can be identified as and needs to be read as realizing a question).

8. Single brackets enclose explanatory comments on linguistic or non-linguistic behaviour, often on the basis of notes made at the time of recording.

9. Double brackets enclose inaudible sections. Where double brackets enclose transcribed text, the transcribed forms are not clearly and surely heard.

10. Double oblique lines are used to show overlapping of speaker turns. The next speaking turn begins where the double oblique // appears in the text. Entirely overlapped speech is shown by enclosing such form in *single* obliques at the beginning of the next 'full' speaking turn. Where a string of such wholly overlapped forms occurs, each point of overlap is given a subscript number which corresponds with a number marked on the appropriate (enclosed) stretch of text that follows.

11. Participants in the travel agency data:

C. A client, identified by a two-figure number at the beginning of the transcribed encounter. Occasionally, *C1, C2,* etc, have to be used to denote other clients who contribute to particular encounters. But encounters are essentially dyadic.

S. An assistant – Sue – who is involved as the principal assistant in all fifty-one encounters and in all of the conversational data.

P., Cl., Cal., K. Other travel agency staff who occasionally contribute to one of Sue's encounters.

The fifty-one client-assistant encounters that form the basis of certain studies reported in chapters 3 and 5 are available at the University of Birmingham as part of a computerised corpus of English language texts known as 'The Birmingham Collection of English Text', compiled under the direction of Professor John Sinclair.

1

Introduction: dialect and dialect-study

Many academic disciplines can claim to be centrally concerned with the study of dialect and this is at the same time a source of strength and of weakness. Dialect has variously been viewed as a reflection of sociocultural difference and change, as a linguistic index of the sociological differentiation of communities, as data for linguistic theorising and as a prime site for reading the patterns of social interaction. These diverse approaches have produced a vast fund of knowledge concerning the history, geography, linguistics, sociology and psychology of dialect behaviour, though particular disciplines have rarely looked beyond their own immediate boundaries. One theme of this volume is that a more interdisciplinary perspective is beneficial to the concerns of each individual discipline and particularly when the aim is not only to describe but also to explain dialect in use as a pervasive dimension of everyday talk. To justify such a perspective, this introductory chapter adopts a historical view and briefly summarises (in sections 1.2, 1.3 and 1.4) three broad orientations in dialect-research before outlining work specifically relating to Wales (1.5), and the aims and methods of the empirical studies in the later chapters (1.6). The first subsection is an attempt at terminological wood-clearing.

1.1   'Dialect' and 'dialects'

There is a reasonable level of agreement as to how the term 'dialect' should be specified linguistically. It is generally taken (as Chambers and Trudgill 1980:5 take it) to refer to a linguistic variety which is grammatically, lexically and phonologically different from other varieties. As such, the term 'dialect' subsumes the term 'accent', which refers to a 'variety of pronunciation' only (cf. Hughes and Trudgill 1979:2). For the purposes of defining 'accent', the term 'pronunciation' itself needs specifying – most appropriately in Wells' sense (1982, Vol.1:1) including rhythmic, intonational and other prosodic features as well as segmental phonology and phonetics. Petyt (1980:21ff) argues for a minor modification to these definitions, preferring to classify certain phonological features as 'dialect', but otherwise supports the definitions given for 'dialect' and 'accent'. The main advantage of this sort of linguistic characterisation is its neutrality – its clear implication that standard as well as non-standard, urban as well as rural, contemporary as well as outmoded linguistic varieties can be considered dialects. We are all dialect-speakers, however predisposed people may be to use the term 'dialect' exclusively of rustic, often stigmatised and apparently quaint forms of a language. Of course, dialect is a social as well as a linguistic phenomenon and we cannot define the term without specifying that dialects are language varieties (or 'lects') distributed across ('dia-') geographical or human 'space'. We most naturally think of dialects as geographically delimited, but much attention has been directed to social dialects and accents which relate to various strata of society within a given geographical area. Halliday, in fact, uses the term 'dialect' very broadly to refer to any variety of language 'according to the user' (cf. 1978:35) – a definition which allows dialect to include varieties differentiating males/females, age-groups and even individuals, as well as hierarchical socioeconomic classes. For Halliday, dialect constitutes one of the two general planes of linguistic variation, the second being *register* – variation 'according to the use'. Whereas a dialect is 'what you speak habitually' and expresses diversity of social structure, register is the stylistic or contextual dimension – 'what you are speaking at the time' – and expresses diversity of social processes (ibid.).

As soon as we begin to study dialect in use rather than from a narrow, self-contained, descriptive linguistic perspective, it becomes obvious that the various social and contextual dimensions of dialect are inextricably intertwined. Dialect features (like those to be described in chapter 2) often – indeed typically – function in more than one social dimension. In Cardiff, as we shall see, it is not uncommon to hear words like *time* and *five* pronounced with the vowel variant [ɔɪ], with a rounded and less open starting-point than in most English varieties. Even in isolation, this nonstandard dialectal feature may be socially significant. It may mark the speaker as a Cardiffian, although by no means unequivocally, since many English dialects will have the same feature. At the same time, though, it will be unlikely that the speaker is from the highest socioeconomic group, where nonstandard features like [ɔɪ] in this context are rare. This is the sort of observation illustrated in Trudgill's well-known schematic representation of dialect variation (cf. Hughes and Trudgill 1979:6), as follows:

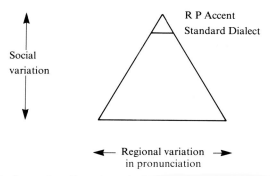

As this simple figure implies, there is little regional information available when the speaker is from the highest social group and does not regularly use non-standard forms. However, non-standard usage may also reflect other social categories such as age or sex and an unexplored range of attitudinal states from desire for social advancement to political allegiance, so that ultimately there is no clear association between linguistic usage and any one social or social psychological variable. This is not to deny that dialectal forms act as social makers in various ways (cf. Scherer and Giles 1979), but to emphasize that the reading of social markers is highly dependent on contextural factors.

Indeed, the register and dialect planes of variation are themselves inter-related, as Halliday acknowledges. This is true not only in the obvious sense that the speakers of some dialects predictably find themselves in particular speaking contexts, as standard speakers tend to fill higher administrative, commercial and professional jobs. But also, when speakers manipulate their dialects in different contexts by dialectal switching or shifting, the dialect forms themselves have contextual significance in the register plane. As Halliday puts it (loc. cit., 34), 'the dialect comes to be an aspect of the register'. Again, then, dialect is not unambiguously associated with any one plane of variation, but with several simultaneously. The empirical studies reported in chapters 2, 3, 4 and 5 try to tease out some of these patterns of association in the use of Cardiff English.

The greatest problems of definition arise when we try to distinguish one dialect from another or a dialect from a language (cf. Hudson 1980, Chambers and Trudgill 1980 and Petyt 1980, where these problems are fully discussed). Sociolinguistic studies (see section 1.3) have repeatedly shown that the use of language in society is shot through with patterned variation at all levels, to an extent that it is difficult to find empirically justified definitions of *a* language, *a* dialect, *an* accent, even *an* idiolect. Certainly, 'a dialect' will subsume far too much interpersonal and intrapersonal linguistic variation for it to be describable as a simple linguistic entity. Still, it is useful to be able to talk of 'the Cardiff dialect' or 'the south Wales accent' as if they were homogeneous linguistic entities for ease of reference. Indeed, we can argue that these terms do have some perceptual integrity if they sum up aspects of individuals' or groups' linguistic experiences and identities. They may even have some linguistic validity in one of three more abstract formulations. We could claim that Cardiffians constitute a speech-community because they draw on the same linguistic resources: they make different selections from the range of Cardiff dialect-features, some selecting very few on some occasions, others selecting almost all on most occasions, but from the same 'fund'. This is a reasonable but ultimately weak definition of a speech community because it fails to exclude large, even international 'communities' of, say, English-speakers. The definition is considerably strengthened by adding secondly that the members of the community share a set of norms and rules for using the resources available to them, all shifting their pronunciation in the same direction, for example, in the same circumstances (cf. Labov 1966:7 and Romaine 1982:13ff). A third definition is possible, one that builds on the beliefs and attitudes that community-members hold about their language. As Corder (1973:53) suggests, 'a speech community is made up of people who *regard themselves* as speaking the same language. In Cardiff this is the group of people who identify themselves as Cardiff-English speakers and who moreover share an appreciation of the social significance of using varieties of Cardiff English. As a result, the concept of speech community is less neat and implies that individuals may select themselves in or out of the speech community as they like. But it may also be a more realistic definition, throwing the emphasis back onto the symbolic function of dialect – dialect, standard or non-standard, as a marker of identity, a means of locating oneself in multi-dimensional space (cf. Hudson 1980:13). This is another sense, then, in which dialect is everyone's concern – in that we all establish our social personas and define ourselves partly in relation to and by means of social and geographical dialects. As communicators, we are all 'dialect-sensitive'.

These are the justifications for referring to what is an inherently varying dialectal system as 'Cardiff English' and 'the Cardiff dialect'. Still, some other, more basic, reservations need to be expressed. No urban community is linguistically homogeneous even in the modified sense suggested above. Like other cities, Cardiff is an intriguing, essentially fluctuating admixture of individuals, social and ethnic groups and nationalities. For this reason, the term 'Cardiff English' should be taken to be the range of linguistic varieties most centrally associated with the indigenous, relatively perman-ent inhabitants of the principal inner-city areas. In fact, this is the population from which informants are drawn for all of the empirical studies to be reported. No attempt is made to delimit the boundaries of Cardiff English in any precise way. This would be unwise, because dialects are widely acknowledged to form geographical continua with one focal dialect-area progressively shading into its neighbours. (cf. Chambers and Trudgill 1980:6). Nevertheless, informal observation suggests that the principal features of 'Cardiff English' extend to other urban centres around the capital along the south-east Wales coastal belt – Barry and Penarth to the south-west of Cardiff and Newport to the east.

The primary focus here is less on such geographical concerns than on the symbolic function of dialect – dialect as the carrier of semiotic value, as a measure of social identity and of social distance (cf. Halliday 1978:159). From this perspective, Cardiff English dialect features are to be seen as intrinsically trivial linguistic features whose use in social contexts significantly reflects and symbolises a whole range of national, regional and social identities, attitudes and allegiances (Giles 1977a) as well as more individual and ephemeral, genuine or assumed attitudes, affective states and personality-traits (Giles and Powesland 1975). Later chapters will show how this social 'loading' of dialect characteristics makes them available both for the relatively permanent marking of sociostructural positions and for the essentially dynamic negotiation of statuses and roles during spoken interaction.

1.2   *Traditional dialectology*

Dialect is everyone's concern. Yet, traditional studies of dialect did little to dispel the myth, still widely subscribed to in everyday usage, that there are two broad categories of speakers: ourselves and 'the dialect speakers'. The traditional dialectology or dialect geography, epitomized in Britain by the painstaking, meticulous work of Harold Orton and his co-workers on the Survey of English Dialects (SED),[1] was an exercise in linguistic ecology, dedicated to preserving endangered linguistic species. Its focus was largely historical; the broad aim was to 'demonstrate the continuity and historical development of the language [and] . . . serve as a historical baseline against which future studies [could] be measured' (Orton *et al.* 1978, quoted in Trudgill 1983:33). We might get the impression that what might be thought of as 'real' or 'pure' dialects (meaningless concepts in linguistic terms) are themselves a property of the past, or if not the past, perhaps the just living. If we set out to capture the 'oldest kind of traditional vernacular' (Orton *et al.,* loc.cit.), it follows that we must search out those dialect-speakers least 'tainted' by linguistic and social change: older speakers whose linguistic usage was fixed as long ago as possible, who have lived their lives in simple, relatively static communities away from the urban melting-pots. Typically, these speakers will be males – the sex more closely associated with linguistic non-standardness (cf. section 3.3, below).

We are tempted to believe that these are 'the dialect-speakers', the Non-mobile, Older, Rural Males (or NORMs, cf. Chambers and Trudgill 1980:33) who have principally informed the traditional dialect surveys. Dialect itself appears as an archive of quaint, outmoded linguistic fossils, the 'traditional vernacular, genuine and old' (Orton 1960:332). This is a valid enough dimension of dialect-study and arguably the dimension which holds the most immediate appeal. There is an undoubted rustic fascination about documented regional lexical forms like those for DONKEY: *cuddy*, *fussock*, *pronkus*, *dicky*, *nirrup*, *moke* and *neddy* (SED Book . *13. 16. and Wakelin 1977:70)* and for COUCH-GRASS : *stroil*, *strap-grass*, *spear-grass*, *squitch*, *twitch*, *whilks*, *crouch*, *scutch*, etc. (SED II. 2. 3. and Wakelin 1977:77). Indeed, for many, dialect-mapping is only part of the more general task of mapping cultural and sub-cultural differences and trends (cf. Weinreich 1954). Morphological relics like the so-called 'weak' – *(e)n* plural suffix in words like *een* (EYES, SED VI. 3. 1.), *flen* (FLEAS, IV. 8. 4.), *shoon* (SHOES, VI, 14. 22.) and *housen* (HOUSES, V. 1.1, and cf. Wakelin 1977:109) are manifestations in (almost) contemporary usage of earlier states of the English language. Perhaps they intrigue us in the way they bring together the humble, rural associations of the dialect-speaking NORM and the revered historicity of Old and Middle English.

It is precisely in the historical dimension that the tenacity and versatility of the traditional dialectologist is most evident – in tracing the etymological derivations of words and usage-patterns, in identifying archaic survivals and foreign influences, in hypothesizing about geographical, social, cultural and linguistic causes of change or stability, drawing on an encyclopædic fund of detailed dialectal information. As many contemporary researchers are pointing out (cf. Trudgill 1983 and Petyt 1982), despite the radical changes in the aims and methods of dialect-research that were to take place in the 1960s, traditional dialectology still has a role to play and should not be seen purely as the linguistic counterpart of butterfly-collecting. For example, the large amount of data collected for the SED can provide a valuable reference point for modern studies of linguistic change where the fields of investigation overlap. Traditional linguistic geography raised a number of questions which can now be re-examined in the light of modern techniques under the heading of 'geolinguistics' (cf. Trudgill 1983, Chapter 3), and in general, the diachronic approach to dialect is increasingly seen by some as a necessary complement to, if not the fundamental rationale for synchronic studies.

But a major shift in emphasis within dialectology was to be expected for many reasons. With better communications and increased geographical and social mobility, the communities and the individuals valued and investigated by traditional dialect geography became generally less numerous and even less representative of Britain as a whole. As rural communities developed, it became more difficult to sustain the fiction of dialectal 'purity' (always a dubious notion) and certainly more difficult to describe the 'pure' dialect forms. In the view of some researchers, rural dialect differences were themselves decreasing; rural dialects were converging and beginning to disappear:

> '. . . by the time dialects began to be systematically studied, . . . [the] trend towards linguistic divergence had been replaced in . . . rural communities by a trend towards convergence. The younger speakers no longer focused on the village, and so in their speech they were already moving away from the more highly differentiated forms of the village dialect.'
>
> (Halliday 1978:155)

Again, if dialect research was to be truly systematic, more attention had to be paid to the principle of representativeness. However rigorous researchers were in devising questionnaires to elicit lexical, syntactic, morphological and phonological/phonetic data, and however meticulous fieldworkers were in the transcription or recording of informants' responses, on whatever scale, traditional methods could be challenged on grounds of validity. Eager researchers plying enthusiastic NORMs with leading questions like 'What do you dig the ground with?' (SPADE and its variants) or gap-filling tests such as 'Coal is very useful but gold of course is even . . . ' (MORE USEFUL, etc., cf. Wakelin 1977:52) might easily lead to over-reporting: supplying dialect words or constructions remembered from a range of sources, perhaps claiming to make (or not make) distinctions which would interest the dialectologist. If the broad aim is dialect preservation, this criticism is less serious, but it still raises doubts about the status of the dialect features being documented. Whose dialects are these?

Informants selected to be *un*representative could tell us nothing about dialect varieties actually in use in contemporary society. Since the 1930s, linguistics had argued that the current manifestations of language in use need detailed (though perhaps not exclusive) consideration. By the 1960s, therefore, the time was ripe for a more synchronic approach to dialect investigation which would match up more closely to the principles of social scientific methodology; in particular, the principle of representativeness.

Quite clearly, the list of 'dialect-speakers' did not end with NORMs, and popular conceptions of contemporary British dialects in fact tend to focus on the large urban centres: Cockney (London), Scouse (Liverpool), Geordie (Newcastle), etc., despite the social heterogeneity and instability of such communities. Taking this view of dialect, since most of us live in the cities and towns, it was natural to assume that most of us must be dialect-speakers, identifying ourselves to others, locating ourselves geographically and socially through our speech. This categorisation seemed to leave only those who claim to use standard English consistently; what of them? Firstly, research has failed to identify a single individual in any community whose speech is uniformly standard in all dialectal respects. Then again, standard English (if we can identify and describe it) meets all the linguistic and social criteria for being considered a dialect. In this sense also, then, dialect is communal property, since every speaker – urban or rural, young or old, at any point in history – is a dialect-speaker. Modern approaches to dialect-study are based on this assumption.

1.3   *Urban sociolinguistics*

When attention was turned to majority urban populations, there was little direct carry-over from traditional dialectology. The intention of capturing the traditional dialect of a region was itself less relevant in the context of complex, heterogeneous cities. We may loosely talk of 'the Liverpool dialect', 'the Bradford dialect', 'the Cardiff dialect', but as we have seen, these expressions are extreme idealisations and not representative of the linguistic variation each of the areas subsumes. There are certainly dialectal features which generally characterize an urban area, but no individual will use all of them all of the time; some speakers, indeed, may never use some of the features. In general, geographical delimitation of the dialect area is less central to our understanding of urban dialect than the *internal different-iation* of linguistic usage within the area.

The cities demanded dialectological study for more than the obvious reason that most people live in and around urban areas. Whereas rural dialects were declining under the centralizing pressures of mass communications and geographical mobility, urban dialect was and is more than holding its own, so dialect research needed to account for the persistence and even growth of non-standard dialect forms in urban communities. As Halliday says (1978:184), we cannot draw on the traditional explanation that dialect differences are maintained through physical isolation and lack of communication. The very different speakers we find within an urban complex do indeed speak to one another, at least in these rather formal, public contexts that Gumperz has labelled 'transactional interactions'

(1975:35 and cf. section 1.6 below). Rather, dialectal features persist because they serve significant communicative purposes for their users, and dialect-research needed to develop a methodology which would begin to capture the social significance of dialect-use and variation in urban communities.

The focus on linguistic differentiation and its social implications under the heading of urban sociolinguistics, is primarily associated with the pioneering and extraordinarily influential work of William Labov in New York City and in Martha's Vineyard, Massachusetts in the early 1960s. What sociolinguistics is, could be and should be has been amply discussed (e.g. Hymes 1972b, Labov 1972a, Pride 1974, Bright 1975, and particularly Trudgill 1974b, 1978, 1983) although, as Dell Hymes says, 'no-one has a patent on its definition' (1972b:315). For some researchers, sociolinguistics in its most 'uncontroversial' sense is the study of language and society '. . . where the objectives are wholly linguistic' (Trudgill 1978:2), while others will define the term far more broadly to encompass all aspects of 'the study of language in relation to society' (Hudson 1980:1). For Labov's work, the term was at least appropriate[2] in that it emphasized the need to study the social contexts of language use and implied that sociological issues need to be addressed before we can make adequate statements about linguistic processes.

A central insight of Labov's early work (1966, 1972a) was that detailed description and quantification of the speech of individuals and social groups in urban communities could reveal *patterned* linguistic variation. Investigating this patterning was given priority over all other linguistic concerns by some writers:

> 'The key to a rational conception of language change – indeed of language itself – is the possibility of describing orderly differentiation in a language serving a community.'
>
> (Weinreich, Labov & Herzog: 1968:101)

One of the two central cases of this patterning is what Labov termed the *social stratification* of language. Aspects of language use were said to be socially stratified if they could be positively correlated with recognizable, measured social strata or hierarchial levels; the clearest instance of such strata are those relating to socioeconomic status or 'social class'. Of course, our own experience tells us that aspects of language co-vary with factors such as education, occupation, income, abode – the cluster of variables we label 'social class'. But Labov set out to chart the precise extent and nature of the correlation using the rigorous methods of social scientific survey research.

The seminal 1966 New York study developed a procedure for studying sociolinguistic variation in urban communities that has come to be regarded as a standard or classical method. Its basic form has been replicated, though with various extensions and modifications, in investigations of many other communities including British urban areas (e.g. Trudgill 1974a, 1978; Macaulay 1976, 1977; Milroy and Milroy, 1978; L Milroy 1980; Cheshire 1982) and has strongly influenced almost every dialect-study, including the present study of Cardiff English, since the early 1970s. The procedure involved random sampling of the population being investigated and systematic recording of speech samples from the selected individuals, often in an interview setting. In all survey research, a form of random sampling (cf. Babbie 1973, Federer 1973) is needed to preclude bias in the selection of data and so that findings may reasonably be taken to be representative of the broader community after the usual statistical checks have been made. The standard procedure uses interviews because a randomly selected set of informants cannot easily be observed in naturally occurring, everyday situations, and because interviews offer the possibility of controlling the activities being observed.

The Labovian approach requires careful attention to be paid to the detailed methods to be followed during the survey-interview. Labov (cf. 1972b) has developed a set of methodological principles which allow us to predict aspects of the linguistic behaviour of informants being interviewed. In particular, Labov's 'principle of style-shifting' postulates that all speakers have a repertoire of styles of speaking: there are no single-style speakers. The 'principle of attention' claims that the various speaking-styles can be ordered along a single dimension – of formality-informality – and will be selected depending on the amount of attention a speaker pays to his/her speech. The 'principle of formality' recognizes that whenever a speaker is systematically observed, for example in a tape-recorded interview, more than the minimum attention will be paid to speech; in such circumstances, we cannot expect to gather samples of 'vernacular' or 'base-line' speech.

As later chapters show, some of the assumptions underlying Labov's methodological principles are open to criticism, as it is possible to see the procedure of gathering speech-samples through interviews as unnecessarily limiting. Nevertheless, these methods allowed Labov to establish a second basic plane of variation in which sociolinguistic patterning was evident: the *stylistic* or contextual plane which revealed *stylistic stratification*. Layers or strata of speech-styles could be produced, albeit rather artificially, by carefully manipulating contexts within the framework of the interview. By varying the activities which informants were involved in, Labov (1972a: 79ff) was able to isolate a word-list-reading style, a general reading-style, a 'careful style' and a 'casual style', ranked from most to least formal. The 'careful style' was 'the type of speech that normally occurs when the subject is answering questions which are formally recognized as "part of the interview"' (ibid.); the 'casual style' was produced by opportunism or deception: recording those moments when there was a break in the interview or when an informant could be distracted by an emotionally loaded question.

The linguistic correlates of social and stylistic stratification needed to be measured as precisely as possible and in a way which would allow quantitative indices to be computed. For these purposes, the concept of the *linguistic variable* was developed. A linguistic variable is a set of variants which are tied to an underlying form – that is, they are linked by some defined 'sameness' – but whose distribution is uneven across different contexts of use. To take a very familiar case – the phenomenon popularly known as 'G-dropping' – we can treat (ng) as a linguistic variable with the two variants /ŋ/ (the standard pronunciation) and /n/. /ŋ/ and /n/ are equivalent in that they do not affect the referential meaning of the words in which they occur: *somethin'* (/'sʌmθɪn/) is of course referentially identical with *something* (/'sʌmθɪŋ/). G-dropping is a very common feature of non-standard British speech, and the choice of /n/ rather than /ŋ/ will correlate with certain interpersonal factors (lower rather than upper socioeconomic class) and certain intrapersonal factors (informal rather than formal use). In this case, the variable can be shown to be a *socio*linguistic variable since its use is predictive of some social contexts; it is socially diagnostic.

To quantify the (ng) variable, it is necessary to (i) identify the linguistic environments where both variants can occur (e.g. including unstressed final syllables: *running*, *swimming*, but excluding stressed monosyllables: *rang*, *sing*, where /n/ is not a possibility); (ii) identify the total number of environments where the (ng) variable occurs in the corpus of data to be quantified; (iii) count the total number of actual occurrences of each variant; (iv) express the score as the ratio of actual occurrences (usually of the less standard variant) to potential occurrences, often translated into a percentage-figure.

This basic procedure can in principle be used with a whole range of linguistic variables – more complex phonological variables, morphological, syntactic and probably discoursal variables (cf. Sankoff and Thibault 1977, Lavandera 1978, Dines 1980, Coupland 1983), with relatively minor mathematical and other methodological extensions. Still, by far the most significant sociolinguistic advances have been made through work with phonological variables. One explanation for this can be seen in the set of criteria that Labov provides for the selection of linguistic variables (Labov 1972a:7ff):

'It would be appropriate to ask at this point what are the most useful properties of a linguistic variable to serve as the focus for the study of a speech community. First, we want an item that is frequent, which occurs so often in the course of undirected natural conversation that its behaviour can be charted from unstructured contexts and brief interviews. Secondly, it should be structural: the more the item is integrated into a larger system of functioning units, the greater will be the intrinsic linguistic interest of our study. Third, the distribution of the feature should be highly stratified: that is, our preliminary explorations should suggest an asymetric distribution over a wide range of age-levels or other ordered strata of society.'

The second of these criteria reflects Labov's commitment to the linguistic importance of variationist research. The first and third relate to the required distribution of the variable and its variants and on purely practical grounds favour phonetic/phonemic features. Phonological segments are obviously more frequent than grammatical or lexical features and, as Labov says, are more 'useful' as a result. This consideration is particularly important, though also problematical as we shall see, when we are looking at moment-to-moment stylistic shifts in dialectal usage in the speech of individuals, rather than charting broad patterns of variation across large aggregates of individuals.

But there are theoretical considerations too. The fact that individual phones and phonemes are themselves (referentially) meaningless gives us a strong definition of the 'sameness' which ties variants together. Intrinsically meaningless elements of pronunciation are, we might say, 'free' to bear social and/or stylistic significance. On the other hand, if we want to consider lexical forms as variants (e.g. *yes* and *aye*, cf. Douglas-Cowie 1978), we have first to establish that the forms are indeed equivalent: if *yes* and *aye* cannot be shown to have the same potential contexts of use, they cannot strictly be considered variants of a single variable. This problem surfaces in an obvious way when we read traditional dialectological accounts of the distribution of words like *bogey, bogle, buglug, bugbear, boggard*, etc. (Wakelin 1977:69) which are glossed as meaning 'hobgoblin, object of dread, . . . scarecrow'. Traditional methods, starting from the forms themselves and going on to chart their distributions, cannot give us information about linguistic variation in Labov's strict sense because we are not in a position to treat the forms under examination as variants of a defined variable. Phonological features, then, together with certain low-level grammatical features (like present-tense verb suffixes in Reading, studied by Cheshire 1978, 1982), fit most neatly on theoretical as well as practical grounds into Labov's category of linguistic variables.[3]

More generally, it is possible to argue that phonological features *should* be given priority in contemporary dialect-research, independently of the arguments above. The decline of the traditional rural vernacular has taken a heavy toll of dialect vocabulary and our society's emphasis on literacy and a standard written code (cf. Stubbs 1980) has imposed strong pressures against non-standard grammar. It is the pronunciation-system, far less easy to codify and less consciously monitored by speakers themselves, that has primarily been left to bear dialectal significance. And phonological variables are particularly well-suited to carrying out this task. Not only are phonological variables frequent for speakers to use and for researchers to count, as Labov has pointed out, but their frequencies brings its own flexibility. *Relative* frequencies have been shown by Labovian sociolinguistic studies to carry some indexical significance in their own right. That is, frequential indices of phonological behaviours (such as 'G-dropping' or 'aitch-dropping') can be employed to differentiate social groups or social situations, over and above the qualitative variation across variant forms of a particular variable. In fact, phonological sociolinguistic findings are represented almost exclusively as frequency-data – the relative frequencies (expressed as percentages or on some other defined scale) of certain variants in certain contexts. Graphs like that shown in figure 1–1

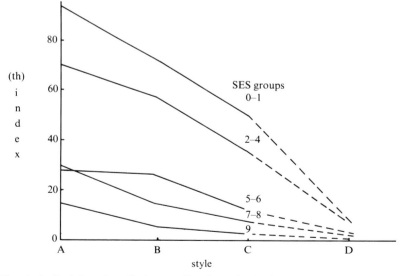

Fig. 1–1: Social and stylistic stratification of (th) in New York City. Styles: A-casual speech; B–careful speech; C–reading style; D–word-list style. SES groups: 0–1 'lower class'; 2–4 'working class'; 5–6, 7–8 'lower middle class'; 9 'upper middle class'. Redrawn from Labov 1972a: 113.

.........arize frequency-data across a range of interview contexts for a range of socioeconomic groups, and constitute the evidence to support the concepts of social stratification and stylistic stratification.

1.4   *Some recent emphases*

To talk of a 'standard' Labovian approach to urban dialect-study is not to claim that Labov presented his work as definitive. Contributions as major as Labov's are always liable to be called 'classical' because of the number of replicatory studies they spawn. Labov himself emphasized the principles that lay behind his work rather than the research methods themselves, and looked forward to the development of new sociolinguistic techniques:

> 'It . . . seems likely that the principles behind the methods outlined here will provide a foundation for future sociolinguistic studies'.
> (1972a:109)

Certain recent developments and new emphases have led some researchers to talk of 'post- or neo-Labovian socio-linguistics' (Romaine 1982:2, and cf. Hudson 1980:138ff). The volume edited by Romaine (1982) contains a number of studies of linguistic communities which are too internally diverse to be analysed by Labov's methods in New York. In particular, she argues that British 'Old World' communities cannot be expected to show the same patterns of social and stylistic stratification, and that defining social class-groups or status-groups is not necessarily the best way of revealing patterns of linguistic differentiation. Also, we need to pay more attention to what happens with individual rather than aggregates of speakers in more natural situations, and to the complexities of particular linguistic varibles.

These developments are taking place within the field of sociolinguistics, but researchers working under the label of social psychology have also become increasingly involved in the development of variationist studies. Labov had brought dialect-research into the realm of social science by matching the methodological standards of contemporary sociology, and social psychologists are now keen to explore the psychological processes involved in the selection and use of linguistic varieties. Perhaps inevitably (given the way in which academic disciplines defend their own boundaries and make exploratory raids into the territories of others), these new emphases were first expressed as criticisms of the standard Labovian research-paradigm.

Since the mid-1970s, Howard Giles and his co-workers have pointed to a number of significant weaknesses in Labovian methods and assumptions as seen from a social psychological viewpoint (cf. Giles 1977b, 1979; Giles and

St Clair 1979; Scherer and Giles 1979; Smith, Giles and Hewstone 1980). The central criticism is that Labovian sociolinguistics relies on taxonomy and description rather than being built around theories which can predict patterns of linguistic behaviour. In other words, the study of dialect has satisfactorily developed from an exercise in linguistic preservation to one in representative *description*, but has still to develop its powers of *explanation*. As Smith *et al.* (1980:285) say, 'it is certainly now time for an attempt to be made to move from the what, when and where to the *why* of sociolinguistic phenomena'. To understand why dialects persist in urban communities, why social groups are linguistically differentiated within a community, and above all why individuals choose particular dialectal features on particular occasions, we need to identify social psychological factors relating to human experiences and motivations and how these interact with aspects of the speaking situation.

Giles and others are particularly critical of the way that sociolinguistic survey research undervalues the individual's contribution to linguistic variation and treats subjects as automata, spewing out particular quantities of linguistic variants in relation to their socio-economic status and situational classifications. Giles and Smith, for example, argue persuasively that '. . . sociolinguistics . . . should reconsider its view of speech behaviour as if it were a blob of clay moulded by situational constraints' (1979:64). The same objection underlies the rather uncharitable view expressed by Halliday (1978:108), that 'sociolinguistics sometimes appears to be a search for answers which have no questions'. It might be fairer to say that Labov has begun to answer many of the central descriptive questions relating to linguistic variation, how some language communities are structured and how dialects change over time, and now we can move on to more interpretive questions.

'Why' questions cannot ultimately be satisfactorily answered through correlational studies, where social categories and linguistic phenomena are separately defined and their co-variation is examined. Labovian methods are essentially correlational, and the success of these methods led one reviewer to see 'covariance' as the necessary form of sociolinguistic study:

> 'The sociolinguist's task is . . . to show the systematic covariance of linguistic structure and social structure – and perhaps even to show a causal relationship in one direction or the other.' (Bright 1975:11)

Others, even within sociolinguistics, have taken the opposing view:

> 'The drift of sociolinguistic evidence . . . suggests . . . not only some limitation of interest in but also the ultimate impossibility of explanation by correlation.'
>
> (Pride 1974:1612)

Going beyond correlation means extending sociolinguistics towards what Dell Hymes has called 'socially constituted linguistics . . . the fundamental challenge' (1977:196). The aim, according to Hymes, must be first to identify the social functions individuals need to fulfil and then to '. . . discover the ways in which linguistic features are selected and grouped together to serve them' (ibid.).

Hymes' priorities are in many respects those of social psychologists working in the linguistic field, whose work revolves around explanatory and testable theories which predict linguistic behaviours and their outcomes in specified attitudinal and motivational contexts. The social psychological paradigm known as interpersonal speech accommodation theory (cf. Giles and Powesland 1975, and sections 4.4 and 5.1.2, below) is one of the best documented attempts to approach linguistic variation from the starting-point of human experiences and motivations. Essentially, the theory predicts that people who are keen to gain the social approval of the persons being addressed, and/or want to communicate more effectively will make their speech in many ways more similar to the addressees' speech as they perceive it; they will 'accommodate' to their addressees linguistically. On the other hand, people who want to distance themselves from their addressees and to emphasize their own distinctiveness will shift their speech in the opposite direction, away from the addressees'. These predictions allow us to look for 'converging' or 'diverging' speech-patterns, reflecting speakers' attitudes and intentions. Dialect offers great potential for marking speech convergence or divergence, as speakers modify or maintain aspects of their pronunciation, their grammar and so on, just as sociolinguistic methods offer the fine-grained analysis of stylistic variation needed to fully appreciate the communicative processes at work during speech-accommodation. Dialect research will be in a position to be even more fully integrated into the social sciences when the theoretical rigour of social psychology and the methodological sensitivity of sociolinguistics are allowed to interact with one another. This sort of interdisciplinary interaction is exemplified in the two case-studies reported in the final chapter.

1.5   *Dialect-research in Wales*

The Welsh language has been the focus of most language- and dialect-research in Wales. This is understandable, of course, given the political, administrative, educational and cultural issues involved in discussing the future of the language against a background of steadily declining numbers of Welsh speakers.[4] The extent of research into Welsh dialects since 1934 is seen in a detailed bibliography compiled by Gwenllian Awbery, published in *Cardiff Working Papers in Welsh Linguistics*, 2 (1982). The scope of these studies is most impressive, covering most areas of Wales, examining most linguistic levels and with recent studies adopting the methods and viewpoints of traditional and modern dialectology and sociolinguistics. An increasing amount of attention is now also being paid to English dialects in Wales, the so-called Anglo-Welsh dialects, although there is as yet nothing like the depth and coverage of the Welsh-language research.

As an important contribution to traditional dialectology, we can point to David Parry's work for the *Survey of Anglo-Welsh Dialects* (1972, 1977, 1979a, 1979b). The survey, begun in 1968, was closely modelled on Orton's *Survey of English Dialects* and set out to record the dialect characteristics of English-speaking Welshmen aged sixty years and above in selected rural areas. Within south-east Wales – the focus of Volume 1 of the survey – the selected localities closest to Cardiff and Newport were Peterston-Super-Ely (six miles from Cardiff) and Marshfield (five miles from Newport). In this way, and given the usual concentration on unrepresentative speakers, the Survey tells us little about dialect-usage in the major urban complexes. Great care needs to be taken, then, in interpreting Parry's remarks about the south-east Wales dialects 'as a whole' (cf. Parry 1972), because the dialect characteristics of the majority populations of the area are excluded from that entity. Nevertheless, Parry's work has firmly established the need for detailed analyses of varieties of Welsh English.

A fragment of Cardiff English, phonetically transcribed by Jack Windsor Lewis, appeared in 1964 (and cf. Windsor Lewis, unpublished), and a description of 'the sounds of the dialect of Canton, a suburb of Cardiff' by Lediard (1977) was included as an Appendix to Parry's Survey of south-east Wales. In 1977, Inger Mees conducted a thorough study of the pronunciation of a group of Cardiff school-children along Labovian sociolinguistic lines. The children were aged between 9 and 11 years when tape-recorded for this study, and Mees (1983) is able to offer an interesting developmental perspective by analysing the speech of the same informants some four years later. (Mees' work is briefly reviewed in section 3.3.1 and aspects of her detailed phonological characterization of Cardiff English are referred to in chapter 2). Connolly (1982) offers a detailed analysis of the segmental phonology of Port Talbot (West Glamorgan) English. In a 1971 paper, Parry presents an informal overview of the lexical, syntactic, intonational and (segmental) phonological features of Newport English. Beyond these studies, some recent overviews have considerably extended our knowledge of English in Wales. A series of papers by Alan Thomas (1980, 1983, 1984, 1985) have catalogued many features of Welsh English and helped to trace their origins. John Wells' comprehensive three volumes of *Accents of English* includes a section (1982 Volume 2, 5.1) on Wales (cf.

also Wells 1970). The work of Mees, Thomas and Wells provides a very useful background for the present study of Cardiff English. But it must be clear that urban Welsh English and Welsh English in general are underinvestigated. The lack of research is particularly noticeable when set against the numerous studies of the bilingual situation in Wales, sociological and social psychological investigations of Wales and Welsh identity (reviewed in Chapter 4) and the healthy state of Welsh-language research (referred to above). Yet, all of these fields of study would benefit from a better understanding of how the majority Welsh populations use their language. For example, while no one would disagree with the view that a national language such as Welsh can be the corner-stone of national identity, there is evidence that regional accents of English in Wales can also mark national identity and allegiance (cf. Bourhis and Giles 1976, Bourhis, Giles and Tajfel 1973). Discussions of Welshness and 'the Welsh experience' could profitably build on the studies of Welsh English. Again, it is ultimately impossible to give an adequate account of *either* Welsh *or* English in contemporary Wales in isolation from other language. Just as dialectal varieties of Welsh English can be shown to have varying degrees of relatedness to varieties of Welsh, so the description of contemporary Welsh needs to chart the effects of language contact, the spread of transfer phenomena like structural and lexical borrowing and code-switching (cf. Thomas 1982). At present, our knowledge of Welsh English varieties is not adequate to contribute fully to studies like those mentioned above. There is no clearer evidence of this inadequacy than the repeated attempts to treat Welsh English or perhaps south Wales English as a homogeneous variety. As argued in section 1.2, it is in any case more appropriate and profitable to look for patterned sociolinguistic *hetero*geneity in dialect than for *homo*geneity, but many published accounts recognize very little variation even among major regions of Wales.

1.6   *Aims and methods*

A cursory glance at Cardiff English and an ear to the opinions of Cardiff-speakers themselves are enough to raise serious doubts about the characterizations of Welsh-English or south Wales-English at the end of the previous section. It has become part of the folk mythology of Cardiff (cf. chapter 4) that 'Cardiff is a language on its own', with its own history and associations and its ambiguous relationship with Welshness. The studies in this volume are intended as a contribution to the detailed study of Welsh English and the considerable variation its subsumes. The general aims are to give an account of the distinctive characteristics of contemporary English-dialect-usage in the capital city of Wales and to outline ways in which Cardiff English varies in response to social factors and in the conveying of social meanings during interaction. The research is sociolinguistic in the sense that its analytical procedures are largely those of William Labov and others (as outlined in 1.2 above). But later chapters also draw on the work of Giles and other social psychologists in the fields of language attitudes, identity-marking and interpersonal communication in attempting to account for what the use of Cardiff English signifies for speakers on particular occasions.

A wide range of methods has been used to collect data for the studies reported in the following chapters. On the one hand, unsystematically gathered views and opinions (hardly constituting 'data') have sometimes been reported where they are a means of vividly expressing certain popular or media attitudes to Cardiff English. Dialect in Cardiff is such a living issue that it would be wrong to ignore the popular dimension, which can in any event be extremely revealing in its own right. This *ad hoc*ery is counterbalanced by the more systematic approach to language attitudes taken by social psychologists, as reviewed in chapter 4.

The basic dialectal description in chapter 2 is arrived at in the traditional and ultimately unsatisfactory way – by a single individual attempting to reproduce in printed form the linguistic characteristics of tape-recorded source-material. The deficiencies of this approach, particularly when most of the transcription is of phonetic material, should not be underestimated. But in this instance there is at least the reassurance that the linguistic description builds on the documented descriptive accounts of Cardiff English that are available.

The quantitative aspect of Mees' studies (section 3.3.1) uses the classical Labovian method for collecting data – the interview. But most of the quantitative studies in the following chapters are noteworthy for being based on more natural, arguably more 'real' speech. Of course, the question of what constitutes 'real' speech data is not an easy one. Robinson (1979:216ff) discusses the 'layers of reality' surrounding what we like to call 'the truth' in linguistic research, and considers the phenomenological view that social reality is only the product of individual perceptions. But the phenomenological view does not close the door on how linguistic methodology can bring us closer to the goal of naturalism, and this has been the specific focus of attention within sociolinguistics. Labov has convincingly argued (1972b) that idealisation of linguistic data is a problem that is only satisfactorily overcome through *observation*. Still there are different means of observing, some more naturalistic than others. We have already seen (in section 1.2) how Labov's standard interviewing procedure uses to good effect what might otherwise be seen as limitations of the interview setting – the fact that interviewees are likely to be relatively aware of their own speech and will shift aspects of their speech away from their base-line 'vernacular'. Using Labov's classical methods, we are still a long way from achieving the goal of observing unobserved linguistic behaviour – we are still trapped in what Labov has called 'the observer's paradox'(ibid.).

To come closer to 'real' speech, we need to go beyond the interview. As Wolfson argues (1976), interviewees, like all members of the speech community, have strong expectations of how an interview will proceed; that is, the interview is a familiar speech-event (in the sense defined in Hymes 1977) governed by speaking norms. The expectations are that one participant, the interviewer, will lead the discussion and ask a series of specific questions which the other answers, the object being to find out information required for a specific purpose. Wolfson goes on to say that a certain style of speech is required of an interviewee, and is therefore 'natural' in this setting. If the interviewer breaks the rules for this sort of encounter, perhaps by inviting a long, detailed, personal narrative about a time when the interviewee was in danger of death, the interviewee may be disoriented, and the data therefore by definition *un*natural. This will be particularly true of group sessions, which Labov values highly (1972b:115) as '. . . a more systematic approach to recording the vernacular of everyday life', when '. . . the investigators provide the initial setting, but gradually recede from the situation'. Wolfson's strongly stated and convincing conclusion (1976:209) is that '. . . unless it is interview speech we wish to study, we cannot expect to obtain valid results from experiments conducted in the form of an interview'.

In an attempt to meet objections like those of Wolfson, most of the quantitative studies in chapters 3 and 5, drawing their inspiration in part from Labov's department stores survey (1972a Chapter 2), are based on tape-recorded conversations which occurred naturally in a Cardiff city-centre travel agency. The setting was a valuable one for sociolinguistic research partly because of the range of communicative activity it allowed. The central category of travel agency talk is well described as a set of *transactional encounters* between assistants and clients. The term 'encounter' is intended in Goffman's sense as a particularly focused interactive event, 'a physical coming together . . . an ecological huddle wherein participants orient to one another and away from those who are present in the situation but not officially in the encounter' (1961:135). 'Transactional' is the term used by Gumperz (1975:35) to refer to 'one type of interaction which . . . centers largely around certain limited goals such as purchasing such items as groceries or clothing, cashing a cheque at the bank, getting the telephone operator to put a call through, going to the doctor. Participants in such interactions suspend their individuality and act by virtue of their status.' The face-to-face assistant-client interactions also fall under the heading of *service encounters*[5] – communication between a posted server and a served party who are typically unacquainted (cf. Merritt 1976:2,3).

These encounters are a rich source of data for many reasons, but principally because the business of researching, selecting and booking holidays needs to be achieved through talk. Travel agency encounters are not the formulaic exchanges of goods/services that one finds in many shops and ticket-offices; they need to be 'managed' co-operatively, to be opened and closed by the participants, to establish a theme and sustain it through conversation. Travel agency clients represent a fairly wide range of social categories which is of value for studying social differentiation in speech (see chapter 3). At a purely practical level, the physical environment allows tape-recordings of reasonable quality to be made, since particular encounters are usually conducted at fixed serving posts in the travel agency. But travel agency talk is not restricted to assistant-client encounters. A whole range of communicative activities was available for analysis – telephone conversations (to other travel agencies, tour-operators, clients), formal and informal conversations between assistants, even the day-to-day laughter, grumbles and asides that make up spontaneous, human exchanges in most work-settings. It is precisely this diversity of topics and approaches and the way participants switch between them from moment to moment that makes the setting ideal for studying stylistic variation (as in chapters 3 and 5 below).

There is still the observer's paradox. Observing and recording naturally situated talk seems to guarantee it will be 'unnatural'. And of course, the recordings could only be made with the co-operation of the travel agency staff, who were therefore necessarily aware – at least at first – of the presence of an observer and recording equipment. But the predictable observer-effects were minimized in three different ways: First, the period of time over which recordings were made was long enough for the travel agency staff to become fully accustomed to, even to ignore, the presence of an observer and a tape-recorder. Recordings made during the first four days were not used in the analyses. Second, the observer was physically remote from the encounters being recorded and the microphone was positioned unobtrusively (but not concealed). Third, the assistants were assured that the main aim of the study was to record and analyse the speech of clients. This had the effect of reducing self-consciousness from the outset. Again, the sheer amount of work done by assistants at most times demanded their full attention. In the end, there is no doubt that the travel agency staff were not conscious of being recorded; their recorded conversations included spontaneous laughter, jokes, even conspiratorial remarks and made reference to a whole range of informal topics – social events, friends, food and dieting.

In the recording of clients' speech, there seemed to be no alternative to the procedure of collecting data before individuals were informed of their involvement (a procedure which is not rare in sociolinguistic research, cf. Labov 1966, Schegloff 1968, Merritt 1976). Otherwise the acknowledged presence of an observer would inevitably have redefined the situation for the participants and distorted their linguistic behaviour. This is the most direct way of overcoming the observer's paradox and the only guarantee of natural data; but it raises the question of ethics. There is no doubt that individuals have the right to decide whether they are treated as 'subjects' – whether their own speech is used in linguistic research. In this case, the question centres on whether it is acceptable to ask their permission *after* rather than before making tape-recordings, which allows the large step to be taken in the direction of real data. There is probably no general answer, only particular considerations in particular cases. A major factor is the integrity of the researcher in discarding any recorded materials he/she is not given permission to use. Even more crucially, there is the initial selection of the setting for making recordings. There are many settings where the nature of the interaction is predictably private and where the imposition of even asking permission to make recordings is ethically questionable – for example, doctors' surgeries or courtrooms, although even these have been the settings of linguistic research (cf. Candlin, Leather and Bruton 1976, Coulthard and Ashby (mimeo), Sudnow 1965, Cicourel 1968). The booking of holidays is not intrinsically of such potential consequence, and this is borne out by clients' reactions. In the event, no individual refused to co-operate, and almost all subjects were interested in the research and keen to be included and to provide the background information asked for in short interviews as they left the travel agency.

A non-interactional speech-situation involving Cardiff English was required for the second case-study of stylistic variation (to be reported in section 5.2). While the travel agency encounters proved valuable for investigating the interpersonal dimension of style predicted by speech-accommodation theory, the analysis of style-shifting during what is essentially a monologue would allow individually-based processes such as the marking of aspects of identity and self-presentation to be studied. For this purpose, section 5.2 presents data from a broadcast radio request-show. The problematical notion of naturalness again surfaces here, and it is impossible to claim that the speech produced in the radio-study is fully spontaneous or natural. It is clearly quite heavily monitored speech and does not allow confident generalizations to be made from the radio-show findings to other speaking situations. The significant point is that the data, once again, are at least uninfluenced by the fact of being observed for research-purposes, so that we can identify processes of sociolinguistic variation which are 'natural' in their own terms.

As a consequence of these methodological choices, most of the studies presented in the volume have the benefit of being based on naturally occurring data, and this methodological advance must increase the validity of the findings. There are corresponding *dis*advantages, particularly in the fact that uncontrolled data preclude strict sampling procedures and other manipulations of independent variables necessary to arrive at fully generalizable conclusions. It is also inevitably the case that the studies conducted are tied neither to a single corpus of data nor to a single, narrowly defined population of subjects. This eclectic approach, focusing on the dialect-usage of a wide variety of individuals from a broadly defined Cardiff speech-community (cf. section 1.1), at least allows a valuable breadth of coverage – it takes in various individuals, social and professional groups, across various domains of language use. In general, the volume is built on the belief that, for the study of dialect in use, a commitment to less controlled, more naturalistic data is necessary if we are to progress our understanding of the role of dialect in day-to-day talk and be convinced of the applicability of previous research findings to everyday life. As Labov's 'principle of convergence' states, '. . . the value of new data for confirming old data is directly proportional to the differences in the methods used to gather it' (1972b:118).

2

Cardiff English

Contemporary sociolinguistic studies do not always manage to characterize the range of linguistic features constituting the dialectal resources available to the community being investigated. This is for two reasons. In practice, these studies are forced to select a relatively small number of dialectal features for detailed quantitative analysis as linguistic variables (see 1.2 above). In such studies, sociolinguists do not generally intend to give an account of urban dialect characteristics as much as to identify the social significance of certain linguistic *markers* (in the broadly defind sense of Laver and Trudgill 1979). Secondly, there is a theoretical objection. If we see a speech community as a rather abstract entity subsuming a great deal of internal differentiation, then it is impossible to provide a simple description of, in this case, 'the Cardiff dialect'. The speech of any group of individuals will be heterogeneous, and so will that of even a single individual, in that it will contain a mixture of relatively standard and non-standard variants of different variable features. Moreover, particular speaking-situations – such as the travel agency where tape-recordings for some of the Cardiff studies were made – will select a limited range of speakers and speaking-styles (see chapter 3). These considerations make it extremely unlikely that any one individual will produce a consistent, maximally broad variety of Cardiff English.

Still, there are justifications for trying to describe just such a variety, despite the artificiality involved. Firstly, we need a preliminary description of the non-standard features to be found in Cardiff English before we try to set up linguistic variables for detailed study. Also, provided we are careful not to claim that our hypothetical maximally broad variety *is* Cardiff English, assembling dialect features to be found in the community gives a clear overview which will allow the resources of Cardiff English to be compared with those of other dialects. This is the approach adopted by John Wells (1982) in his description of Welsh and other accents, and the approach I adopt below.

2.1   *Phonetic and phonemic features*

In 1977, Inger Mees listed the contrastive **vowels** of Cardiff English with their standard (RP) equivalents as follows:

Cardiff	RP	Cardiff	RP	Cardiff	RP
/ɪ/	/ɪ/	/iː/	/iː/	/əi/	/aɪ/
/ɛ/	/e/	/eː/	/eɪ/	/əu/	/aʊ/
/a/	/æ/	/ɛː/	/ɛə/	/ʌi/	/ɔɪ/
/ɑ/	/ɒ/	/aː/	/ɑː/		/ɪə/
/ɤ/	/ʊ/	/ʌː/	/ɔː/		/ʊə/
/ə/	/ʌ/ /ə/	/oː/	/əʊ/		
		/uː/	/uː/		
		/øː/	/ɜː/		

This analysis shows that, in traditional terms of phonological systems (cf. Wells 1982, Volume 1), Cardiff English differs from RP in its use of a single phoneme /ə/ where RP has /ʌ/ and /ə/, and in sometimes treating RP centring diphthongs /ɪə/ and /ʊə/ *(near, beer; pure, fewer)* as phoneme sequences (/iː/ + /ə/ ; /uː/ + /ə/). Although the symbols are, strictly speaking, arbitrary, Mees' phonemicization suggests some significant differences in the phonetic realisation of these groups of sounds. Certain short front vowels tend to be more open in Cardiff English than in RP, such as [ɛ] for RP /e/ in *help, ten, next* and [ɪ] representing RP /ɪ/ in words like *bit, little, hid*. The degree of openness with /ɪ/ can be enough to lead to non-Cardiffians mis-hearing Cardiff *bit* as *bet*, *pit* as *pet*, and so on. The table above phonemicizes the Cardiff equivalent of RP /æ/ (in *as, hand, back*) as /a/, and [a] or [a̠] realizations are certainly frequent. But broad Cardiff /a/ (i.e. the form usually used by speakers who use clearly non-standard variants of other variables) is [æ] or even [ɛ] which is *closer* than the usual RP realisation. [æ] for short /a/ in fact seems to have the same stereotypical function as long /aː/ (cf. below). Short back vowels in Cardiff are typically unrounded (as indeed are all short vowels), which explains the choice of symbols /ɑ/ and /ɤ/ for RP /ɒ/ as in *pot, bottle, long* and /ʊ/-*put, soot, pudding*. /ə/ is found in stressed syllables in Cardiff in addition to the unstressed syllables to which it is restricted in RP – so we find Cardiff /ˈməni/, /ˈləki/ *(money, lucky)*.

  Cardiff long vowels can be extremely distinctive. Where RP has /ɔː/, as in *morning, caught, thorn*, Cardiff typically has an unrounded centralized form [ʌ̈ː], justifying the choice of /ʌː/ in the phonemic table. The RP vowel /ɜː/ in *nurse, heard, bird* is often more fronted and more close in Cardiff. Mees phonemicizes /øː/, although there need not be full lip-rounding, and [ë:] is the appropriate phonetic transcription in many instances. The close vowels /i:/ and /u:/ as in *eat, Ely, even* and *fool, two, move* are generally noteworthy for their lack of diphthongization and centralization when realized phonetically. That is, the RP tendency to produce [ɪi] and [ʊu] sequences for these phonemes (cf. Wells 1982, Vol. 1) is not common in Cardiff. Cardiff pronunciations of words involving RP /u:/ are also interesting for the different way they often assign phonological units in words spelt with 'u' or 'w': although fool is [fu:l] (not unlike RP), *nude* and *you* are generally [nɪŭd] and [jɪŭ], as in other Welsh accents of English. This feature arguably results from Welsh substratal influence (cf. Thomas 1984), /ɪu/ (spelt 'iw') being a phoneme of Welsh. On the other hand, whereas many Welsh accents of English also have the diminuendo [ɪŭ] diphthong in words of the *sure, cure, during, insurance* set (which have /(j)ʊə/ in traditional RP shifting to /(j)ɔ:/ in contemporary RP – cf. Wells 1982, Vol. 1 :162), non-standard Cardiff English has either /ʌ:/ or the sequence /u:ə/. Mees (1983:78ff) quantified /ʌ:/ and /u:ə/ incidence across particular lexical items and found some evidence of patterning. *Sure* almost always took /ʌ:/, with the remaining words studied falling into two classes – those in which the vowel is preceded by a consonant + /j/ (*cure, pure, during*) and those where it is not (*insure, tourist, tour*). In words in the *cure* category, /ʌ:/ increases in frequency from low social status to high social status; in the case of *insure* words, the upper middle-class speakers use fewer /ʌ:/ forms than the other classes. In any case, although the vowel selected in Cardiff may be non-standard in relation to RP, it is interesting to note that it is closer to RP than the more typical Welsh English diphthong. The RP centring diphthong /ɪə/, in parallel with /ʊə/, can have a characteristically Cardiff non-standard realization other than the /i/ + /ə/ phoneme sequence implied by the phoneme-table. As Mees points out (1983:67-8), a small set of lexical items including *near, merely* and *here* may have /jø:/ realizations as a further possibility – /njø:/,/'mjø:li:/ and /jø:/, the last of which can realize *year* and *ear* as well as 'aitch-dropped' *here*.

The quality of the long /a:/ vowel in Cardiff (as in the word *Cardiff* itself, and in *half, part, calm*) is distinctive both acoustically and socially as the main stereotypical feature of Cardiff English. As Mees comments, the RP realization of /a:/ is an advanced cardinal five [ɑ:], ' . . . but this is hardly ever heard in Cardiff. It is usually fronter, most commonly a cardinal four [a:], but closer realizations also frequently occur' (1977:15). It seems that no other British accent has realizations of this phoneme closer than [æ:], although Wells notes (1982 Vol.1:134) that they are found in North American English. When Cardiffians and others comment on this feature and when they mimic Cardiff speech, they will even realize it as around cardinal two [e:], although I have not heard this quality in any normal (non-stereotyping) speaking-context. [ɛ̃:] realizations are heard in the broadest varieties of Cardiff English – generally, the speech of working class males in informal contexts – with [ã:] and [æ̃:] being probably the most frequent variants. The nasalization shown in transcription is also significant and, if perceptually linked to Merseyside velarised speech (cf. Wells 1982 Vol 2:373, Knowles 1978), may be a factor in some Cardiff speakers' views that Cardiff English resembles North West English dialects (see below). It would be difficult to overestimate the speech community's awareness of Cardiff long and short /a/s as stereotypical features (– more accurately as a single feature, since the 'short' vowel is often lengthened in Cardiff speech and is apparently subject to a similar pattern of sociolinguistic variation). The salience of the (a:) variable in Cardiff is heightened by its occurence in a number of lexical forms which relate to focal elements of Cardiff local culture. Most obviously the word *Cardiff* itself; also the national rugby stadium in the heart of the city – *Cardiff Arm's Park* – and the revered local brew – *Brain's Dark* (/ə ˈpəɪnt əˈda:k/). The contemporary Cardiff folk-hero, singer and broadcaster Frank Hennessey,[1] has as one of his catchwords *remarkable* ([riˈmæ̃:kəb]]), and, as his radio programme jingle, a sung fanfare dominated by the vowel-quality [æ:] in *Hark hark the lark in Cardiff Arm's Park!* At one level, these lexical forms are a vehicle for the phonological variable; but their availability in turn reinforces and compounds the social significance of the variable itself. In this instance, regional pronunciation and local experience have a mutually encouraging, we might say symbiotic, relationship.

RP /eɪ/ *made, maid, name* and /əʊ/ *know, coal, note* are phonemicized as /e:/ and /o:/ for Cardiff English by Mees, and she describes their realizations as 'very narrow diphthongs', with /o:/ sometimes realized as a steady state vowel with the quality of an advanced, slightly lowered CV 7. I would prefer to retain a diphthongal phoneme to represent the /eɪ/ and /əʊ/ groups of sounds, however, to avoid giving the impression that the maximally non-standard forms in Cardiff English are always monophthongs. In fact, the social significance of the /əʊ/ phoneme (as analysed by Mees herself) attaches to the starting-point of the glide rather than to the choice of monophthong/diphthong. Standard speakers have a mid central starting point [ə] for their /əʊ/, whereas non-standard Cardiff speakers have [ö]. Some non-standard Cardiff speakers do, in fact, produce substantial glides in their realizations of RP /əʊ/ and /eɪ/, although this marks them off from many speakers from other areas, and from some older Cardiff speakers, who tend to have monophthongal forms in these positions. Other Cardiff diphthongs too are distinguished from RP by their starting-points. RP /aʊ/ *now, coward, Trowbridge*, is best phonemicised as /əʊ/ in Cardiff English, indicating the centralization of the first element of the glide – in the area covered by schwa. RP /aɪ/ (*I, light, nine*) is also appropriately represented by /əi/ in Cardiff English because of the frequent central starting-point, although an even more retracted and slightly rounded starting-point [ɔɪ] is heard in very non-standard speech. The phoneme-table gives /ʌi/ as the Cardiff equivalent of RP /ɔɪ/ (*noise, voice, toy*), rightly suggesting that there is rather less clear lip-rounding at the start of this diphthong in Cardiff English than in RP.

Wells suggests that there are three broad sets of words involved in the /a/ versus /aː/ contrast; he labels these the *TRAP* (including *man, mass, shall, tax,* etc.), *BATH* (*class, grass, dance, fast*) and *PALM-START* (*calm, father; large, bar*) categories. *TRAP* words select the short vowel, *PALM-START* words select the long vowel and *BATH* words show variation, with *class, grass* usually long and the pronunciation of *chance, fast* being subject to socially significant variation (1982, Vol.2:387). Hughes and Trudgill (1979:28) suggest different lexical sets for /a/ and /aː/, and the complexity of the situation can be seen in table 2–1 below partly on Hughes and Trudgill's classification.

Table 2–1: The general incidence of short (S) and long (L) /a/ vowels in selected areas of Britain.

Lexical set	RP	North England	Cardiff	South-West Wales
(i) *pat, bad, cap*	S	S	?S	?S
(ii) *path, laugh, grass*	L	S	L	?L
(iii) *dance, grant, demand*	L	S	?S	S
(iv) *part, bar, cart*	L	L	L	L
(v) *half, palm, can't*	L	L	L	L

The question-marks reflect the 'confused and variable' situation described by Wells (above); that is, there is scope for more research into conditioned variation in L/S vowels in different lexical sets across different British communities. But it is also true that Hughes and Trudgill's categories (i) to (v) do not form natural sets in South Wales English. For example, maximally non-standard *dance* in Cardiff usually has a relatively short variant while *grant* typically has a form of /aː/; similarly, West Wales *bad* can often be long while *cap* is inevitably short. The Cardiff situation is complicated firstly by the generally quite long phonetic realizations of even the so-called 'short' vowels, which means that the /a/ - /aː/ contrast is not a clear one for some speakers. (In 1977, Lediard recorded a long /aː/ even in *bag.*) Then again, the extremely strong stigmatization of [æ]-type realizations, particularly when lengthened, leads Cardiff speakers to vary both the quality and length of this cluster of sounds when they style-shift. Mees (1983:74ff) concluded that there was evidence of sociolinguistic variation in her data between short /a/ and long /a:/, since the short vowel was more frequent among lower status groups. For example, her lowest social group consistently used long /a:/ only in *laugh* (of 20 words in a word list) while her highest group consistently used /a:/ in *laugh, pass, forecast, passed, task, after* and *rather*.

There are fewer **consonantal** than vocalic distinctive characteristics of Cardiff English. Mees suggests (1977:30) that the fricative /x/ and the alveolar lateral fricative /ɬ/ could be considered to have places in the Cardiff consonantal system. However these forms are best treated as very rare borrowings from Welsh, particularly since Cardiff speakers go to great lengths to avoid them in their pronunciation (see section 2.3). The phenomena popularly known as 'aitch-dropping' and 'G-dropping' are both very common in Cardiff English. Mees considers /h/ a marginal Cardiff phoneme, which is hardly surprising when we examine the restricted function of the phoneme in British dialectual usage in general. Stubbs (1980:39) concludes an analysis of /h/ by saying that 'not only is its functional load low, but in addition its distribution in phoneme sequences is unusual, it is not integrated into the phoneme system, and it is phonetically unusual'. In fact Stubbs claims that the /h/ phoneme has only a marginal status in English as a whole. Even so, very few speakers in my data consistently avoid /h/ in those contexts where it can be 'dropped'. Instead, they use the feature as the more standard variant of a sociolinguistic variable, with social and stylistic significance. This variability is seen in most word-initial environments, particularly of course with the modal auxiliaries *have, has, had* and the personal pronouns. Medial environments *(ahead, behind)* have different possibilities and some initial environments *(hotel, historic)* need to be treated as special cases (see section 3.2 below). The alveolar nasal /n/ often replaces velar /ŋ/ in Cardiff English in unstressed positions, mainly in realizations of the morpheme *-ing*. Mees found that the morpheme *-thing* in compounds *(anything, something, nothing)* was often /θɪŋk/ in her data. But this may well be because her informants were children aged 9–11. Non-standard Cardiff adults regularly produce the alveolar nasal in unstressed compound *-thing* morphemes, as with *-ing*.

A characteristic realizational feature in Cardiff is the voicing of normally voiceless alveolar stops [t] between vowels *(got a, lot of)*. Although this is not uncommon in other varieties of English, Cardiff speakers produce a voiced tap or flap [ɾ] as a further slightly different non-standard variant. As Mees notes, the same tap is frequently produced as a variant form of phoneme /r/ intervocalically and after consonants /b,v and θ/ *(very; broke, every, three)* and occasionally in initial position *(run, Rhiwbina)*. This is the case even when the /r/ in question is an intrusive form, such as *I saw (/r/) an aura*. The tap does not seem to be related to the typically Welsh trilled variant [r], and is acoustically very different from it despite the similarity in the articulatory mechanisms involved. As in RP, but unlike many other Welsh accents of English, Cardiff English shows allophonic variation between 'clear' [l] and 'dark' [ɫ] forms of the phoneme /l/ in complementary distribution. In fact, word-final /l/ in Cardiff can be particularly heavily velarised and even syllabified, so that children in the city parks can be heard to shout [göʊɫ] and [fəʊɫ] *(goal* and *foul)*.

Processes of elision and assimilation are normal in all varieties of English (see Gimson 1972), but as Mees notes (1983:90) there is a markedly higher frequency of occurrence of them in all styles of Cardiff speech, enough to consider them a dialectal feature. Her detailed analysis includes assimilations of place (e.g. /t/ → /p/ in *that person*), voice (/z/→/s/ in *was standing*), and more significantly of manner (e.g. /ð/ → /l/ in *all that*), and elisions (e.g. of final /t/ in *but we*). Simplification of final consonant clusters is very common, particularly involving the voiceless alveolar stop /t/. The linguistic environments where alveolars are commonly lost are: continuant consonant + /t/, followed by a word with an initial consonant other than /y/ or /h/ *(next day, left turn)*, including the negative form -*n't (didn't, come, won't work)*; word-final /t/ + /s/ clusters formed by the reduction of *is* or *has (that's* /ðas/, *it's* /ɪs/). Some extreme examples of the elision of phonological segments are found – as in /sraɪt/ *that's right*, /'ɔɪdn̩'ʊ / *I don't know*. Again, we could use the term elision to characterize the pronunciation of the common dialect form of the tag *isn't it?* /'ɪnɪt/ (phonetically often ['ɪn̩ʔ]). But there is no real justification for treating /'ɪnɪt/ as derived from the 'full' form /'ɪzn̩t'ɪt/, particularly since Cardiff speakers do not seem to move toward the 'full' form during style-shifting (cf. section 2.2 below). Another possibility of elision exists with final alveolar stops in utterance-final position (e.g./ða/ in *I don't eat that)*. Mees observes (1983:120) that in her data /t/ elision also occurs in non-utterance-final environments, regularly before consonants and at times before vowels. But she also finds /t/ elision to be restricted to a small set of high-frequency (and, as we would expect, predominantly monosyllabic) words, including *it, bit, get, let, at, that, but, lot, got, out*, etc. Yet another possibility with utterance-final alveolar stops is to prolong the hold-phase and then release with slight affrication.

Affrication is worth mentioning in its own right as a Cardiff consonantal characteristic. As in Liverpool (cf. Knowles 1978, Wells 1982) stop consonants at the beginning of a syllable can have a perceptibly 'noisy' affricated release, as in the word *Cardiff*, which can therefore sometimes be phonetically transcribed as [kxæ̃:dɪf]. Probably, it is the affrication here that a local journalist noted (Cardiff Post, 1983, February 24th) and ingeniously transcribed using normal English alphabetic symbols as 'Kiaadiff'. Sometimes (cf. Mees 1983:82), the stops themselves may lack complete closure, so that only a fricative is heard – e.g. [pʰakəv 'xa:ʤ] *(pack of cards)*.

2.2   Other features

Beyond the segmental phonological characteristics listed above, some broad varieties of Cardiff English have **prosodic and paralinguistic** features which are indexically important in identifying speakers as non-standard Cardiff English speakers, differentiating them either from RP or from other Welsh accents of English. Only tentative observations can be made about most of these features. As Wells says (1982, Vol.1:91), our ignorance about the rhythmical characteristics of local accents is still very great. Some Cardiff speakers, and certainly those who mimic a broad Cardiff accent, assign stress within connected speech very differently from the RP model offered by Gimson (1972: 260ff). In standard English, says Gimson, an utterance is delivered as a series of close-knit rhythmic groups, with the rhythmic beats occurring at fairly equal intervals of time. The speed with which the unstressed syllables are uttered will be varied to fit in with the primary 'stress-timed' rhythm. Of course, particular patterns of stress will vary depending on the precise context and the function of the discourse, which makes it very difficult to identify deviations from the 'normal' rhythmical pattern of RP. Still, some Cardiff speakers do seem to move towards a more even stressing of syllables within connected speech, giving a staccato effect. We can compare Gimson's example (:260)

They couldn't have	chosen a	better	time for their	holiday
• ● • •	● ••	● •	● • •	♪ ••

with this fragment from the speech of an older Cardiff woman (noticeably non-standard in her segmental phonology):

but er	of course	I don't know	what	kind of	twang	we got	I	don't	know
/bər ɸ:	ə kʌ:s	əɪ də nɔʊ	wɒ	kəɪnd ə	twaŋ	wi gɑr	əɪ	də	nɔʊ/
● •	• ♪	● • •	●	● •	●	♪ •	●	●	●

One effect of this distribution of stressed syllables is the impression of rapid speech, although the number of syllables or words per second may not be greater than in other accents. But it is interesting in this context that Wells suggests that 'there exists a general tendency for urban speech to be faster than rural speech' (1982, Vol. 1:87). Certainly, there is scope here for detailed research of less idealized speech-data than that examined by Gimson.

There is widespread agreement that many Welsh accents of English differ markedly from RP in their intonation. Parry (1972:155) makes the observation that the similarity between Welsh (language) intonation patterns and those of South-East Wales (SEW) ' . . . is so remarkable over so wide an area . . . that it constitutes one of the most obvious characteristics of all that strike the average English ear as a mark of the Welsh colouring of the SEW dialects.' We must remember, though, that Parry's study was essentially of rural south-east Wales, and Wells (1982, Vol.2:392) notes that the situation in Cardiff is different from that in, say, the Valleys. One feature recognized as a general Welsh-English tendency (Thomas 1984:183), however, is found in Cardiff. Thomas points out that, as in Welsh itself, Welsh English allows pitch-movement to occur on syllables which follow non-final stressed syllables (standard English English requires stress and principle pitch-movement to co-occur). This tendency leads to some unstressed syllables being as prominent as the stressed syllables they follow. In just this way, Cardiff speakers can be heard producing pitch-variation such as :

where the major pitch-pattern on the second (unstressed) syllable of *Valleys* is not normally possible in RP.

One intonation contour in particular can be considered a dialect-feature specifically of Cardiff English – the use of the Low Rise tune, preceded by Low Head (Tone Group 6 as classified by O'Connor and Arnold 1961:30). Of course, this pattern occurs in all varieties of English, but can be taken to be a Cardiff feature by virtue of its relatively high frequency. Particularly, it seems to be a conversational device used to show incompleteness and to hold the listener's attention, so that it often appears in longer discourses such as explanations or narratives. O'Connor and Arnold summarize the 'meaning' of this intonation pattern as ' . . . inviting further contribution to the conversation from the listener' (1961:48). But Cardiff speakers seem to use the pattern to invite vocal signs of agreement or other non-verbal feedback responses from the listener within a discourse. The tune, in fact, is likely to *deter* an interlocutor from making a full contribution, other than perhaps a request for clarification, because it is clear that the speaker has more to add. A good example is the following extract from a young male speaker's account of a film he has seen (occurences of the tune are marked by 'TG6' below the nuclear syllable, with the duration of the Tone Group delimited by vertical lines):

| . . . *their original plan* | *was to take this Japanese prisoner* | *who*

they captured earlier on | *back with them* | *to get the information*
                                    TG6   TG6

| *but now they'd already* | *they already knew the information* | *so they* |

decided to kill him | *and meanwhile this hardnut Bamford* | *he like*
            TG6

liked this prisoner | *and they'd already* | *beaten the prisoner up*

| *thinking he'd been pinching fags* | *because Bamford had given him*
                          TG6

ten snouts as they called it | . . .
   TG6

The use of Tone Group 6 here compels the listener to show his/her understanding and appreciation of the narrative elements as they are put forward by the speaker and to produce a string of appropriate facial expressions, head-nods and grunts of acceptance to match each final low rise. It is not clear whether this effect would be produced in listeners more used to the Tone Group 6 as a dialect feature.

    Cardiff English shares a number of non-standard **morphological and syntactic** chatacteristics with many (perhaps most) regional dialects of English. The most recent detailed accounts of such characteristics are Hughes and Trudgill's overview (1979:13ff) of common non-standard British grammatical features and Cheshire's sociolinguistic study (1982) of Reading grammar, and it will be useful to take these works as a starting-point. Cheshire's work is particularly relevant because she indicates at many points that the features she finds in Reading are characteristic of most dialects of the South-West of England. The same features in Cardiff English may therefore be analysed as reflecting South-Western (English) influence, particularly when they are *not* found in most other English dialects in Wales.

    As in Reading, Cardiff present-tense verbs often differ from standard English forms. The central aspect of non-standardness here is the extension of the inflected verb form (written as '-s') to the whole present tense paradigm *(I likes it; we lives in Splott; they squeaks when I walks)* in addition to the third person singular environment where it occurs in standard varieties of English. This extended use of *-s* can also occur with the 'full' forms of the irregular verbs BE and DO *(they's awful; we does it often)* and occasionally with HAVE *(we never has homework)*. Cheshire notes that the *-s* form of HAVE *(has)* never occurs in Reading when the verb acts as an auxiliary *(they have been; they've been)*, and indeed in Cardiff the usual non-standard form when unemphasized is *they been*, analysable either as phonological elision or as a further morphological variant. On the other hand, the inflected form of auxiliary DO *(does)* is found (in Cardiff and occasionally in Reading), as in *they does try like*.

In the absence of a detailed quantitative study of present-tense verbs in Cardiff, replicating Cheshire's work, it is difficult to comment on the linguistic constraints on the use of inflected forms. But the complement constraint that Cheshire finds in Reading – which inhibits the use of *-s* inflections in a present-tense verb followed by a complement where subject and tense are marked (:40) – does not hold throughout the Cardiff community. We find utterances like *we knows we're Cardiffians* and *I knows what I likes*. But both these examples were recorded in the speech of older male speakers, and Cheshire comments that the constraint is not operative for older Reading speakers. The Reading form *dos* (/duːz/) does not occur in Cardiff except in the expression *fair dos* (/fɛː duːz/) meaning 'give her/ him/etc. due credit', where the /z/ seems to be a realization of the plural morpheme and not a verbal inflection.

A converse non-standard form – the *absence* of the *-s* inflection with the third person singular subjects – also occurs both in Reading and Cardiff with the auxiliary verb HAVE *(he've gone; no he haven't)*. Negative third person forms of auxiliary HAVE (as in the case of the last example) are, however, difficult to analyse because of the way they are realized phonologically. Sequences like /iːˈaŋ ˈgarə ˈtʃɑns/ can be seen to represent *hasn't, haven't* or even *ain't* (cf. Cheshire:54ff) in *he——got a chance.* Non-inflected forms of DO in Cardiff are a related non-standard third person verb feature, as in *he don't come here; he swears he do.*

What was referred to above as the central pattern of non-standardness in this morphological area – extending the contexts where *-s*-inflected forms are used – also surfaces in the past tense forms of BE, where *was* is found outside the first and third singular environments, where it is standard *(I was; he was)*, as in *you was, we was, they was*. However, the use of *were* with first and third singular forms *(I were; she were)* that Cheshire attests in Reading is not, to my knowledge, found in Cardiff, except occasionally when negated *(he weren't)*. Some other past tense forms are non-standard because they are identical to the (standard) non-third-person present-tense forms, as with *he give me a quid; they run off; he come over here* (and cf. standard English past tense *hit*). Past-tense *come* and *done* on the other hand, is non-standard in that, like most standard past-tense forms in English, but not *came* and *did*, they are identical to the standard past participle forms. In Cardiff, I have not heard the over-generalized past-tense forms *gived, holded, swinged,* etc. that Cheshire records in the speech of Reading teenagers and that Wakelin (1977:122) considers to be 'widespread in dialect'.

Several other grammatical features noted both by Cheshire and by Hughes and Trudgill occur in Cardiff. Since it seems that these features and their distributions are characteristic of the non-standard varieties of most urban British dialects, they are probably best seen as British social dialect characteristics rather than as marking regional provenance. In this category we can identify:

– negative concord *(I haven't had nothin', my love; there isn't* /ɪnn/ *no-one in)*;

– *never* as a past tense negative *(I never did nothin'* – standard *I didn't do anything; I never!* = a denial);

– *them* as a demonstrative adjective *(I hates them things)*;

–absence of plural marking with some quantified nouns after numerals *(forty pound; fifty quid; six foot of rope* – but cf. also the standard form *five foot three* used to indicate length or height);

– using adjectival forms with adverbial function *(Shop Local!* – a commonly seen advertisement in Cardiff corner-shops; *she drives lovely)*;

– reduction of complex prepositions to adverbial (rather than 'pure' prepositional) components *(he run out* [standard *out of*] *the door; round* [*round at*] *Dave's place; over* [*over to/over in*] *Canton; up* [*up to/up in*] *Ely)*;

– regularizing of the reflexive pronoun paradigm *(he did it hisself* [standard *himself*]; *they did it theirselves* [standard *themselves*]).

The only regional associations that these Cardiff forms have is a negative one, in the sense that they can occasionally differentiate Cardiff English from the minority of dialects of English which do *not* contain them. The point is not trival, though, since English dialects in Wales which are more heavily influenced by the Welsh language than Cardiff English is, will not show some of the features listed. A case in point is the complex of non-standard present-tense forms discussed above, including *I likes it; they does try; he've gone,* which are not found in most dialects of south-west Wales. Within Wales, then, some non-standard grammatical forms with very wide British currency can indeed still mark a speaker's regional provenance (see section 2.4 below).

On the other hand, there are certain non-standard Cardiff grammatical features which are characteristic of Welsh English as a whole, and less common outside Wales. The invariant tag *isn't it?* in non-third person environments *(you're going home now isn't it?)* is sometimes used in stereotyping Welsh English. Thomas (1984:192) says the feature is 'of fairly common occurrence in rural varieties of Welsh English'. But it is also commonly heard in Cardiff English, as in the following continuous fragment:

> *they've all got they're all different kinds of languages isn't it?*

As is generally the case, in the absence of a detailed analysis of a large number of instances, it is impossible to identify any constraints operating on the use of this feature. Certainly, the feature shows variation, since the quoted speaker in the same discourse goes on to produce the standard tag *didn't they?*

> *like to say for the valleys they they speak here different again to us don't they?* (quoted above)

One possible explanation for this variation is, of course, that standard and non-standard tags are variants of a contextually sensitive sociolinguistic variable. But another is that invariant *isn't it?* where its occurrence is non-standard, fulfils a different syntactic function from the tag which shows agreement. It is possible that the *it* of non-standard *isn't it?* refers anaphorically to the whole preceding utterance rather than specifically to the previous noun-phrase subject (i.e. *they* in both the above examples). It may be functionally equivalent, then, to *isn't that so?* or French *n'est-ce pas?* or the *yes?* tag that Thomas identifies (1984:192) as a northern Welsh English feature. It is even possible that there is *no* formal anaphoric link between *isn't it?* and the preceding utterance, since the tag is typically realized phonologically by the sequence /'ɪnɪt/ and speakers and listeners do not necessarily analyse it at a clausal unit incorporating the pro-form *it*. If this analysis is correct, alternation between standard tags and invariant *isn't it?* is not sociolinguistic variation in the strictest sense but semantically motivated choice.

Of the grammatical features listed as Welsh English features by Thomas (1984), only one other is common in Cardiff English and *not* common in many non-Welsh dialects of English. This is predicate fronting, as in *hurt she was; awful I thought it sounded*. Thomas implies this is a pattern modelled on Welsh syntax and it is certainly common to find parallel Welsh examples of clefting from the predicate, as in *bachgen drwg yw Gwyn* (literally, 'naughty boy is Gwyn'); *ar y ford y mae'r llestri* ('on the table that are the dishes', i.e. 'the dishes are on the table') (Awbery, pers. com.). The feature does, of course, appear in standard English too, where it is explained as 'thematic' fronting or 'marked theme' (cf. Quirk and Greenbaum 1973:412ff). Its status as a Welsh dialect feature therefore depends on its higher frequency in Wales or, more accurately, its use in a broader range of environments, yet to be empirically established. Predicate fronting may be a quite rare instance of Welsh substratal influence on Cardiff English, weighing against the large number of cases where such influences on other dialects of Welsh English are *not* typical of Cardiff speech (see section 2.4, below).

One final grammatical feature is again shared by Cardiff English and many other Welsh English dialects: the use of compound forms of the standard positional and directional adjuncts *here* and *there – by here, by there*. These forms are sometimes realized as if they were simple rather than compound forms – /bəɪˈjøː/,/bəˈðɛː/ – but *are* heard in Cardiff in phonologically standardized realisations such as /baɪˈhɪə/,/baɪˈðɛə/. Standard English of course, allows adverbial compounding of this sort with *here* and *there (over here, over there)*, but not in conjunction with *by*. Some Welsh dialects show a parallel structure with *where? – where by? (where's it by?)*, but Cardiff has the well-known non-standard compound *where to?* used to express directional *and* positional meanings – *where to's the hammer?* (standard English – *where is the hammer?*) The particle *to* generally precedes the complement, as in the last example, but can sometimes follow it, as in *where's my wallet to?* This pattern of alternation is structurally similar to the stylistically motivated variation standard English shows between, say, *on what . . . ?* and *what . . . on?* (cf. Quirk *et al*:1973). In Cardiff, it has the interesting consequence that directional uses of *where to?* can be variously heard as standard/non-standard depending on the choice of position for the *to* particle: *where are you going to?* (apparently standard), versus *where to are you going?* (non-standard). In its positional sense, the non-standard Cardiff compound is enshrined as the title of a regular public information feature on the local radio station – *Where To's That Then?*

A number of researchers have made observations on the **lexical and discoursal** aspects of Welsh English, although contemporary British urban dialects tend to be *least* clearly marked at these linguistic levels (cf. section 1.2 above). Parry's rural study threw up a number of Welsh words which he found to be used in English speech. In south-east Wales, he found *flummery* (from Welsh *llymru –* 'a porridge dish'), *tollent (taflawd* – 'hay-loft') and *tump (twmp* – 'hillock') to be 'used in the English speech of the whole area' (1972:149). Parry also documents sporadic use of many other dialect words deriving from the West Midlands *(askel –* 'newt', *cratch –* 'hay-loft', *hopper* – 'seed basket', *larper/lumper –* 'a young boy', etc.); from the south-west of England *(dap –* 'to bounce', *pine-end –* 'gable-end', *pilm* (cf. Cornish *pilm) –* 'dust', *plud –* 'puddle', etc.); and from both of those areas *(oont –* 'mole', *quist* 'woodpigeon', *sally –* 'willow', *clem –* 'to starve', etc.). Trudgill and Hannah (1982:30) identify the items *eisteddfod* (the annual Welsh arts festival), *del* (a term of endearment) and, again, *llymru* as Welsh loan-words used, they claim, in standard Welsh English. They also note the less widespread (but still, it is claimed, standard Welsh English) forms: *delight* (in the sense of 'interest'), *rise* ('to buy a round of' drinks, for example) and *tidy* ('good', 'nice'). Thomas (1984:193ff) lists *all* of the above lexical items as Welsh English dialect forms, labelling *dap, pine-end, pilm* and *plud* 'south Welsh English words' and noting that *delight, tidy* and *rise* (plus *off –* 'angry' and *lose –* 'miss') are 'typical of southern Welsh English'.

Very few of these items deserve to be called lexical dialect features of Cardiff English. It is always difficult to establish that particular dialect-features are *not* part of a community's repertoire, particularly in respect of lexical features which are linked to restricted domains of usage. Cardiffians may have limited opportunities to talk of hay-lofts, seed-baskets and newts, and any corpus of observed speech may in any case exclude the particular lexical items by chance. Direct questioning of informants is the only reasonable alternative. All the lexical forms labelled Welsh English forms by Thomas were compiled to form a short, informal questionnaire, put to fifty randomly selected native Cardiff speakers in street-interviews. The subjects were asked if they (a) recognised and (if so) (b) used any of the listed words; if they did use them, (c) in what contexts and with what senses. The methodological limitations here are obvious, but at least it was arguably likely that subjects would over-report rather than under-report their knowledge and use of the listed words. No background information (on age, class, abode, etc.) was systematically collected except to check that all informants were Cardiffians by birth and long-term residents. Nevertheless, all subjects questioned were middle aged-to-old, subjectively judged.

None of those interviewed claimed to recognize any of the following forms: *flummery, tollent, askel, cratch, larper/lumper, pilm, oont, quist* and *sally*. Also, *delight* and *rise* were never recognized in the senses referred to above. *Hopper* was known by a minority of informants as 'a tipping grain-container' (not strictly a 'seed-basket'); *pine-end* was recognized, again by a minority, but also seemed to be in general use by those who were familiar with the term. About half the informants acknowledged *tump* in senses covering 'a hillock', 'a bump in the road' and 'a mound of grass', but very few claimed to use the word on a day-to-day basis. *Eisteddfod,* but never *del* or *llymru* (which were not recognized), was confirmed to be a standard Welsh English term in general usage. *Lose* in the sense of 'miss' e.g. *(he lost the bus)* was recognized by some as a 'West Walean' but not a Cardiff usage; *off* was fully accepted, but more in the sense of 'hostile' than 'angry'. A large majority of informants recognized *tidy* to have a wide range of uses as a term of general approval *(a tidy looking girl* 'nice-looking'; *he's a tidy sort of chap* 'decent'; *a tidy job* 'a job well done'); some felt the word did not have a direct translation equivalent.

Questioning about *dap, plud* and *clem* (as listed above) elicited some interesting responses. Although no subjects recognized *plud* as a nominal ('puddle'), two claimed to recognize (and use) *pluddle* as a verbal form in the context *to pluddle through a pool* ('to walk through water'). Again, *clem* was never recognized, but about a quarter of those questioned 'corrected' the form to *clamming* in the colloquial standard English sense of 'dying' – *I'm clamming for a smoke*. All informants knew (and claimed to use) *dap* meaning 'plimsole' but most also recognized (and claimed they had in the past used) its verbal sense of *to dap a ball* 'to bounce'. Some were more specific and explained that 'dapping' meant 'bouncing once and catching' rather than 'to bounce repeatedly'. Many said they used 'dap' in a third sense to signify a person's height – *dap* 'short'; *a dapper fellow* 'a short fellow'; *a dap of a lad* 'a small boy'; *he's that dap* (with non-verbal specification) 'he's that tall'. Finally, four informants were familiar with *dap* as a verb 'hit' *(I'll dap you)*.

These findings show that there are lexical dialectal features in Cardiff English, though the features are rarely if ever unique to Cardiff. As expected, the rural dialect vocabulary identified first by Parry has not apparently survived in urban Cardiff speech and loans from Welsh are rare. Where Cardiff dialect vocabulary is recognized by Cardiffians, they often also recognize that the forms are increasingly infrequently used. Also the dialect words identified often have different senses or more specific contexts of one from those suggested in the literature. Interestingly, informants questioned in the street-interviews were able to volunteer a few phrases which they felt were more central to Cardiff speech than most of the lexical items they were asked about. *She don't half kid her mitt she do* (transcribed uncertainly here into conventional orthography), meaning 'she fancies herself', 'she thinks she's better than she is', was offered by one informant and recognized as a common Cardiff expression by many older subjects. Some explained that *her mitt* denoted 'her hand', which in turn signified 'herself'; hence, *she don't half kid herself* was also recognized as a rendering of the same meaning. Again, *it's something to <u>do</u> with them, isn't it?* (which, if differently stressed, has a readily interpretable meaning in Standard English) was identified as a Cardiff feature by virtue of its sense 'it's an intrinsic characteristic', 'it's of their nature' (e.g. of children squabbling). *He's half tidy* was widely said to be in use as an expression of general approval.

2.3   *Cardiff Welsh or Cardiff English?*

The Welsh capital city has an ambiguous relationship with the Welsh language. As the capital, Cardiff is the focal point of many administrative, educational and cultural activities strongly associated with the Welsh language, its history and development. The National Museum of Wales, the Welsh Folk Museum, the headquarters of the Welsh television and radio channels, the Welsh Office and the colleges of the University of Wales, to name just a few examples, are to be found in or around the capital; Cardiff has a number of thriving Welsh-language schools and Welsh is taught as a school subject throughout the area. Indeed, Cardiff has some of the trappings of a fully bilingual community – most noticeably its bilingual road-signs, public notices and administrative forms.

But the Welsh language is rarely heard on the streets in Cardiff and when it is, it is very unlikely to be in the mouths of long-established, indigenous Cardiffians. Census figures show that only a small (though apparently increasing) proportion of the region's population report themselves to be 'Welsh speakers' – 5.8% and 2.5% of the population of South Glamorgan and Gwent at the 1981 census (Welsh Office 1983). Since a national language will often be the touchstone of national identity – language, as Fishman (1977:25) puts it, being 'the recorder of paternity, the expresser of patrimony and the carrier of phenomenology' – it is not surprising that monolingual Cardiffians also seem to take an ambiguous position in respect of their own Welshness. Clearly, Cardiffians are Welsh men and women, born within a stone's throw of the national rugby stadium in the capital city; but at the same time the majority will use the adjective 'Welsh' as an attribute of an out-group – 'Welsh people', even 'those Welsh people'. Cardiffians are Welsh, but there is a group identifiable to many of them as 'the' Welsh who are perceived to have a stronger claim to Welsh identity. This perception may have a historical basis, reflecting the circumstances in the nineteenth century under which Cardiff grew dramatically to its current size and importance (see section 2.4, below). But there is undoubtedly a linguistic dimension too, in that the Welsh language is a less significant force in Cardiff and the urban south-east coastal belt than in most of the rest of Wales. This is true in respect of *both* the use of the Welsh language itself *and* its influence on the English of the region.

To talk of monolingual English speakers in Cardiff is not to imply that the indigenous Cardiff population never confronts the Welsh language.

There is a small but significant set of contexts where, in day-to-day-interaction, Cardiffians need to use fragments of Welsh; more accurately, fragments which are Welsh by origin and would be treated as Welsh by Welsh-language-speakers. These include personal names (such as *Carys* /'karıs/, *Siân* / ʃa:n/, *Llewelyn* /ɬəu'ɛlın/, *Dafydd* /'davıð/), and place-names, as in the case of street-names in the city including *Cwrt-Yr-Ala* /'kɷrtər'ala/ *Road, Crwys* /krɷis/ *Road, Llanmaes* /ɬan'maıs/ *Street, Heol-y-waun*/ 'he:ələ'waın/), city-district names (including *Llanedyrn* /ɬan'ɛdırn/, *Cyncoed* /kın'kɔid/, *Llandaff* /ɬan'da:v/, *Pentwyn* /pɛn'tɷin/), and the names of villages and towns outside the city (such as *Pentyrch* /pɛn'tırχ/, *Pontypridd*/ pɔntə'pri:ð/, *Radyr* /'radır/, *Llantrisant* /ɬan'trısant/ and *Llanelli* /ɬan'ɛɬi/); loan-words from Welsh which have no ready English equivalent (such as *eisteddfod*, mentioned above) form a further category. The phonemic transcriptions above (based on the phoneme inventories for contemporary Welsh in south Wales compiled by Awbery (1984)) give a general impression of many Welsh (language) speakers' pronunciation of the listed proper names.

The phonological system presupposed by the transcriptions of course differs in certain respects from the system we find in most non-Welsh varieties of English. For example, as shown above, Welsh has the voiceless lateral fricative /ɬ/ (as in *Llanelli, Llewelyn, Llandaff*) alongside the voiced lateral /l/, the voiceless uvular fricative /χ/ *(Pentyrch)*, the diphthongs /ɷi/ *(Pentwyn, Crwys)* and /əu/ *(Llewelyn)*, the monophthong /ɷ/ *(Cwrt)* and the extra contrasts between /e:/ and /ei/ *(Heol)*. In addition, there is the perceptually significant realizational difference that Welsh /r/ is rolled ([pɛn'tırχ] – *Pentyrch)*, and the many correspondences between Welsh orthographic symbols and phonemic items which do not apply in English (e.g. 'ff' = /f/; 'f' = /v/; 'si' = /ʃ/; 'dd' = /ð/; 'w' = /u:/, /ɷ/ or /w/; 'y' = /i:/, /ı/ or /ə/).

These are often some of the phonetic, phonemic and orthographic obstacles to Welsh-like pronunciation that confronts most people who do not speak Welsh. But it is very significant that within Wales, many people who do not speak Welsh *do* have the linguistic resources for producing Welsh-like pronunciation sequences in such cases. For example, speakers from Llanelli, even if they do not speak Welsh, have no hesitation over the non-English lateral fricative /ɬ/ in the their town's name [ɬan'ɛɬi] though they may 'anglicize' their pronunciation of it in other ways – perhaps as [ɬən'ɛɬı]. Most of the monoglot (English-speaking) Welsh who have migrated eastwards or southwards to Cardiff or who visit the city expect to hear 'Welsh' (non-anglicized) pronunciations of street- and district-names like those listed above. Just as the Welsh language is a living influence on English pronunciation in most northern and western areas of Wales (cf.

Thomas 1984:178 and section 2.4, below), many of the phonetic, phonological and orthographic rules of Welsh live on in the competence of
English-speaking monolinguals from these areas in the restricted contexts
where Welsh pronunciation is required. It is a special case of linguistic
transfer – from Welsh into English – where speakers to an extent
consciously resist the natural tendencies to integrate their pronunciation of
Welsh proper-names into the dominant English system (cf. Baetens-
Beardsmore 1982). In resisting such integration, these speakers are
supported by a pervasive argument that proper-names should be pronounced 'correctly', which in this case means in accordance with the
accepted rules of standard Welsh. This view is actively promoted by the
media in Wales. Television and radio news-readers, for example, are
generally careful to switch from near-RP to near-standard-Welsh phonology in pronouncing Welsh place-names and personal names within an
English discourse.

The indigenous population of Cardiff pronounces Welsh proper-names
very differently. In a recent study (reported in Coupland 1984b, 1985a),
tape-recorded street-interviews were conducted with 125 randomly chosen
Cardiff inhabitants in four areas of the city. The interviewers claimed to be
interested in Cardiffians' local geographical knowledge and quizzed the
subjects about the names of streets in their localities, city-district-names
and the names of selected towns and villages around Cardiff (marked with
numbers on a map). All the apparently Welsh and partially Welsh place-
names pronounced by each subject were phonetically transcribed and
grouped to show the range of pronunciations associated with each name.
The most frequent pronunciations of selected place-names are shown in
Table 2–2 (variants are transcribed in the order most-to-least frequent).

The findings show massive 'anglicization' of Welsh place-names in
Cardiff in a number of respects. Firstly, there is very little evidence of
Cardiffians transferring aspects of the Welsh phonological system into
their speech in pronouncing apparently Welsh place-names. The Welsh
lateral fricative /ɬ/, corresponding to orthographic 'll' is very rare in the
data where it is often represented by English /l/ (cf. examples 2,7,8,13,25
etc.). The only exception is example 27, consistently pronounced with a
lateral fricative – ['gɛɬi'gɛ:]. No pseudo-Welsh clusters like /θl,fl,kl/ were
recorded, although these are sometimes used by speakers from outside
Wales (as noted by Wells 1982, Vol. 2: 389). The Welsh uvular fricative /χ/
(Welsh orthographic 'ch') occurs only once in the data. It is generally
replaced by /k/ (examples 2,4,31,40), although a velar fricative [x] is
sometimes produced as a close approximation to standard Welsh /χ/ in
three of the four listed names. The written sequence 'wy' is variously
represented in Cardiffians' speech as /ʊɪ/ (as in English RP *ruin*), /ʊwɪ/, /ɔɪ/

Table 2–2: Summary of the most frequent variants of street-names in four areas of Cardiff, city-district-names and local town-/village-names, in broad phonetic transcription

Street Names

A. *GRANGETOWN*

1.	*Coedcae St.*	'kɔɪd'kəɪ	'kʌɪg'kəɪ	'kɔɪg'kɛɪ
2.	*Llanbradach St.*	lam'bɹadəx	lam'bɹadək	ɬam'bɹadək
3.	*Cymmer St.*	'kəmə	'kʊmə	
4.	*Clydach St.*	'klɪdək	'klɪdəx	
5.	*Bargoed St.*	'baːgɔɪd	ba'gɔ̃ɪd	
6.	*Penhevad St.*	'pɛn'ɛvəd	pən'ɛvəd	
7.	*Llanmaes St.*	'lan'mɛɪs	'lam'mɛɪs	

B. *ELY*

8.	*Heol-Y-Berllan*	'ilə'bɜːlan	'hiəl bə'lan	'hilə'bɜːlan
		'hiəl bə'lɛɪn,	'hiɑl bə'lan	etc.
9.	*Caerau Rd./Lane*	'kəɹɹe	'kaɹɹə	
10.	*Heol Trelai*	'hil tɹə'ləi	'hiɑl trə'ləɪ	etc.
11.	*Heol-Y-Gaer*	'hil ə 'gɛː	'hiɑl 'gɛː	'hilɒ 'gɛː
12.	*Heol-Pant-Y-Deri*	'il 'pantə'dɛɹi	'iəl 'pantə'dɛɹi	
13.	*Heol-Y-Castell*	'iəl 'kas'tɛl	'ilə'kas'tɛl	'hiɒl'kas'tɛl
14.	*Cwrt-Yr-Ala Rd.*	'kʌːtˤə'ralə		
15.	*Heol Carnau*	'iəl 'kaːnəi	'ka:nɔ̃ɪ	
16.	*Heol Eglwys*	'iəl 'ɛglɔɪs	'iəl 'ɛglʊʷi	

C. *WHITCHURCH*

17.	*Heol-y-waun*	'hɛɒl ə 'waɪn	'hiəl 'wəɪn	ili wʌːn
18.	*Heol Coed Cae*	'hiəl 'kʌɪʔ'kəɪ	hɛɪəl 'kɔɪd'kɛɪ	
19.	*Heol Waun-Y-Nant*	'hil 'wəɪn i 'nant	'hɛɒl'waɪn ə 'nant	
20.	*Clas Newydd*	'klas 'njʊʷɪd	'klas 'njʊʷəθ	
21.	*Clas Heulog*	'klas 'haɪlɒg	'klas 'həɪlɒg	
22.	*Plas Treoda*	'plas tɹi'oda	'plas tɹi'ʊʊdə	
23.	*Lon Madoc*	'lɒn 'madək		
24.	*Cradoc Road*	'kɹadɒg 'ɹʊʊd		

D. *CATHAYS*

25.	*Llanishen St.*	'lan'ɪʃən	ɬan'ɪʃn̩	
26.	*Talygarn St.*	'talɪ'gaːn	'tælə'gɑːn	
27.	*Gelligaer St.*	'gɛɬɪ'gɛː		
28.	*Crwys Rd.*	'kɹʊɪs	'kɹʊwɪs	'kɹɔɪs
29.	*Brithdir St.*	'bɹɪθdə		
30.	*Hirwain St.*	'hɜːwɛɪn		
31.	*Pentyrch St.*	'pɛn'tɜːk		

City Districts

32.	*Llanedeyrn*	lanˈɛdɪn	ɬanˈɛdɪn	
33.	*Cyncoed*	kɪŋˈkʌɪd	kɪŋˈkɔɪd	kɪŋˈkɔʊəd
34.	*Rhiwbina*	ɹʊˈbəɪnə	ɹuˈbəɪnə	
35.	*Llandaff*	ˈlandəf	ˈlanˈdaf	etc.
36.	*Llanrumney*	ˈlanˈɹəmni	ˈlanˈɹəmmi	
37.	*Pentwyn*	ˈpɛnˈtʊɪn	ˈpɛnˈtˈʊɪn	
38.	*Llanishen*	ˈlanˈɪʃn̩	ˈlənˈɪʃən	etc.
39.	*Gabalfa*	gəbˈalvə	gəˈbalfə	

Towns/Villages

40.	*Pentyrch*	pɛnˈtɜːk	pɛnˈtɜːx	pɛnˈtɜːχ
41.	*Penarth*	pənˈaːθ	pɛnˈaːθ	pn̩ˈaːθ
42.	*Dinas Powis*	ˈdɪnɪs ˈpəʊɪs		
43.	*Pontypridd*	ˈpɒntɪpɹiːð	ˈpɒntəˈpɹiːd	ˈpɒntəˈpɹiːθ
44.	*Creigiau*	ˈkɹəɪgə	ˈkɹaɪgə	ˈkɹəɪgaɪ etc.
45.	*Radyr*	ˈɹadə		
46.	*Llantrisant*	ˈlanˈtɹɪsənt	ˈlanˈtɹɪsn̩t	
47.	*Caerphilly*	ˈkəˈfɪli		

and /wɪ/ (examples 28,37), never by the Welsh crescendo diphthong /ɔi/. Orthographic 'w' (in example 14) corresponding to the Welsh monophthong /ɔ/ is reassigned to Cardiff English /ʌ:/. In Welsh, the /r/ phoneme occurs before vowels *and* in other environments; but in the place-names data, as in RP English, non-prevocalic /r/ does not appear (examples 3,5,8,11, etc.) In other words, then, when pronouncing apparently Welsh place-names, Cardiffians generally keep within the bounds of the characteristically English pronunciation rule-system, which differs from Welsh both in its inventory of phonemic contrasts and in the particular linguistic environments across which its phonemes are distributed.

Secondly, it is clear that what we might call the 'Cardiff Welsh' forms in table 2–1 are generally 'anglicized' in the direction of Cardiff English, and many of the dialectal phonetic and phonological characteristics of Cardiff English discussed in section 2.1 show up here. So, we find /h/ variably 'dropped' in *heol* names (examples 10,11,12,13 etc.) and from its medial position in *Penhevad* (example 6). The open, unrounded vowel symbol [ʌ;], representing the orthographic symbol 'w' in *Cwrt* (example 14, referred to above), was the one chosen as the phonemic symbol for Cardiff English equivalent to RP /ɔ:/. The final diphthong in example 15 is in one instance transcribed phonetically as [ɔɪ], which was noted in section 2.1 as a variant to be assigned to the Cardiff phoneme /əi/ corresponding to RP /aɪ/. Again,

Cardiff /r/ between vowels is often flapped [ɾ] rather than continuant [ɹ], and this feature appears in 'Cardiff Welsh' in examples 12 and 14 (though not 9). In dialectal terms, then, Cardiffians treat the 'Welsh' sequences no differently from English. It seems that we can find Cardiff English dialect features even in the pronunciation of (what we have up to now been considering to be) 'Welsh' place-names.

Thirdly, and most interestingly, the transcriptions in table 2–1 show another dimension of the 'anglicization' of Welsh. In many instances, Cardiff speakers produce forms which cannot be explained *either* by the phonetic/phonological differences between Welsh and English *or* by the influences of Cardiff English dialect. For example, a number of speakers said [ba'gɔɪd] (example 5) and some produced similar realizations of *Cyncoed* (example 33) – [kɪŋ'kɔɪd, kɪŋ'kɔʊəd]. Yet, the phoneme /ɔɪ/ is available in both standard Welsh and RP English, and Cardiff English has the corresponding phoneme /ʌi/. Why, then, do some speakers feel the need to add prominence to the second element of diphthong/phoneme-sequence? Why is the second syllable stressed in example 5 – [ba'gɔɪd], rather than the first (as in Welsh and most English versions of this name)? A similar case is the production of /d/ and /θ/ in place of Welsh /ð/ in example 20, when English itself frequently has /ð/, sometimes even in final position (*tithe, blythe*). Again, we find [(h)il, '(h)iəl, '(h)ial, '(h)ilə, '(h)ili, 'hilɒ and 'heɪəl] for *heol-y* sequences in the data, when only the last of these is a predictable anglicization of the Welsh pronunciation. A few speakers produced the voiceless fricative /f/ in *Gabalfa* (example 39), although [v/ is the Welsh form and available in RP and of course in Cardiff English.

This third group of realizations makes it obvious that many of the forms in the table are *not* in fact modelled on Welsh pronunciation. They are highly variable spelling pronunciations (or attempted spelling-pronunciations) based on very limited awareness of Welsh spelling conventions. As such, they cannot strictly be considered examples of 'anglicization' – a term which implies derivation from a source language. When a Cardiff speaker pronounces Welsh orthographic 'f' as /f/, that person is clearly unaware of the link between the symbol and Welsh /v/ (or at least of any need to represent that link in this instance) and is, presumably, treating the word itself as an English sequence. With orthographic 'oe' (*Bargoed, Cyncoed*) and 'eo' (*Heol*), there is a reasonable expectancy that the names are non-English since English orthography does not frequently permit these letter-sequences in these environments ('oe', 'eo' between consonants; 'dd' in word-final position). And it is precisely with these names that we find inconsistency, even idiosyncracy in pronunciation. Some speakers opt for a 'best solution' generally within the bounds of English spelling-rules: /d/ for written 'dd' (20,43), [ɔʊə] to represent 'oe' (in 33, *Cyncoed*) – perhaps on the analogy of the word *coed*ucational. Some make partial concessions to non-English conventions: realizing 'dd' as a fricative, but fortis /θ/ rather than (Welsh) lenis /ð/ (again, cf. examples 20,43); realizing *coed* (33) as [kɔɪd], an 'interlingual' form, standing between predictable Welsh and English pronunciations (cf. Selinker 1972). In some instances, there seems to be nothing short of a breaking down of graphological-phonological correspondences according to *any* rule-system. We find [ə] for written 'iau' in *Creigiau* (44), ['hilɒ 'gɛ:] for *Heol-y-Gaer* (11) and ['hiəl bə'leɪn] for *Heol-y-Berllan* (8). The last example here may be a false identification of Welsh *llan* (meaning 'church') with English *lane*, just as it is said that Cardiffians have sometimes associated *Pen-yr-heol* ('top of the road') with *Penny Royal*.

The broader significance of these tendencies in the pronunciation of apparently Welsh place-names lies in the area of language-attitudes and ethnic identity – to be discussed in chapter 4. The immediate conclusion is that Cardiff pronunciation is notable for its lack of concession to and recognition of the Welsh language. Street-, district-, town- and village-names whose Welshness is evident to many Welsh people and preserved by them in their pronunciation, are predominantly aligned with English phonological and orthographic rules in Cardiff speech. This process of remodelling is, in many cases, so complete that the Welsh-language basis of the forms is no longer apparent and the names themselves cease to be in any meaningful sense 'Welsh'.

2.4   *Cardiff English and Welsh English*

This section attempts to assess the distinctiveness of Cardiff English among varieties of English in Wales as a whole. This enterprise needs some justification, in the light of comments made in chapter 1 and at the beginning of this chapter about the artificiality of constucts such as 'the Cardiff dialect'. I have admitted to using this phrase as a short-hand means of referring to the central non-standard linguistic resources available to Cardiff speakers. As such, Cardiff English is not at all clearly delimited in its own right and subsumes much inter- and intra-personal variation, of the sort to be exemplified in chapters 3 and 5. This variation will be an obstacle to any dialect description which sets out to find homogeneity within a speech community, within a social group, even within the speech of a single individual. But despite wide recognition of these difficulties, some researchers have claimed or implied that there is dialectal uniformity over communities even broader than the city of Cardiff. For example, some social psychologists have conducted experiments involving 'the Welsh accent' or 'South Welsh accented speech' (cf. Giles 1971a; Bourhis *et al.* 1973,1975,1976) and have drawn conclusions about the social significance of using and adapting these supposedly identifiable accents. One descriptive linguistic study (Trudgill and Hannah 1982: 27ff) sets out to list features which characterize standard 'Welsh English'. As we have seen, the most detailed description of English in Wales are those by Thomas (1984) and Wells (1982), but even these studies start from the assumption of considerable homogeneity in Welsh English, proceeding to comment on instances where dialectal varieties diverge from the central model or models. Wells, for example, comments on the clearly distinctive dialect-area of south-west Dyfed and the Gower penisula before focusing on 'the more typically Welsh accents of English' (Vol. 2,:379). Thomas identifies two basic models of Welsh English – a 'northern' and 'southern' model. He takes the 'southern' model as a starting point for the description of Welsh English, principally noting rural south-western and northern variants (:178/9).

Of course, both Wells and Thomas make some specific references to Cardiff English in the course of their descriptions, but all of these studies risk underestimating the distinctiveness of English spoken in and around the capital city. There are very good social, economic and demographic reasons in history to expect that Cardiff English may be as distinct from other varieties of English in Wales as it is from, say, dialect varieties of the south-west of England. The lowlands of south-east Wales, as a coastal borderland, were always prone to the influence of invading nations – Romans, Vikings, Normans, English and Flemings. Strong English influence in the area has been detectable since the Act of Union in 1536, when Glamorgan and Monmouth were incorporated into the English realm, with Cardiff as a regional centre. From that time on, strong trading links with the West of England were maintained. Cardiff's astonishingly rapid growth during the nineteenth century is particularly significant:

> Cardiff owes its existence to the age of steam-coal in the second half of the 19th century; it was a creation of the Victorian era. Between 1801 and 1841 it had grown from an insignificant village of 1,870 people to a small township of 11,400. (B.Thomas 1960:111)

In the sixty years from 1851 to 1911, the pace of expansion was phenomenal (cf. Jenkins 1854). The volume of coal exports went up fourteen-fold, and there was a corresponding growth in investment in railway and port facilities to handle the huge flow of traffic. By 1911, those living within the boundaries of Cardiff City Borough numbered 182,000. Watkins (1962) documents the rapid and thorough anglicization of south-east Wales over this period resulting from such expansion. The increasing industrial and commercial activity brought its own pressures to consolidate the predominance of English in the area. But the pattern of immigration into the area did so more directly. The 1911 census showed that only *half* the people living in Cardiff had been born there (B. Thomas 1960:113). Of the 182,000 people accounted for, about 30,000 had been born elsewhere in Wales, 46,000 had immigrated from England (many from the Midlands and the South-West), about 5,000 from Ireland and Scotland and 5,000 from foreign or British Empire countries – most of them coloured males who settled in the area around the docks (ibid.; cf. also Lewis 1960).

The influx of population, predominantly working-class males, threw many wide-ranging speech-varieties into Cardiff's dialectal melting-pot. Gradually, these influences will have been assimilated by the variety of Welsh English that characterized the Cardiff area before the Industrial Revolution to form the patterns of dialectal variation we can now call Cardiff English. Claims made about the derivation of Cardiff dialect-features on the basis of a synchronic description are necessarily speculative, but it is at least interesting to identify points of overlap or close similarity between Cardiff English and other dialects of English that may have influenced its development (see table 2–3; references are to Wells 1982, Vol 2, and to Hughes and Trudgill 1979). Derivational explanations of the sort suggested by the table are most plausible when the linguistic features in question do not appear in most other Welsh English dialects. In fact, it is the case that *most* of the features listed in table 2–3 do not appear in Wales other than the south-east: rounding of the RP long mid central vowel /ɜː/ to [øː] or /œː/; unrounding of RP /ɒ/ to /ɑ/; [ɒɪ] (or [ɔɪ]) realizations of RP /aɪ/; possible loss of contrast between short /a/ and long /aː/; voicing or flapping to /t/ intervocalically (whereas other English dialects in Wales often lengthen the consonant – [tː]; affrication of initial stops; and certain of the non-standard grammatical forms discussed in section 2.2, such as non-third-person -*s*-inflected present tense verbs.

Independently of the question of derivation, there are other respects in which Cardiff English does not align itself with other Welsh English varieties. Some features appear in Cardiff but not otherwise widely in Wales, including close realizations of /aː / ([ɛː], [æː], which are unusual in Britain as a whole (cf. Wells 1982, Vol 1: 134); also unrounding of RP long /ɔː/ to /ʌː/. Often, Cardiff English shows features which are more characteristically English English than Welsh English. In this category, we find the availability of /jʌː/ sequences as an alternative to typically Welsh English /ɪuə/ in *cure, pure,* etc.; the diphthogal phonemes in words of the lexical sets *pane, pain; toe, tow* (/peɪn/; /təʊ/) whereas many south Wales varieties have the extra contrasts /eː / – /eɪ/; /oː/ – /oʊ/ which establish *pane – pain* and *toe – tow* as minimal pairs; the RP pattern of vowel 'reduction' in unstressed environments, as in the case of /ɪ/ or /ə/ in the final syllables of *helpless, ticket, village* (cf. Thomas 1984: 179), where many south Wales

Table 2–3: Points of overlap or similarity between Cardiff English and selected other dialects of English.

South West	References
– lengthening of 'short' vowels, including /a/ with possible loss of phonemic contrast /a/ – /a:/	Wells : 345; H + T :47
– unrounding of RP /ɒ/ to [ɑ]	Wells :347
– variant forms of RP /aɪ/ include [əɪ] and [ɒɪ]	Wells :347
– possible integration of RP /ʌ/ with /ə/	Wells :348
– the complex of morphological and syntactic features discussed by Cheshire 1982 and in section 2.2 above	
West Midlands	
– RP /aɪ/ realized as [ɔɪ]	Wells :364; H + T :54
– RP /ɜ:/ and /ɜə/ rounded to [œ:]	H + T :54
Merseyside	
– affrication of initial stops	Wells :372; H + T :61
– flapping of /r/ as [ɾ] intervocalically and post-consonantally	Wells :372; H + T :62
– RP /ʊə/ realized as [ɪuə], [ɪwə] or (commonly) as /ɔ:/ in *cure* etc.	Wells :373
– flapping of intervocalic /t/ to [ɾ]	H + T :62
Ireland	
– unrounding of RP /ɒ/ to [ɑ]	Wells :419
– possible opening of front vowel /ɪ/ to merge with /ɛ/	Wells :423
– lengthening of 'short' /a/	Wells :423
– realizations of RP /aɪ/ include [əɪ], [ʌɪ] and [ɒɪ]	Wells :426
– fricative realization of /t/, postvocalically and sometimes prevocalically	Wells :429
– voicing of intervocalic /t/ as [t̬] or flapping as [ɾ]	Wells :430

dialects have /ɛ/; alveolar rather than dental realisations of /t,d,n/; weak rather than strong aspiration of /p,t,k,s/; glottal reinforcement of stops ([kʰəʔpʰ] rather than [kʰəpʰ]); 'clear' and 'dark' /l/ in complementary distribution (rather than clear [l] in all environments). We should also include in this category the thorough anglicization of Welsh sequences in Cardiff which, we have seen, is entirely unrepresentative of the situation in Wales as a whole.

The above is the descriptive linguistic evidence to support the view that Cardiff English is by no means typical of Welsh English dialects. Certainly, it is not typical of the varieties described in the literature under the heading of Welsh English. Thomas (1984) rightly claims that the South Wales industrial communities share a number of dialectal features and need to be considered apart from 'less evolved' Welsh English dialects which are far more strongly influenced by the Welsh (language) substratum. On the other hand, Thomas' comments on 'accent variants' within his 'southern' model of Welsh English do not recognize most of the 'non-Welsh-English' features listed above. Welsh substratal influence on Cardiff English is in fact minimal, as we would expect from the historical sketch given above.[2]

Some final comments should be made about the relationship between Cardiff English and what Trudgill and Hannah (1982) describe as Standard Welsh English. While it is doubtful whether a regional standard variety can be adequately defined as the variety 'normally employed in writing and normally spoken by "educated" speakers of the language' (:1), there are grounds for arguing that an identifiable standard variety does exist in Wales. No empirical work has been done, but there is widespread popular recognition in Wales of the concept of 'the educated Welsh voice', which is *not* simply the voice of the educated, whoever they may be. It is essentially a phonological concept, referring to the pronunciation of English in a way which shows a specifiable amount of subtratal influence from the Welsh language but otherwise approximates to RP. It may include short /a/ in place of RP /ɑ:/ in *last, dance*, etc.; resistance to RP-type vowel 'reduction' in unstressed syllables; maintenance of the /e: / – / eɪ/, /o:/ – /oʊ/ phonemic contrasts; replacement of RP /ɪə/ and /ʊə/ diphthongs by /iːə/, /uːə/ sequences (in *fear, poor*); strong aspiration of plosives; 'correct' Welsh phonetics, phonology and orthographic interpretation in the pronunciation of transferred Welsh sequences (cf. Trudgill and Hannah:27ff).

However, some of the vocalic and consonantal features referred to by Trudgill and Hannah, as with the lexical forms *del, llymru, delight, rise* and *tidy* discussed in section 2.2, are *very un*likely to be considered.standard forms by Welsh people. The lengthening of intervocalic consonants, as in ['mən:i] – *money* – is in fact a feature used in stereotype of *un*educated Welsh English. Again, absence of /g/ in *language, longer* (/laŋwɛʤ/, /lɒŋə /) is heavily stigmatized. Standard Welsh English *tooth* may well be /tʊθ /, but *comb* is never (to my knowledge) /kʊm/ and is non-standard when pronounced /kuːm/ (:29).[3] In any event, Cardiff English bears no close relation to standard Welsh English pronunciation as this is characterized above. The features considered standard are, in most cases, just these which Cardiff English does *not* have. Conversely, most features identified as specifically Cardiff English features are negatively evaluated and avoided by 'careful' speakers in 'careful' contexts (see chapter 3). Because Cardiff English is generally far removed from the Welsh language as a living and even as a substratal influence, it cannot so easily be used to mark a speaker's 'Welsh' (as opposed to 'Cardiff') identity. For this reason (see chapter 4), Cardiff English has not naturally played a part in the revival of ethnicity in Wales and has in no way benefited from it. Thomas comments (1984: 178) that the model for the more 'evolved' dialects of the urban south Wales communities is the same as that for most other varieties of British English – RP and Standard (English) English – and this must be particularly true of Cardiff English. If so, we can expect this fact to be reflected in the patterns of internal differentiation that Cardiff English reveals.

3

Dialect and Social Structure

The most solid achievement of contemporary sociolinguistics is its ability to demonstrate and exemplify patterned linguistic variation in urban speech-communities. Central examples of this patterning are the social stratification and the stylistic stratification of language referred to in section 1.3 which show up as positive correlations between social and linguistic variables. This chapter will show that correlational studies of this sort can reveal patterned linguistic variation in the use of English in Cardiff when some of the linguistic features discussed in chapter 2 are quantified in various contexts. Nevertheless, there are various problems associated with correlational studies, and some of these, relating to the selection and quantification of independent variables, need to be examined first. (More general limitations of the correlational approach itself are discussed in the last section of this chapter.)

3.1   *Establishing independent variables*

In research into the relationship between social and linguistic parameters, it is not at all obvious which parameter, social or linguistic, and indeed if *either*, should be held as a constant, as the independent variable to be correlated with a defined dependent variable. The historical background to the development of sociolinguistics favoured a method which used 'social' facts as independent variables, since the intention was to provide evidence of patterned *linguistic* variation. But now that the existence of such patterned variation is firmly established, sociolinguists can accept that neither the social-to-linguistic nor the linguistic-to-social approach is theoretically more sound and that each can reveal its own insights. Nevertheless, it is the social-to-linguistic design that is most frequently adopted. In part,this reflects the clearly expressed priorities of some researchers (e.g. Trudgill in the Introduction to *Sociolinguistic Patterns in British English*, 1978) and doubtless other sociolinguists' views on their own areas of special competence – essentially in linguistics rather than sociology.

There are problems of validity associated with both research designs. As in Pellowe and Jones' study (1978) of intonational variation in Tyneside speech, it is possible to establish linguistic groupings as the independent variable and then examine whatever social correlates are to be found. The Tyneside study is, in fact, able to reveal correlations with sex and age of speaker and with family residence patterns. But as Macaulay says, '. . . the mere possibility of grouping several speakers into a "lect" does not prove that this is a linguistically *significant* group' (1978:142, emphasis added). Although detailed quantitative linguistic analyses can give us a good deal of confidence in the linguistic 'facts' we describe, the perceptual dimension – how speakers and listeners perceive or do not perceive the categories that are set up – remains unexplored.

More usually, correlational sociolinguistic research establishes independent variables on the basis of social classifications of various sorts. Such classification can be uncontroversial and objectively valid – as when speakers are grouped into males/females or into age-bands. Even here, though, it might be possible to see some subjective measure of, say, age as a potentially more significant variable: age as it is perceived and perhaps reflected in communicative strategies – so-called 'contextual age' (cf. Rubin and Rubin 1982). The classical Labovian approach, as it was described in chapter 1, is founded on particularly problematical social classifications in using socioeconomic status groupings and categories of situational types. In both of these cases, we cannot take the pre-existence of objective classifications for granted; we must recognize that 'social class' and contextual categories are not necessarily 'out there' before the study is conducted, and are no more than *models* of possible patterns of social organization. This perspective suggests that independent variables should be set up in accordance with specific criteria. Relevant criteria include:

(1)   that the independent variable should be of general *prima facie* relevance to the dependent variable. For example, it is quite plausible that sex should be associated with differences in phonological behaviour, since accent conventionally marks social roles and role-relationships. Trying to correlate dwelling-type with phonological behaviour would be more dubious by this criterion.

(2)   that the *categories* arrived at in constructing the independent variable should be potentially relevant to (i.e. be likely to show differentiation in) the independent variable. For example, if we set up educational background as a variable, we should recognize that taking versus not taking public examinations is a major distinction involving possible differences in attitude to formal education and therefore to standardness in language use. By contrast, the cut-off point between leaving school at fourteen and at

fifteen is less likely to be of such significance. Hypotheses like these may be supported or modified in the light of empirical findings.

These are common sense criteria and will be influenced by practical considerations like the size of the sample and the extent of variation it subsumes. But the criteria point to the fact that social and linguistic structures are not independent and not immutable. Social classifications – of people or of speaking contexts – may largely *depend on* patterns of linguistic behaviour; the initial classifications proposed may be supported or challenged by the correlational evidence itself. Because we may have to redefine the independent social categories in this way, a third criterion should be met:

(3)   that the categories arrived at in constructing the independent variable should be recoverable in the interpretation of the findings. That is, we should be able to relate our interpretations to readily identifiable aggregates of individuals or to natural contextual types. With social variables like age, categories are easily recoverable, but this is not necessarily the case with 'social class' which is idiosyncratically defined and quantified in the sociolinguistic literature.

Sociologists recognize the problems associated with the notion of class; cf. Littlejohn (1972:105):

'. . . in current sociology various conceptions of class are in use, class as an abstract economic function, as a collection of individuals sharing a common place in a hierarchy of social prestige or in the division of labour, and class as a collective representation.'

Marx distinguished two aspects of class – *class in itself*, the objective circumstances set for people by their position in the system of production, *and class for itself*, the collective consciousness and subsequent organization of individuals in response to their objective circumstances. This distinction is supported by a three-way distinction attributed to Max Weber into *class, status* and *power*. 'Class' in this latter sense is close to Marx's 'class in itself', referring to a 'group of individuals' '. . . accretion of economic advantage under the conditions of the commodity and labour markets' (Runciman 1966:38). 'Status' is concerned with social estimation and prestige, while 'power' clearly refers to the extent of a group's sovereignty, independent of its objective economic circumstances or its status in the community.

There can be little doubt that class distinction in a general sense continues to be a potent factor in contemporary British urban society (cf. Bottomore 1965, Littlejohn 1972, Westergard and Resler 1975) and therefore predictably plays an important role in motivating internal linguistic differentiation in British speech-communities. The problem is to devise a means of quantifying class in a meaningful way so that it can be used as a variable in correlational research. In Labovian sociolinguistic work, class has often been defined as a cluster of features and measured by quantifying individual social parameters like occupation, education, income, housing and locality which can be combined into a composite index of social class. Although the intention behind this method is to provide an objective assessment of class (cf. Trudgill 1974a:34), this approach arguably compounds the *subjectivity* involved in selecting and weighting individual social variables at the expense of others. We end up with an abstract numerical index of social class which does not directly relate to any identifiable group of individuals in the community.[1] Overall, it is preferable to accept that no assessment of class can be fully objective and work with individual social parameters (such as occupation group and educational background) which are relatively 'tangible' variables in their own right, but clearly contribute to the cluster of variables we call 'social class' or more appropriately (cf. Robinson 1979) 'socioeconomic status'.

Establishing contextual types as an independent variable, is an even more uncertain affair. Despite Labov's success in revealing the 'stylistic stratification' of speech within the interview-setting (see section 1.3, above), his method is clearly able to capture only a tiny part of that variation in language that may be labelled 'stylistic' or 'contextual' or 'diatypic' (cf. Gregory and Carroll 1978). Firstly, Labovian interviews allow only a very narrow definition of 'social context', when the sub-categories identified are 'casual', 'careful', 'reading' and 'word-list' styles. Only the first two of these are naturally occurring spontaneous speech-styles, as Labov himself points out (1972a:97), and we need to extend the study of stylistic variation to more naturalistic speaking-situations. Secondly, it is not necessary to assume that speech-styles will always show stratification – orderly differentiation in a single plane related to 'formality' (cf. Joos 1961) or 'amount of attention paid to speech' (Labov 1972a). Of course, this pattern of 'vertical' differentiation *will* be revealed by many social dialect features; it is presumably the uneven distribution of dialect forms across social classes that imbues these forms with social meanings and makes them available for meaningful style-shifting. But speakers can achieve more than this stylistically, as foreseen by Crystal and Davy in their outline of the scope of stylistic analsis:

'As a starting-point, we would say that the aim of stylistics is to analyse language habits with the main purpose of identifying, from the general mass of linguistic features common to English as used on every conceivable occasion, those features which are restricted to certain kinds of social context; to explain, where possible, why such features have been used, as opposed to other alternatives; and classify these features into categories based upon a view of their function in the social context. By "features" here, we mean *any* bit of speech or writing which a person can single out from the general flow of language and discuss – a particular word, part of a word, sequence of words, or way of uttering a word. A feature, when it is restricted in its occurrence to a limited number of social contexts we shall call a *stylistically significant* or *stylistically distinctive* feature . . .' (1969;10ff).

This programme of research acknowledges that stylistic variation reflects a wide spectrum of human motivation and conveys many different communicative effects beyond those that can be tapped by classical Labovian methods.

As with the social plane of variation, there is also the problem of establishing levels or categories of stylistic variables. Naturally situated speech does not often present itself neatly parcelled into contextual types, and there is a good deal of subjectivity involved in deciding what does and what does not constitute a change of context. Firth (1957) suggested four dimensions within his notion of a 'context of situation':

'– the spatio-temporal situation of persons in context . . . e.g. on a bus . . ., passing in the street.
– the activities of participants, e.g. buying a suit of clothes . . .
– speech functions, e.g. boasting, cursing . . .
– biographies of interlocutors, e.g. specific trade or profession, geographical and class origins . . .'

Applying Firth's analysis to the travel agency context (where some of the data reported in the next section were gathered), we might expect to find only one basic contextual type. Talk in the travel agency is spatio-temporally bounded; the activities of the participants generally centre around transacting travel agency business; certain speech functions recur (e.g. eliciting information, giving information, greeting, leave-taking, etc.); the 'biographies' of clients clearly differ, but the travel agency assistants are by definition of a 'specific trade or profession'. In reality, the extent of stylistic variation in the travel agency, particularly in the speech of the assistants as we shall see, is striking. To begin to detect it, however, we need to identify a range of micro-contexts – more detailed than Firth suggests – defined as combinations of situational components of the sort described by Crystal and Davy (1969), Ervin-Tripp (1964) and Hymes (1972a). But once again, contextual types are by no means definitive, merely the result of a subjective view about which situational components might be marked stylistically. As the travel agency studies will show, any deterministic approach which seeks to correlate pre-established social/stylistic categories with linguistic variants ultimately limits the explanatory potential of the research.

3.2 *Phonological sociolinguistic variables in Cardiff English*

As was noted in chapter 1, correlational sociolinguistic studies most commonly count frequencies of variants of segmental phonological variables to establish dependent measures. We have seen that there are many factors – some practical, some theoretical – favouring the analysis of phonological variables, but that the fundamental methods involved must be recognized to be problematical in various ways. We shall return to these problems in the interpretative section at the end of this chapter when an attempt is made to assess the significance of the quantitative studies of language and social structure in sections 3.3 and 3.4. This section identifies a number of phonological features which are socially and stylistically diagnostic in Cardiff and defines their use as variables in the studies that follow.

Variable (ng) So called 'G-dropping' – the alternative between velar and alveolar realizations of written 'ng' in words like *running, something, ceiling, meeting* – is an obvious candidate for detailed variation study as a pervasive British social dialect feature. Some comments have already been made about the (ng) variable (see section 1.3, above); the feature has been analysed in many British quantitative studies, including Trudgill 1974a; Mees[2] 1977, 1983; Douglas-Cowie 1978 and Reid 1978. The alveolar (non-standard) variant can be produced in all unstressed environments (in *something*, but not in *thing*; in *making*, but not in *King*) although it is probably most commonly associated with verbal *-ing* suffixes. As Mees notes (1977:34), assimilated variants do complicate the analysis of (ng) somewhat. In particular, the bilabial nasal [m] is common as the phonetic realization of 'ng' before a word beginning with a bilabial stop (as in ['sli:pɪm'pa:tnə] – *sleeping partner*). In such cases [m] realizations clearly need to be grouped with /n/ variants rather than /ŋ/. In passing, we can recognize that the alveolar variant does not have a totally consistent association with low prestige. Some people may still associate /n/ forms with aristocratic speech as in the stereotypical *huntin', shootin'* and *fishin'*; if so, for them the alveolar form of (ng) may be seen to carry its own prestige in some contexts.

Numerically, following the quantitative procedure described in section 1, velar variants are zero-scored and alveolar-type variants are assigned a score of 1:

(ng)	–	/ŋ/	–	0
	–	/n/	–	1

Expressed as percentages, 100 represents consistent non-standard usage and 0 consistent standard usage across a corpus of spoken text.

Variable (h) Preliminary observations of Cardiff speech show that /h/ is variably present/absent in the speech of many individuals, as it is in many varieties of English (cf. section 3.1 above). Since English /h/ occurs only in syllable-initial, prevocalic positions, it can be characterized as a strong, voiceless onset of the vowel in question (Gimson 1972:191). A voiced variant [ɦ] can occur between voiced sounds (as in *anyhow, behind, ahead*) and, as Mees notes, varies in perceptual prominence. For this reason, medial environments of (h) are ignored in the travel agency studies. Another decision to be taken is whether to include so called 'weak' forms which frequently lose /h/ in RP – *have, has, had* pronouns and pronominal adjectives (Gimson 1972:192). Mees excludes these forms from her 1977 analyses. In the travel agency data, however, clients and assistants 'aitch-drop' variably even with these 'weak' forms, so all potential occurrences of word-initial /h/ are included in those studies. The only exceptions are the set of items (including the frequent lexical item *hotel*) which can occur after *an*, when they are of course pronounced without /h/ by some standard speakers wanting to display their awareness of the forms' supposedly French etymology.

(h)	–	/h/	–	0
	–	zero	–	1

Variable (a:) This variable allows us to account for the qualitative variation to be found in Cardiff pronunciation of words like *carpet* RP /'kɑːpɪt/), *hard* (RP /hɑːd/), *after* (RP /'ɑːftə/) and the word *Cardiff* itself (RP /'kɑːdɪf/). As we have seen (in section 3.1.), there are many different pronunciation types in Cardiff English equivalent to RP /ɑː/, varying from an RP quality to an almost half-close front vowel [æː]. Mees converted this variation continuum into the following numerical scale (also shown diagramatically on the vowel trapezium in figure 3–1):

(a:)	–	0	[ɑ̞ː]
(a:)	–	1	[Aː] (where [A] represents a central, fully open phone)

(a:)   –   2   [a̱ː]
(a:)   –   3   [aː]
(a:)   –   4   [æː], [a̠ː]

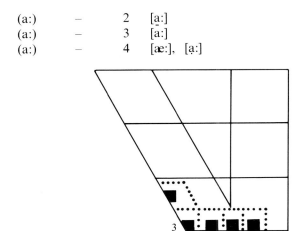

Fig. 3–1: Range of values for variable (a:), (after Mees 1977), with shaded areas indicating each variant's place of articulation

After applying this scale to the variants of (a:) produced over a stretch of spoken text, index-scores are calculated (following the usual procedure for three - or more term variables outlined in Labov 1972a) which range between 000 for consistent use of [ɑː] to 400 for consistent use of [æː] or [a̠ː]. As we have seen, this qualitative variation with the (a:) variable is complicated in Cardiff by the question of vowel length (cf. section 2.1 above). Cardiff English does not make as clear a distinction (quantitatively) between long /aː/ and short /a/ as RP does between /ɑː/ and /æ/; when the short and the long phonemes *are* distinguished, they are allocated to lexical items differently from RP. As a gesture in recognition of this complication, Mees excludes the words *chance, class* and *fastest* from her analysis since these words were sometimes pronounced with short [a] in her data.

Variable (ai) The RP diphthongh /aɪ/ in words such as *like, time, nine, quite* was phonemicized as /əi/ for Cardiff English in chapter 2. This reflected the Cardiff tendency to centralize the first element of the diphthong. Building on this observation, Mees established a three-term index-scale for (ai) as follows (again, shown diagramatically in figure 3–2):

(ai)   –   0   [äɪ]
(ai)   –   1   [ɐ̈ ï]
(ai)   –   2   [ə̞ ï]

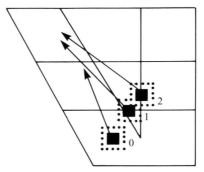

Fig. 3–2: Range of values for variable (ai), (after Mees 1977).

Interestingly, Mees does not refer to the [ɔ̈ɪ] variant which was described (in section 2.1) as the least standard realization of RP /aɪ/ in Cardiff, and which seems to be common in working-class male speech. After coding, Mees produced indices on a scale from 000 (consistent [äɪ] usage) to 200 (consistent [ə̣ ï] usage).

Variable (au) Like RP /aɪ/, the RP diphthong /aʊ/ in *now, Trowbridge*, etc. can have a central starting-point in Cardiff, in the area of schwa. This is the basic plane of phonetic variation that Mees uses to establish another 3-term variable, although the characteristic of the three variants (below) shows simultaneously varying realizations of the final element of the diphthong – from [ʊ] in the most standard variant to [ü] in the less standard variants. Figure 3–3 shows the phonetic space occupied by these variants diagrammatically.

(au)	–	0	[äʊ]
(au)	–	1	[ʙü]
(au)	–	2	[ə̣ü]

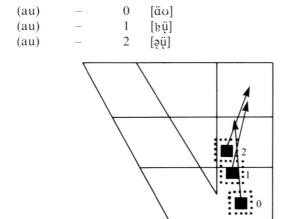

Fig. 3–3: Range of values for variable (au), (after Mees 1977).

Once again, index-scores potentially range from 000 for consistent [äʊ] usage to 200 for consistent [əʉ] usage.

Variable (ɔʊ)   The RP diphthong /ɔʊ/ in *know, coal, note* words often has a more retracted starting-point in Cardiff. This again suggests that a phonological variable can be set up based on the phonetic quality of the first element of a diphthong. In fact, Mees includes monophthongal [ö:] forms in her category of less standard variants, setting up a two-term variable as shown below, both in phonetic transcription and in the vowel trapezium in figure 3–4:

(ɔʊ)   –   0   [əʊ]
(ɔʊ)   –   1   [ö̈ö̈],[ö̈ʉ],[ö:]

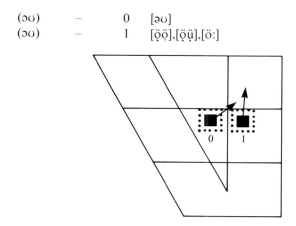

Fig. 3–4: Range of values for variable (ɔʊ), as analysed by Mees (1977).

The usual 0–100 index-scale can be set up on the basis of this two-term variable with lower index-values again representing more standard overall use of variants. The same variable is used to index differentiation in some of the travel agency data, although the monophthongal variant that Mees refers to is not attested there. As in Mees' study, centralization-retraction of the first element of (ɔʊ) is defined as the significant phonetic dimension, but it is also recognized that the retracted first element may by unrounded [ʌ̈] or rounded [ɔ̈] in non-standard usage. For the travel agency studies, then, variable (ɔʊ) is defined slightly differently, as follows:

(ɔʊ)   –   [əʊ]   –   0
(ɔʊ)   –   [ʌ̈ʊ], [ɔ̈ʊ]   –   1

Variable (r)   Cardiff English variably employs a single-tapped form [ɾ] as opposed to the standard post alveolar continuant [ɹ] and its own variants (voiced or devoiced fricatives following plosives). The tapped variant appears to be most common and most noticeable intervocalically (context (i)), so it is necessary to calculate percentages for different environments separately. The tap can also be realized in word-initial position (context (ii)) and less frequently in post-consonantal position. Percentage-scores calculated in the normal way for each of the principal environments of (r) may be averaged to produce a composite (r) index, still expressed as a percentage. In each environment:

(r)	–	[ɹ], [ɻ], [ɹ fricative]	– 0
(r)	–	[ɾ]	– 1

Variable (C Cluster). Simplification of final consonant clusters, particularly involving voiceless alveolar plosives, is a common feature of British English. It is noted even in descriptions of RP, but appears to be particularly prevalent in certain styles of Cardiff speech. As with (r), it is necessary to examine different types of cluster simplification separately. The linguistic environments in which alveolars are commonly lost are:

(i)   continuant consonant + /t/, followed by a word with an initial consonant other than /y/ or /h/ (e.g. *next day, left turn*), but excluding the reduced negative forms -*nt* (e.g. *didn't, can't*);

(ii)   the negative forms -*nt* followed by a word with an initial consonant;

(iii)   word-final /t/ + /s/ clusters formed by the reduction of *is* or *has* (e.g. *that's, it's*), where loss of the alveolar is particularly characteristic feature of Cardiff English.

In all cases, percentage-scores can be obtained on the basis of the following numerical allocation:
(C cluster) – alveolar elided   – 1
(C cluster) –   – 0, if the full form remains, or is replaced, for example, by [ʔ] or an assimilated form (e.g. ['ðaʔ'θɪŋ], ['laːsp'pɔʊst]).

Variable (intervoc. t) Between unstressed syllables or following a stressed syllable (particularly across a word-boundary), intervocalic /t/ may be realized in Cardiff as a voiced allophone [d̥] or as a tap [ɾ]. Cardiff is by no means the only dialect-area in Britain to show this feature. Wells (1982) takes the tapping of /t/ to be the origin of what he calls the T-to-R rule operating in the middle and far north of England (:370); /t/ voicing is also said to be 'very typical of Dublin working-class accents, particularly with men' (:430). Taken together, it is arguable that /t/ tapping, /t/ voicing and T-to-R constitute a pervasive social (rather than regional) dialect feature of British speech. For the studies to be reported below, percentage-scores are calculated on the following basis:

(intervoc. t)	–	/t/	–	0
(intervoc. t)	–	[t̮], [ɾ]	–	1

Mees in fact argues that non-standard (intervoc. t) variants occur almost exclusively with a limited lexical set of short, frequent words – those including *bit, get, lot*, etc. that were discussed in relation to /t/ elision at the end of section 2.1 – where the /t/ occurs at a word-boundary (e.g. *lot of, get a*). Word-medial intervocalic /t/ (e.g. *notice, fighting*) is less prone to voicing/tapping. Although these lexical and phonological constraints on the (intervoc. t) variable are not recognized in the definition of the variable given above, Mees' frequency-count of all sub-variants shows that an overwhelming majority of all syllable-final /t/s (between 85% and 90%) occur in the word-final/monosyllabic word category (Mees 1893:120). Therefore, very little numerical precision is lost in this case by adopting a relatively gross definition of a phonological variable.

3.3   *Dialect and socioeconomic class: 2 studies*

3.3.1.   *Social stratification in children's speech*

Inger Mees' study of aspects of the speech of Cardiff schoolchildren in 1977 was the first application of Labov's quantitative sociolinguistic methods to Cardiff data. She analysed tape-recordings of fifteen children, aged 9–11 years, reading a passage specially adapted to be easily read by children of that age-group. The children were selected from a sample of eighty children at school in nine city-districts. The fifteen children selected had lived all their lives in Cardiff and the parents of most of them were also Cardiffians. The fifteen were assigned to three social classes on the basis of their father's occupations, as assessed by the Office of Population Censuses and Surveys Classification of Occupations (1970):

Class 1 –	Professional and managerial (R.G. 1,2,3,4)
Class 2 –	Other non-manual workers including office-workers (R.G. 5,6)
Class 3 –	Manual workers, skilled and unskilled (R.G. 9,11,12).

Table 3–1: Averaged index-scores from six phonological variables for fifteen children, five in each of three socioeconomic classes (from Mees, 1977).

Index-scale		FATHER'S SOCIOECONOMIC CLASS		
		1 Professional & Managerial	2 Other non-manual	3 Manual
(ng)	%	006	043	083
(h)	%	000	000	020
(a:)	0–400	032	068	316
(ai)	0–200	110	142	163
(au)	0–200	060	110	170
(ɔʊ)	%	007	063	096

Index-scores for six phonological variables averaged across the five children in each social group are shown in table 3–1. Despite the small number of informants in each cell of the table, we see a consistent pattern of variation between the children's use of each of the sociolinguistic variables and their fathers' occupational class. As Mees says, this pattern confirms the general conclusions of other British studies which have pointed to the social stratification of language in urban communities. Moreover, the results show that even before the age of ten, children have assimilated consistent patterns of phonological variation and use them to mark their social provenance.

Beyond this general correlational pattern, however, individual variables pattern quite differently. Even from the table, we can see that some variables produce a 'shallow' gradient of more standard – less standard pronunciation: in particular (h) and (ai) where only about a quarter of the quantitative 'space' between maximally standard and maximally non-standard is used. Others ((ng), (ɔʊ) and perhaps (a:)) use almost the full range. The index-scores for *individual* children are even more revealing. They show that, with some variables, categorical (rather than variable) selection of variant is the norm.[3] So, with (ng), nine of the fifteen children show no variation in their choice of [ŋ] or [n], as shown in table 3–2.

Table 3–2: Individual index-scores for fifteen children in three social classes for variable (ng) (from Mees, 1977).

Index-scale	FATHER'S SOCIOECONOMIC CLASS		
	1 Professional & Managerial	2 Other non-manual	3 Manual
%	028 000 000 000 000	085 028 014 000 085	014 100 100 100 100

The (ɔu) variable presents a very similar picture, with twelve of the fifteen children using all standard or all non-standard variants. In fact, *all* children select (h) variants categorically; fourteen use standard /h/ consistently. On the other hand, variables (a:), (ai) and (au) are *never* used categorically in Mees' data.

Mees interprets these differences in the patterning of individual variables as the result of the different degrees of social significance attaching to those variables. In general, 'aitch-dropping' of course is a heavily and overtly stigmatized social dialect marker, so /h/ is carefully preserved in the reading-styles of all but one of the children in the context of a relatively formal interview at school. We might expect this to be true of (ng) and (a:) in Cardiff. Although non-standard variants of both these variables are used on quite a large scale by the schoolchildren, their overt stigmatization might be said to show up in the degree of categorical usage that we find. Those children who are aware of the stigmatizing of /n/ (mainly in class 1) studiously produce /ŋ/; those who are not (mainly in class 3) regularly say /n/. With (a:), the two 'non-manual' classes produce quite consistently (but not categorically) low scores, reflecting predominantly RP [ɑ:] and [A:] realizations of the long vowel and it is again reasonable to argue that the stigmatization of non-standard forms of (a:) is only apparent to the 'non-manual' speakers.

But inferring degrees of social significance from quantitative data alone is an uncertain affair. It is entirely plausible, for example, that *all* speakers are fully aware of the social stigma attaching to non-standard forms of (ng) and (a:) in Cardiff, but that some have overriding motives for continuing to produce these stigmatized forms. The question 'stigmatized *by whom?*' is also a relevant one, because what for one group is a marker of low social status or poor education may well be another group's symbol of in-group identity and allegiance. Again, there is the difficulty that statistics in the first instance reflect the methods used to produce them. A case in point is the (ɔʊ) variable which was defined in section 3.2 as a two-term variable without any clear phonetic scale detectable across the four variants listed. We have one RP-type variant [əʊ] and three equal-ranking less standard variants. Given this classification of the variant-forms, very different from the gradual phonetic progression we find with (a:), it is not surprising that we find high index-scores in the two 'lowest' social classes. Therefore, it is probably premature to draw Mees' conclusion (:44) – 'that this variable is heavily stigmatized for this particular class [class 1]. For the other two it has no great social significance.' (Interpretive problems of this sort associated with quantitative studies of sociolinguistic differentiation are taken up more fully in section 3.5.)

In her 1983 dissertation, Mees offered a more detailed study of thirty-six children (including those who took part in the earlier study), principally in respect of specified contexts of variables (r), (h), (ng) and (syllable-final /t/). Since the same children were tape-recorded for both studies, Mees was able to examine variation in her speech-data over time, as well as in relation to socioeconomic (occupational) class, sex and context. In brief, Mees found the significant differences expected across the three socioeconomic classes and the two speech-contexts (reading a text and formal interview-speech) with variables (r), (ng) and two contexts of (h): the lower classes and the interview-context were associated with more frequent occurrences of non-standard variants. Also, with (r) and (h) but *not* (ng), males generally produced less standard speech than females. On the other hand, glottalization of syllable-final /t/, which is a stigmatized form in most British English accents, seems to be a relatively *high* prestige feature in Mees' Cardiff data. The same variables showed very little overall difference in the children's speech at age ten and age fourteen. But as Mees says, 'the slight differences which were found indicated that the lower middle class females move slightly towards the prestige norm as they grow older, whereas the working class males tend to move away from the standard. As a result, the class distinctions become more marked' (1983:275).

3.3.2.   *Social stratification in the travel agency*

At this point we can turn to a study of the social stratification of language in Cardiff which builds on Inger Mees' work but uses data gathered in an entirely different setting. The basic methods used to gather data in the travel agency were discussed in section 1.6, where the advantage of working

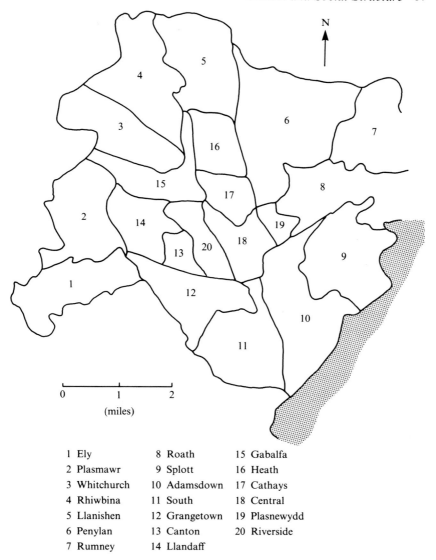

1 Ely	8 Roath	15 Gabalfa
2 Plasmawr	9 Splott	16 Heath
3 Whitchurch	10 Adamsdown	17 Cathays
4 Rhiwbina	11 South	18 Central
5 Llanishen	12 Grangetown	19 Plasnewydd
6 Penylan	13 Canton	20 Riverside
7 Rumney	14 Llandaff	

Fig 3–5: District wards in the Cardiff City area.

with naturally occurring and situated data were stressed. It would clearly be valuable to determine whether the patterns of social differentiation that researchers like Labov, Trudgill, Macaulay (and others, including Mees in Cardiff) have revealed through relatively structured interviews show up in the totally uncontrolled, spontaneous speech of travel agency clients. In all, fifty-one encounters were selected for transcription and analysis. The main criterion used in selecting these from the total number of encounters recorded (after the initial 'settling in' period) was that individual subjects should be 'residents of Cardiff'. This was defined as those who had been born in one of the city electoral wards shown in figure 3–5 and had lived in Cardiff for the last ten years or more. In this selection process, eighteen individuals were omitted, as were a further four whose permission to use the recordings was not obtained. However, none of these four in fact refused permission; they were not prepared to stop and listen to the initial explanation of the nature of the research.

Each of the fifty-one adult clients was interviewed briefly as she/he left the office. They were asked for their permission to use the tape-recordings made and then to supply information about their birth-place, area of residence over the last ten years, age, occupation (where possible over the last ten years) and educational background. No names or addresses were asked for, which helped to reassure clients about the confidentiality of the research. Information about education was obtained in the form of coded bands; subjects were asked to specify appropriate code-letters (A–F) from cards. The distribution of the fifty-one subjects across education groups is shown in table 3–3. Occupations were sub-classified into the Office of

Table 3–3: Classification of fifty-one clients into education groups.

	EDUCATION GROUPS					
	Left school at			O-level/ CSE	A-level	College/ Univ.
	13 –	14	15 +			
(M)	0	2	4	6	1	7
(F)	1	8	9	6	1	6
All	1	10	13	12	2	13

Population Censuses and Surveys Classification of Occupation' (1970) 'social class' groupings. This classifies occupations into six groups:

I   Professional, etc. occupations
II   Intermediate occupations
III   Skilled occupations
      (N)   non-manual
      (M)   manual
IV   Partly skilled occupations
V   Unskilled occupations

Each individual's occupation is listed under the appropriate 'social class' group heading in table 3–4, together with sex coding. In this listing, permanently unemployed females are coded according to their husbands' occupations (marked *). The need to treat occupation and educational background as distinct (though related) independent variables was argued in section 3.1 above. For the data reported here, this same need is clearly shown by figure 3–6 which compares the occupational and educational characteristics of the fifty-one clients. Although terminal education age is a good predictor of occupational class at the extremities of the social scale, it seems that occupation groups II and IIIN contain individuals with widely varying educational backgrounds.

The fifty-one clients are obviously not a truly random sample (not a 'simple random sample', cf. Babbie 1973, Federer 1973) representative of the population of Cardiff as a whole. The well-developed sampling procedures used in large-scale survey research are not compatible with the data-collection methods described above because no rigid criteria can be used for selecting subjects. The sample can be described – it is the range of potential clients able to visit the travel agency at the time when recordings were being made – but cannot be specified in advance. As a result, subjects are unevenly distributed across the social categories (in tables 3–3 and 3–4), though, as we shall see, this does not prevent patterns of sociolinguistic differentiation emerging. In fact, the original occupation and education classifications can be quite conveniently 'collapsed' to give reasonable distributions of individuals across the social categories, as shown in tables 3–5 and 3–6. One difficulty is the ratio of females to males in occupation group IIIN and in education group 1, although allowance is made for this unevenness in the interpretation of the social differentiation findings.

Variables (h), (ng), (r), (C cluster) and (intervoc. t) were chosen for the quantitative analysis of the clients' speech. This was principally because consonantal variables are simpler to analyse reliably over very large corpuses of spoken text. (h)'s failure to discriminate the social groups in Mees' study seemed entirely attributable to the speaking context, so the variable was included here. As soon as realizations of the five variables were examined, quantifiable differences in phonological styles began to emerge.

Table 3–4: Classification of fifty-one clients into six occupational groups.

Occupation Groups

I	II	IIIN	IIIM	IV	V
05 Chartered Surveyor (M)	14 Teacher (F)	01 Organisational methods assistant (F)	07 Plumber (M)	13 Prison officer (M)	25 Factory girl (F)
23 Company director (F*) of ch. accnts.	20 Nursing Officer (F)	15 Clerk (F)	08 Engineer (F*)	56 Waitress (F)	
62 Optician (F*)	24 Lecturer (M)	19 Clerk (M)	11 Steelworker (M)	60 Waitress (F)	
63 Engineer (M)	28 Teacher (M)	21 Car salesman (F*)	12 Steelworker (F*)		
65 Doctor (M)	34 Staff nurse (F)	26 Clerk (F)	27 Steelworker (M)		
	35 Company director (M)	27a Clerk (F*)	31 Printer's assistant (M)		
	44 Farmer (F*)	29 Secretary (F)	37 Electrician (F*)		
	52 Area manager (M)	30 Clerk (M)	45 Mechanical fitter (M)		
	53 Nurse (F)	32 Secretary (F)	50 Shop manageress (F)		
	55 Health/Safety Inspector (M)	33 Receptionist (F)			
	59 Sales Manager				

61 Assistant secretary administrative officer (M)	40 Ins. administrative superintendent (F*)	58 Steelworker (F*)
67 Teacher (F)	48 Clerk (F)	62a Bricklayer (M)
68 Union officer (M)	51 Chemist's assistant (F)	66 Mobile Plant driver (M)
	57 Clerk (F)	
	64 Secretary (F)	
(M) – 3	(M) – 2	(M) – 1
(F) – 2	(F) – 14	(F) – 2
All – 5	All – 12	All – 3

(M) – 7	(M) – 7	(M) – 0
(F) – 7	(F) – 5	(F) – 1
All – 14	All – 16	All – 1

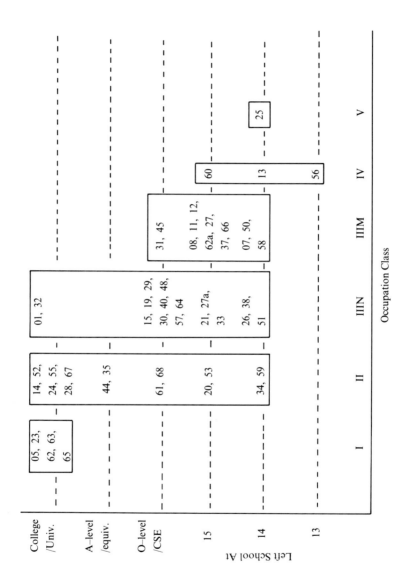

Fig. 3–6: Educational background and occupation characteristics of the fifty-one travel agency clients.

Table 3–5: Three-way classification of the fifty-one clients by occupation.

1 (N = 19)	OCCUPATION GROUPS 2 (N = 16)	3 (N = 16)
Professional & intermediate 'social classes' I & II	Skilled non manual & unskilled 'social class' IIIN	Skilled manual, partly skilled 'social classes' IIIM, IV & V
(M) = 10 (F) = 9	2 14	8) 8) = 51

Table 3–6: Three-way classification of the fifty-one clients by educational background.

1 (N = 24)	EDUCATION GROUPS 2 (N = 13)	3 (N = 14)
No public examinations	O-level/CSE/ A-level	College/ Univ.
(M) = 6 (F) = 18	7 7	7) 6) = 51

Consider the following two extracts. S denotes the assistant (Sue) and C a client; more standard variants are marked with the figure 0, less standard variants with 1; particular variables are identified by symbols which are explained in the key following the extracts. The extracts have been selected to give an impression of the phonological range across different clients in the travel agency data. For this reason, phonological variants in Sue's speaking turns have not been marked in extracts 3–1 and 3–2. Client 23, in fact, does not produce any non-standard variants of the five variables in the extract reproduced above, as shown by the figure 0 below each occurrence of the variable. Client 60, on the other hand produces a high proportion of non-standard variants. Both clients are female, but have very different socioeconomic backgrounds as assessed by occupational class

Extract 3–1
Client 23

line

1. S.   can I help you?

                                    (h)
     C.   um   well we we'd like a holiday
                                         0
                           (ng)
           a week ten days or something between the
                                   0
                         (t)   (ng)
           um   eighteenth April and the beginning of
                    0   0

5.   <u>June</u>   and er

     S.   any idea where you want to <u>go</u>?

               (t)
     C.   we <u>sort</u> of ummed and ahed about <u>Tangier</u>
             0

     S.   yes

               (Cii)   (ri)   (t)
     C.   I don't know whether it but er   but you know we
               0   0   0
                                                   (Ciii)
10.   we've got two small <u>children</u> we've got it's got
                                                       0
                         (t)
           to be somewhere that is s-<u>suitable</u> with nice the
                          0
           (rii)   (t)   (Ciii)
           reason we thought of Tangier it's got quite
           0   0   0
                         (h)
           nice <u>beaches</u> hasn't it?
                          0

     S.   mm the only problem is if you <u>are</u> going to

15. .   Tangier for the <u>children</u> it's very isolated

that's the only problem.

          (t)
C.   what do you mean isolated?
          0

S.   um well you're just going to have the hotel and

the beach that's all you're going to have really

          (Cii)   (ng)
20. C.   I'm sure they don't want anything else.
                   0   0

Extract 3–2
Client 60

line

        (t) (h)   (Ciii)
1. C. I've got a holiday it's the Global book summer one
          1   0   1

for Portugal   ((unintelligible))

S.   oh we've held an option for you have we?

        (Cii)   (ng)
C.   no well you can't can you I'm going in a
          0   1

5.   fortnight's time

S.   oh . . . (another assistant hands over the details)

            (t) (t) (rii)   (h)
C.   oh she's got it all ready // has she?
               1 0   1   1

S.   yeah can I just finish doing this? I won't be

a minute oh I've got it here I think

        (h)   (t)
10. C. I should have come in yesterday but I
         1   1

(Cii)
couldn't er //   (( ))
1

S.   that's right she'd <u>asked</u> if you'd been in //

.   and I said <u>no</u>.

(t)   (ng)   (ng)
C.   /yeah/ oh I've got a <u>stinking</u> cold coming on //
0   1   1

15.   <u>honest</u>

S.   oh <u>have</u> // you?

(Ciii) (t)   (h)   (Ciii)
C.   it's not a cold a <u>head</u> cold it's all in my
1   1   0   1

.   <u>ears</u> and my <u>neck</u> // you know

S.   oh there's <u>awful</u>.

Key to symbols
Bracketed symbols identify particular variables:
(C)   – consonant cluster, i/ii/iii – contexts (i),(ii) and (iii), as defined in section 3.2.
(r)   – variable (r), contexts (i) and (ii)
(h)   – variable (h)
(ng)   – variable (ng)
(t)   – variable (intervoc.t)
0/1 below the text identify more and less standard variants respectively.

and education class. Details of the two clients are given below, together with the percentages of their use of non-standard variants of all five variables over the complete encounters in which they are involved:

Client 23 – Company director's wife (occupation class I); education group F; abode: Llanishen

| (h) | (ng) | (ri) | (rii) | (C cluster) | | | (intervoc.t) |
				(i)	(ii)	(iii)	
0%	0	0	0	0	41.7	33.3	0

Client 60 – Waitress (occupation class IV);
education group C; abode; Llanedeyrn

(h)	(ng)	(ri)	(rii)	(C cluster) (i)	(ii)	(iii)	(intervoc.t)
71.0%	88.2	66.7	14.3	45.5	87.1	88.0	88.5

These two informants represent virtually the extremes of the scale of phonological variation apparent in the travel agency data. We can predict that, between these extremes, we will find regular strata of phonological behaviour which match the social strata that result from, for instance, occupational or educational background classifications.

The speech of all fifty-one clients in conversation with the same assistant was transcribed and analysed, and frequencies of occurrence of the less standard variants of all variables were calculated for each individual. Individuals' percentage were then averaged to produce group means for each variable for three occupation groups, as shown in table 3–7.
Mean deviation – the mean of individuals' scores' deviation from the mean percentage shown in each cell – is quoted to give an indication of the extent of variation within each sub-group. Individuals who produced fewer than four instances of any variable were excluded from the means for that variable, so N-values are reported in each cell, showing the number of individuals on whose speech the group means are based. The relative infrequency of certain forms is problematical, particularly in the case of variables where sub-scores have been calculated for different linguistic environments. Nevertheless, we find strong evidence of social stratification in the clients' use of most phonological variables. Variables (h), (ng) and (intervoc.t) prove to be excellent markers of occupation class. All three contexts of (C cluster) show a certain amount of stratification, with the third context (word final/t/ + /s/ clusters formed by the reduction of *is* or *has*) producing the greatest amount of differentiation. Because all three (C cluster) contexts show stratification, it is reasonable to combine them by percentages to give a single index for all (C cluster). Conversely, the single index for (r) shown in the table is somewhat misleading, seeing that the second (r) context (word initial position) shows no regular differentiation and the first context (intervocalic) can only distinguish 'manual' speakers from others. Values of 'All (r)' are bracketed in the table for this reason.

It is interesting to ask whether a more delicate social classification still shows the pattern of social stratification in table 3–8. Table 3–8 shows scores for the five variables for individuals in all six original occupation groups. Although the N-values are very small in some of the cells, especially

Table 3–7: % ages of less standard variants of five phonological variables in three occupation groups. (% ages are group means of individual % ages.)

	OCCUPATION GROUPS		
	1 Professional & intermediate N = 19	2 Skilled non manual N = 16	3 Skilled manual, partly skilled & unskilled N = 16
(h)	12.9 N = 13 MD = 18.4	16.3 N = 10 MD = 14.5	74.1 N = 11 MD = 22.1
(ng)	7.5 N = 10 MD = 12.0	41.8 N = 9 MD = 26.4	75.6 N = 10 MD = 27.0
(ri) (rii) All (r) by %	29.8 N = 11 MD = 35.2 9.0 N = 5 MD = 10.8 (19.4)	26.8 N = 10 MD = 24.6 4.8 N = 7 MD = 8.2 (15.8)	55.3 N = 11 MD = 36.6 11.9 N = 4 MD = 11.9 (33.6)
(C cluster) (i) (ii) (iii) All(C clus.) by %	37.2 N = 6 MD = 26.1 55.5 N = 9 MD = 14.2 23.7 N = 7 MD = 16.5 38.8	59.1 N = 9 MD = 23.4 68.1 N = 8 MD = 11.4 52.3 N = 7 MD = 20.6 59.8	64.0 N = 8 MD = 19.3 80.3 N = 8 MD = 21.4 73.1 N = 5 MD = 19.5 72.5
(intervoc t)	10.0 N = 9 MD = 13.3	42.1 N = 11 MD = 20.6	66.1 N = 8 MD = 22.0

Table 3–8: % ages of less standard variants of five phonological variables in six occupation groups showing social stratification. (% ages are group means of individual % ages.)

OCCUPATION

	I Professional	II Intermediate	IIIN Skilled non-manual	IIIM Skilled manual	IV Partly skilled	V Unskilled
(h)	16.7 N = 2	12.3 = 11	16.3 = 10	68.9 = 7	88.7 = 3	(66.7) = 1
(ng)	0.0 = 2	9.4 = 8	41.8 = 9	68.9 = 6	73.8 = 3	(100) = 1
(ri)	8.3 = 3	37.9 = 8	26.8 = 10	62.5 = 8	83.4 = 2	(66.7) = 1
(rii)	0.0 = 2	15.0 = 3	4.8 = 7	11.1 = 3	(14.3) = 1	–
All (r) by %	(4.2)	(26.5)	(25.8)	(36.8)	(48.9)	(66.7)
(C cluster) (i)	0.0 = 1	44.9 = 5	59.1 = 9	62.5 = 4	54.1 = 3	(66.7) = 1
(ii)	60.4 = 4	51.7 = 5	68.1 = 8	63.8 = 4	95.7 = 3	(66.7) = 1
(iii)	41.7 = 2	7.8 = 5	52.3 = 7	65.8 = 3	84.0 = 2	–
All (C clus) by %	34.0	34.8	59.8	64.0	77.9	(66.7)
(inter-voc.t)	0.0 = 2	12.8 = 7	42.1 = 11	58.7 = 5	77.6 = 2	(80.0) = 1
Mean of 5 variables	11.0	19.2	37.2	59.5	73.4	(82.7)

for groups I, IV and V, the basic pattern of social stratification again emerges. (ng) and (intervoc.t) succeed in ranking all six groups linguistically as they are ranked socially. If we exclude the (r) variable as a less reliable social indicator, then the perfect patterning of linguistic values and occupational classes is broken only where N-values are too small to be considered significant. In general, it is again the case that different overall levels of phonological standardness characterize different occupation groups in the travel agency data; these groups are ranked very similarly according to occupational and phonological criteria.

Occupation class is only one of many socially relevant dimensions. Information about the educational background of the travel agency clients was also collected, and table 3–9 shows the relationship between education group and phonological behaviour. (Only the most successful variables are included.) The table shows that, with three of the four variables, social and

Table 3–9: % ages of less standard variants of three variables by education group of fifty-one clients.

	EDUCATION GROUPS		
	1 No public examinations	2 A-/O-level /CSE	3 College/ University
(h)	52.1 (169)	19.6 (46)	9.8 (51)
(ng)	65.2 (89)	35.3 (35)	3.3 (30)
(intervoc.t)	60.7 (112)	38.2 (34)	42.2 (45)
all (C cluster)	66.9 (254)	54.8 (88)	39.0 (123)

linguistic variables again co-vary; the clients' educational background is reflected in the rankings by clients' use of variables (h), (ng) and (C cluster). The pattern is broken by the (intervoc.t) variable, although, with (h) too, education groups 2 and 3 are not clearly distinct. But it seems that at least two broad educational groups in the travel agency population are clearly differentiated according to linguistic criteria. The boundary between those who remained in the education system to take public examinations and those who did not is reflected in patterns of phonological behaviour.

A number of sociolinguistic studies have shown regular differences in pronunciation between men and women (cf. Labov 1972a, Shuy 1970, Trudgill 1975, 1983 and reviews by Bodine 1975, Smith 1979 and Kramarae 1982). Smith (:112) draws the conclusion that women are relatively more standard speakers from men from repeated findings that, in a given context and a given socioeconomic group, females regularly produce a higher percentage of more standard phonological (and other) forms than males do. It is important to find out whether and to what extent sex differences in pronunciation are present in the travel agency data, particularly because they are a possible source of error in the findings quoted so far. (As noted earlier, the occupation and education group were not fully matched for sex.) Some of the data shown in table 3–7 were reanalysed to examine the amount of sex differentiation within the groups. As previously indicated, occupation groups 1 and 3 (Professional and Intermediate; Skilled Manual, Partly Skilled and Unskilled) have almost even distribution of males and females. Group 1 includes ten males and nine females; group 3 has eight males and eight females. It is group 2 (Skilled Non Manual) where we can expect the results to be weighted towards the female mean, since females in this group outweigh males by fourteen to two. The mean values of three variables for males and females (separately) in groups 1 and 3 are shown in table 3–10.

Table 3–10: % ages of less standard variants of three phonological variables showing sex differentiation.

OCCUPATION GROUPS				
	Professional & Intermediate		Skilled manual, Partly skilled & Unskilled	
	FEMALE	MALE	FEMALE	MALE
(h)	5.4	25.0	72.7	75.3
(ng)	0.0	12.5	59.5	86.9
(intervoc.t)	3.9	22.2	57.0	81.1

The normal pattern of females using a higher proportion of more standard forms than males shows up well in the table with differences in some cases of over twenty percentage points. From this, we have to conclude that the variable-values for occupation class 2 (skilled non manual) reported above are artificially low, i.e. weighted towards the 'standard' end of the scale, although not so as to interfere with the overall ranking of occupation groups. Similarly, we can now refine our interpretation of the education group results table 3–9 and argue, principally, that the values for Group 1 would be somewhat higher if that group had comprised sex-matched sub-groups.[4]

3.4   *Dialect and situation*

It is useful to conceptualize the correlational patterns shown in the last section as a single plane of sociolinguistic variation (often rather confusingly labelled the 'social' plane of variation). The image is of a two-dimensional plane segmented in various ways to reflect the graduated patterns of dialectal usage across geographical, socioeconomic class, sex or other social groupings. Of course this is an idealized conceptualization, because there is an unlimited number of possible social groupings and the two-dimensional figure permits only two social parameters to be represented – perhaps geographical space and socioeconomic class, as in Trudgill's triangular model discussed in Section 1.1. By adding a third dimension to this plane, as in figure 3–7, we can model linguistic variation across different social contexts. Whereas the 'horizontal' plane relates to variation across language users, the 'vertical' plane here relates to variation across language uses; 'dialect' in Halliday's sense is intersected by 'register'. Once again it is an idealized representation, because there are as many possible categories of social contexts as there are of social groups.

We have seen (in section 1.3) that Labovian methods are able to demonstrate clearly one fundamental relation between dialect and register, between 'social' and 'stylistic' linguistic variation. By consciously manipulating levels of formality and involving subjects in different sorts of activities during interviews, Labov established different 'situations' and showed that correspondingly different levels of phonological standardness were associated with them. Since the situations were arguably ranked in terms of formality or in 'amount of attention paid to speech', it was appropriate to see the situational types as 'stylistically stratified' (Labov 1972a). For a given social (socioeconomic class) group, numerical indices of particular sociolinguistic variables were ranked in the same order as the situations where the data were gathered. Within a given situational type, the ranking of index-values would (with some interesting exceptions)[5]

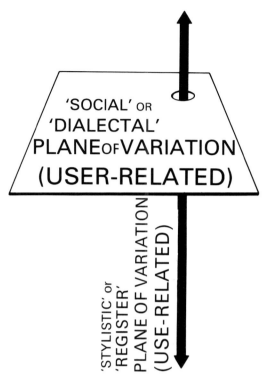

Fig 3–7: Planes of sociolinguistic variation.

reflect differences in socioeconomic status between groups of speakers. The interplay of 'social' and 'stylistic' variation could be summarized as a matrix of indices with values generally increasing in both 'vertical' and 'horizontal' dimensions. Such a matrix could in turn be translated into a graph like that of figure 1–1 (in section 1.3). Using these methods, Labov and others were able to demonstrate that phonological styles could be systematically studied in a quantitative way. There was no suggestion, however, that the methods themselves were definitive. Labov made it clear that he was seeking to establish the 'principles behind the methods' as a foundation for future studies rather than particular methods themselves (1972a: 109). One priority was to take the study of stylistic variation away from Labovian interviews into more naturalistic settings, to begin to explore how speakers shift their speaking-styles in more spontaneous interaction.

A few British sociolinguistic studies have already succeeded in showing naturally-situated stylistic variation. As part of her work on morphological and syntactic variation in Reading (referred to in section 2.2), Cheshire (1978, 1982) analysed children's speech in two settings – adventure-playgrounds and at school. She found that the children used fewer non-standard verb forms at school and perhaps most interestingly that the differences between school and playground speech were greater for girls than for boys. Reid (1978) quantified sixteen eleven-year-old boys' use of two phonological variables across four speaking-situations. The first two situations were typical of the standard Labovian approach – reading from a specially prepared passage and speech recorded in formal interviews. But Reid also recorded individual boys in informal conversation with class-mates and (using radio microphones) playing in the playground. He found that (with one exception) '. . . the process represented by the moves from reading aloud a passage into a tape-recorder, through answering questions posed by an adult stranger, to talking with friends in the presence of an adult, and finally to playing with friends in the playground, is reflected systematically in the increase in indices for both variables, especially when the informants are considered as a single group' (:163). Douglas-Cowie (1978) found that ten adult informants in a Northern Irish village regularly produced more standard speech (in respect of six sociolinguistic variables) in secretly recorded conversations with an English 'outsider' than in paired conversations among themselves in the same setting. She also found that informants who adjusted their speech for the 'outsider' tended to return to a less standard style after an hour of conversation, and that certain topics of conversation (such as occupation and education) encouraged subjects to use more standard forms.

These studies convincingly show that regular stylistic variation is not restricted to consciously contrived research contexts, but is a common, perhaps a universal, feature of naturally situated speech in day-to-day life. In Douglas-Cowie's research there is also the suggestion that studies need to be sensitively designed if we are to explore the nature and extent of this plane of linguistic variation. In particular, lumping together aggregates of individuals in widely discrepant 'situations' leads to rather uninteresting generalizations about stylistic levels. On the other hand, more detailed analysis of individual instances leads to more revealing observations like Douglas-Cowie's about topic and time. As Bickerton (1975: 301) has said, we need to account for '. . . the complex and subtle interplay of forces which brings about the continuous fluctuation in the stylistic levels of actual speech'. Whereas so-called 'social' differentiation in language is a property of the community, stylistic differentiation is essentially a property of the individual. For this reason, there is much to be gained from in-depth study of individual instances of stylistic variation. The Cardiff travel agency recordings proved to be an excellent data-source for a detailed case-study of stylistic variation. As we have seen (in sections 1.6 and 3.1), the travel agency assistants are involved in a very wide range of linguistic activities, and we can expect their speaking-styles to reflect the moment-to-moment situational shifts and fluctuations. The following investigation gives a clear impression of the stylistic range used by one assistant, Sue, in the course of her working day and of how her pronunciation-style shifts in response to a range of social factors. The assistant's pronunciation shows recognizable Cardiff English features in all of its styles, so the style-shifts can be quantified in the usual way using some of the sociolinguistic variables described in section 3.2.

The initial problem is to arrive at a workable classification of situational types within which to quantify the selected variables. To do this, we can draw on well-known taxonomies of situational components, selecting those components which are most relevant in the travel agency setting. Two components – 'participants' and 'topic' – (together with a third – physical 'setting' – which is invariant here) are considered central in the taxonomies of Crystal and Davy (1969), Ervin-Tripp (1964) and Hymes (1972a). Sankoff (1972:35) also suggests that these factors are '. . . the most powerful in predicting language choice.' Another relevant component in the travel agency context is 'channel' or 'medium', to distinguish between face-to-face and telephone talk (coded as $-T$ and $+T$ respectively). By treating these components as systems composed of various terms, we can isolate speaking-contexts defined as unique combinations of stylistic determinants. So, 'participants' comprises Sue's colleagues at work who are also personal friends (F), clients (C) and other travel agents and tour-operators (A) who are addressed over the telephone. Under 'topic' a gross word-related ($+W$) versus work-unrelated ($-W$) distinction is a reasonable first classification. Despite the fact that these three groups of situational determinants have been chosen unsystematically, it is interesting that they correspond generally to Halliday's three-way sub-classification of register – into field ('topic), mode ('channel') and tenor ('participants') (cf. Halliday 1978, Gregory and Carroll 1978). The categories established above can be summarized as follows:

Channel	Participants	Topic
$+T$ / $-T$	F / C / A	$+W$ / $-W$

These dimensions are far from independent, of course, as a choice in one system restricts choices made in the others, sometimes almost by definition, sometimes by chance. For example, the assistant always selects $+W$ topics when addressing C or A, and it happens that, in the data used here, she speaks only to A when on the telephone. Constraints like these allow us to recognize four contextual types, and therefore the possibility of four contextual styles being used, as shown in figure 3–8. In this figure, the four possible styles are given arbitrary labels (in the right hand column) for ease of reference.

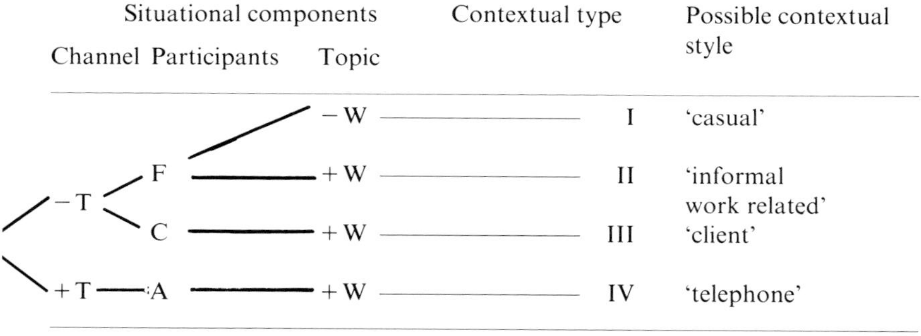

Situational components			Contextual type	Possible contextual style
Channel	Participants	Topic		

Fig. 3–8: The derivation of four contextual types from three situational components.

For the purposes of this investigation, fifteen extracts were randomly chosen from the recordings of Sue's speech. These extracts were then classified into the four contextual types shown in figure 3–8. Four of the fifteen extracts were contextually 'complex': that is, they included changes in channel and/or participants and/or topic, as in the continuous fragment reproduced as extract 3–3, where the contextual types are bracketed to the left of the text. The extract begins with Sue speaking on the telephone to a tour-operator about a work-related topic (channel $+T$, participants A, topic $+W$). At line 7 of the transcript she puts down the receiver and

Extract 3–3 (Sue is on the telephone)
line
1.　Contextual　(IV)　... oh hello   it's H. Travel Cardiff
　　　　type　　　　　your flight London Barcelona?
　　　　　　　　　　twenty three July; the a oh can I
　　　　　　　　　　ring back?   yeah   shall I ring
5.　　　　　　　　　you back?   er how long?   OK
　　　　　　　　　　then fine   bye
　　　　　　　(II)　computers are down   mm everywhere
　　　　　　　　　　you ring lately   I better ring her
　　　　　　　　　　back and tell her not to keep her
10.　　　　　　　　client there hadn't I?
　　　　　　　(I)　how's er Barbara's boyfriend enjoying
　　　　　　　　　　his new job? ...

Table 3–11: Percentages of less standard variants of five linguistic variables in four contextual types (figures in brackets are the numbers of individual tokens).

SOCIOLINGUISTIC VARIABLES

CONTEXTUAL TYPES	(h)	(r) (i) inter-voc.	(r) (ii) initial	All (r) by %	(C cluster) (i)	(C cluster) (ii)	(C cluster) (iii)	All (C clus) by %	(inter-voc.t)	(ɔʊ)	Mean of % ages for five variables
I 'Casual'	85 (27)	71 (7)	9 (11)	40	100 (5)	83 (29)	80 (20)	88	86 (14)	88 (33)	77
II 'informal work-related'	60 (30)	50 (10)	21 (14)	36	73 (11)	71 (14)	44 (9)	63	55 (11)	66 (12)	56
III 'client'	14 (28)	33 (15)	12 (8)	23	40 (15)	52 (23)	26 (27)	39	33 (27)	61 (18)	34
IV 'telephone'	19 (37)	14 (7)	16 (16)	15	38 (8)	71 (7)	18 (11)	42	38 (8)	46 (46)	32

addresses a colleague about computers and clients ($-$T, F, $+$W). At line 11, again to her colleague, Sue shifts topic to discuss a work-unrelated matter ($-$T, F, $-$W). These three combinations of components are analysed respectively as contextual types (IV), (II) and (I), as in figure 3–8, above.

Quantitative indices for five of the phonological variables (described in section 3.2) were then calculated for each of the contextual types across all fifteen extracts. The results are shown in table 3–11. The percentages for the five variables show that three of the four contextual types correlate with significantly different linguistic usage and are ranked overall in the order 'casual', 'informal work-related' and 'client'/'telephone', with the last two types not clearly distinguished. All variables show themselves in this case to be sensitive markers of contextual types with the exception of the initial context of (r) – (rii).

It seems, then, that Sue's stylistic repertoire at work can be statistically characterized with reference to the three situational components – participants, channel and topic, and it is tempting to conclude that she operates with three broadly distinguishable styles: a casual style for general conversations with colleagues, a rather less casual style for discussing work matters (again with her colleagues) and a formal style for use with clients and with other travel agents on the telephone. Of course, frequencies for different variables differ considerably, even when they produce the same rank-ordering of contextual types. This is inevitable, particularly since the less standard variants of some variables – (h), (intervoc.t) and (C cluster) – are overtly recognized, stereotypical Cardiff English forms and are heavily stigmatized, appearing frequently in the 'casual' and 'informal' styles and quite rarely elsewhere. Nevertheless, table 3–11 shows that it is possible to find stylistic stratification across spontaneously recurring, everyday speaking-situations. The structural components of routine social events, no less than the structural components of speech communities, can be marked by levels of dialectal standardness. Not only does dialect mark an individual's (or a group's) habitual position relative to others, but it can also mark his/her momentary activities and preoccupations in day-to-day life.

3.5   *Overview*

The studies of social and stylistic stratification in sections 3.3 and 3.4 have been presented with little interpretive comment. These studies have used similar methods, have provided generally similar insights and are open to the same criticisms. As a result, it will be convenient to assess their validity and significance together in this section. We can only assess a body of research in relation to its aims, and here we run up against what has been held to be an uncertainty in Labovian sociolinguistics – Halliday's view (quoted in section 1.4) that 'sociolinguistics sometimes appears to be a search for answers which have no questions.'Not taking this comment too literally, let us assume that quantitative sociolinguistic studies *do*, in fact set out to answer valid questions, and that these questions are firstly to do with the description of how language varies in society, and secondly to do with why such variation exists and what its implications are. Correspondingly, we need to assess firstly the descriptive adequacy, then the explanatory adequacy of the studies in question.

The quantitative studies have described the co-variation of selected aspects of Cardiff English and some inter-personal and intra-personal dimensions of social structure. Two different populations of Cardiff subjects have been shown to be similarly differentiated according to linguistic criteria (phonological) and social criteria (occupational status, educational background and sex of speaker). These correlational patterns are not any different in kind from those produced in many other quantitative studies of speech-communities. The interest here lies principally in the fact that Mees' subjects were children and in the fact that data for the other studies are naturally occurring conversations rather than interview-speech. It is significant that the untypical research-contexts produce the usual patterns of co-variation. The case-study of stylistic variation shows that it is possible for a speaker's phonology to mark quite fine situational fluctuations in a single physical setting by shifting between stylistic levels. A large number of phonological variables have been shown to be socially diagnostic in Cardiff – in particular (h), (ng), (C cluster), (intervoc.t), (a:) (ɔu) in showing clear social stratification (i.e. they function as 'indicators' in the sense of Labov 1972a); and (h), (C cluster), (intervoc.t) and (ɔu) which are also situationally sensitive (i.e. 'markers', in Labov's sense) at least in the speech of the travel agency assistant. But certain aspects of the methods used to arrive at correlational patterns like these are open to criticisms, which are therefore a challenge to descriptive adequacy. The criticisms fall under four headings:

(a) the quantification of individual sociolinguistic variables
(b) the combining of variables
(c) the grouping of speakers, and
(d) the quantitative approach itself

(a) Firstly, it is an intrinsic weakness of individual phonological variables that they can never be perfectly defined. As we have seen, it is always necessary to specify linguistic contexts which will make variants more or less probable before we make claims about the *socio*linguistic significance of occurrences. But we can never be satisfied that all the possibly relevant contextual features have been considered. The position of sounds in a word (as, for example, with the (r) variable – cf.section 3.2) will often be relevant; stressed versus unstressed contexts similarly (cf. the (ng) variable). But lexical factors may well be significant too. With (h), the lexical item *hotel* was excluded as a special case. But studies of sound-change and lexical diffusion (cf. Chen and Wang 1975) show that many sociolinguistic variables are involved in on-going sound-changes, spreading progressively through the language. Until fine-grained lexical information of this sort is available, the probability of occurrence of particular sounds in particular words cannot be fully established. Again, the full range of stylistic variation in a corpus of text strictly speaking needs to be analysed and compensated for before the speech of individuals or groups can be treated as directly comparable.

Furthermore, it is not always obvious how to establish a particular set of phonetic forms as a sociolinguistic variable. The assumption which underlies the construction of a phonological variable is that phonetic space in some cases corresponds to social space. So, Labov talked of the centralization of (ay) and (aw) connoting a more positive orientation to community values in Martha's Vineyard (1972a:38) and of postvocalic /r/ connoting socioeconomic status in New York City (:58). But in his work in Belfast, James Milroy (1982:35) has identified variables which are too 'complex' to enter relationships of this sort. The (a) system in Belfast – the vowel in words like, *bang, jacket, happen* and *Belfast* – subsumes a wide range of phonetic dimensions,including fronting/backing, rounding, lengthening and diphthongization, and there is no unique association between variation in any one phonetic dimension and social prestige. This is an extreme case, but the general problem inevitably arose with some of the Cardiff vocalic variables: for example (ɔʊ), where the phonetic dimension centralization/retraction of the first element was quite arbitrarily chosen to distinguish classes of variants. Individual sociolinguistic variables have of course proved to be very successful indicators and markers despite these methodological weaknesses, and will continue to be used as diagnostic variables for the studies to be reported in chapter 5, but an investigation based on the quantification of variables of this sort cannot ultimately be said to provide a rigorously and fully objective descriptive account of its data.

(b) As the studies in sections 3.3 and 3.4 show, indices calculated for different variables across the same speech-text can differ considerably, in a way that makes tabulated data difficult to interpret. In practice, we tend to assume that a speaker will produce a *style* of pronunciation rather than a random set of frequencies of variants of different variables. That is, we assume that a high frequency of occurrence of one variant of variable x will be associated with a high frequency of occurrence of the corresponding variant of variable y; consistent 'aitch-dropping' will not, we assume, be associated with consistently standard realizations of, say, (intervoc.t) in a Cardiffian's speech. Rather, we expect to find rules of co-occurrence (Ervin-Tripp 1964) operating across particular variables. In fact, without such co-occurrences, it is not possible to make sense of expressions like 'standard pronunciation', 'less standard style', and so on which form the basis of an adequate descriptive account of sociolinguistic variation.

To test the validity of such expressions, the degree of co-occurrence between indices can be assessed statistically. This was done as an extension to the study of social differentiation in the travel agency population reported above. The fifteen subjects with the highest overall numbers of tokens for the different variables were identified, so that the extent of co-occurrence between variant-scores could be calculated on large samples of speech. These fifteen individuals' scores for variables (h), (ng), (C cluster) and (intervoc.t) were tabulated and inter-correlation coefficients between each paired set of variable-scores were calculated; the results are shown in table 3–12. Over fifteen individuals, intercorrelation coefficients of around

Table 3–12: Intercorrelation coefficients between values of variables (h), (ng), (C cluster) and (intervoc.t) for fifteen individuals.

	(ng)	(C cluster)	(intervoc.t)
(h)	.69	.71	.78
(ng)	–	.67	.69
(C cluster)		–	.70

.7 is evidence of regular co-variation among all four phonological variables considered here. Each variable, of course, has its own range of values across the fifteen speakers. Scores for (h) vary between 0.0 (completely standard) and 95.2 (almost completely non-standard); those of (ng) cover the whole range from 0.0 to 100; scores for (intervoc.t) vary from 0.0 to 83.3; for (C cluster), the range is smaller – from 35.6 to 100. Still within each variable's range, the distribution of scores across the fifteen speakers is fairly consistent. These statistics go some way to supporting our intuitive notion of phonological style and to counteracting the criticism that different variables inevitably lead to inconsistent impressions of sociolinguistic variation.

(c) When we set out to describe sociolinguistic heterogeneity across groups of speakers, there is a tendency to assume homogeneity within the groups themselves. As Berdan (1975) has pointed out, the usual method of tabulating quantitative findings lets this assumption go unchallenged. Indices for social groups are usually presented as averages, which could disguise considerable interpersonal variation within the group. Yet, even if we agree that, for example, 'the working-class accent in Cardiff' is not a neatly-defined homogeneous concept, we may expect it to relate to an aggregate of individual speech-styles clustering around a describable 'centre' or norm. But quantitative sociolinguistic results, presented merely as group-averages, cannot support or challenge this expectation. In table 3–7, mean deviations (the mean of individuals' scores' deviation from the average percentage quoted) were reported, to give an indication of how much heterogeneity each cell subsumed. In general, the mean deviation values are high, many over twenty, showing that there is as much variation between individuals within some of the socioeconomic groups as there is between the most representative members of adjacent groups. If this extent of intragroup variation is normal, we need to be careful not to overstate the categoriality of sociolinguistic differentiation across such groups. From their speech, individuals cannot be unerringly assigned to, say, occupational groups by statistical means any more than they can by impressionistic judgement in everyday life.

(d) Finally, there are cases where an adequate description of linguistic variation is constrained rather than facilitated by the quantitative approach itself. Frequential differences are the heart of Labovian methods, and are generally both successful and appropriate in revealing broad patterns of social differentiation across groups of speakers in different situations. But Labov also argues in favour of frequential data for analysing stylistic variation in the speech of individuals. He claims that, in a spoken sequence, 'the irregular fluctuations' that we find in the use of a particular variable are unanalyzable (1972a:101). His conclusion is that the basic unit of stylistic contrast is 'a frequency set up by as few as ten occurrences of a particular variable' (:109). But this view restricts the study of phonological style to quite large stretches of speech being quantified in isolation from the moment-to-moment 'fluctuations' that are so character- istic of spontaneous speech. At the same time, it underestimates the sensitivity interactants can show to minute details of their own and each other's pronunciation (as will be exemplified in chapter 5). In these cases, a more qualitative approach to the data needs to be adopted,[6] and some of the rigour of Labovian methods needs to be traded for more detailed insights into the ebbs and flows of stylistic variation.

Assuming that Labovian methods are able to describe sociolinguistic variation adequately, notwithstanding the limitations discussed above, their explanatory power, their ability to answer questions about *why* sociolinguistic differentiation occurs and with what effects, is less impressive. Very important exceptions are the contributions that variationist studies have made to linguistic theory (particularly in the development of variable rules) and to our understanding of processes involved in linguistic change. Indeed, both of these interests were central to seminal sociolinguistic works (cf. Labov 1972a, Trudgill 1974a). But, as Giles has said (1977b, 1979), the 'socio' component of sociolinguistics has been lamentably weak in its failure to build explanatory theories of language in society. At the root of the problem is the correlational method itself, which can lead to a static, deterministic approach to linguistic variation (as discussed in section 1.4, above). Social group membership and situational delimitation are depicted as automatically determining a particular linguistic output, and the contribution of the participants themselves is consequently underemphasized. As an experimental technique, correlation will inevitably have a role to play, but it is the correlation of dependent and independent variables in a theoretical vacuum that is being criticized.

Post hoc social explanations of correlational findings *are* put forward by sociolinguists. Labov (1972a :99), for example, argues that style-shifting relates to the degree of attention a speaker pays to his/her speech and he offers some experimental evidence (of the dialectal consequences of masking auditory feedback to speakers) to support his interpretation. Attention to speech accounts quite well for variation across Labov's situations – 'casual', 'careful' and the various reading-styles. But, as we shall see, it cannot account for multi-dimensional variation in speech-style or those plausible occasions when *more* careful self-monitoring leads to *less* standard pronunciation. To explain social stratification findings, Labov has developed the notion of *overt* and *covert prestige*; overt prestige is the prestige associated with standard varieties and openly recognized by high- status groups and, often, the community as a whole. Covert prestige is associated with non-standard speech and is the value tacitly ascribed to it by some low-status groups. These terms relate closely to other interpretive concepts widely used in sociolinguistic studies – *power* and *solidarity* (cf. Brown and Gilman 1972). Overt prestige stems from the power dimension of language-use, while covert prestige is linked to solidarity which reflects social affinity and shared experience. Regionally delimited non-standard speech-forms are able to mark solidarity by virtue of their restricted usage; by this means, they can come to symbolize in-group attitudes and attract covert prestige. Conversely, higher status groups may subscribe more to national norms of power allocation and maintenance; their speech can reflect this attitude because it is not regionally delimited.

With concepts like these we can begin to answer the central question raised by studies of linguistic social stratification: why do non-standard speech-varieties continue to exist (cf. Ryan 1979) in the face of strong centralizing and standardizing social pressures. But social psychologists can justifiably point out that language attitudes and linguistic prestige are proper subjects for social psychological study and, moreover, have been extensively researched in their own right (see Ryan and Giles 1982 for a recent review of this field). Adequate explanations for sociolinguistic variation need to build on this body of knowledge, just as social psychology can benefit from the detailed, linguistically sensitive sociolinguistic approach. This is broadly Giles' position (1977b, 1979) when he argues for a rapprochement between the two disciplines. The social psychological perspective is particularly revealing when the aim is to explain language – in this case, dialectal variation – *in use* as a communicative resource to speakers and listeners on a routine basis. We have seen how the survey-approach to speech-variation, identifying broad patterns of variation 'from above', can obscure the detailed behaviour of particular individuals and particular dialectal elements. Chapters 4 and 5 try to redress the balance by exploring the probable and some of the actual attitudinal, evaluative and symbolic dimensions of Cardiff English and examining their contribution to dialect-variation in specific instances.

4

Dialect as Communication :
Attitudes, Identities and Strategies

Seeing linguistic selections as the correlates of pre-existing social categories is only one among many possible approaches to the study of dialect variation. This 'plan-view' of dialect – where the researcher identifies broad patterns of social differentiation in the data 'from above' – may well be the most appropriate perspective for large-scale survey work of the sort for which Labovian methods were originally developed. Inevitably, though, as we saw at the end of chapter 3, this approach is explanatorily weak; it fails to address questions relating to *why* systematic dialect-variation exists and persists. In the context of stylistic shifting, the 'top-down'approach is particularly blinkering, since speech-style is essentially the domain of the individual, serving to encode individuals' varying responses to and motivated contributions to particular speaking situations.

This chapter tries to articulate an alternative approach to dialect variation, developing a more individualistic, motivational perspective. It is the perspective recently promulgated by social psychologists, as summarized in the words of Smith, Giles and Hewstone (1980: 287):

> 'Of particular relevance to sociolinguistics is the notion that individuals' speech patterns are not simply and only reflections of their large-scale demographic memberships but also of their cognitive organization of the situation. Language can be viewed, then, as a dependent variable of complex social construing . . . Yet important data for this construal process are the linguistic features of the interactant. This allows social categorizations, inferences, and evaluations of the interactant and the situation to be made that are cognitively organized with present expectations, past experiences, belief and value systems and the like. In this sense, language behaviour also acts as an independent variable for cognitive organization.'

The starting point is the view that dialect varieties are at least potentially value-laden. Axiomatically, *to speak is to be judged* – both as individual and as social group member. Moreover, where such judgements or classifications are robust and durable, *to speak is to represent* – either types of individual or, again, social groups. When speakers are able to make productive use of these associations, *to speak is to manipulate judgements and representations* – to manage the persona presented to an interlocutor and/or control the development of the encounter. Once we recognize that particular dialectal features can be symbolically charged, we can begin to understand why speakers may select or avoid selecting these features in specific contexts. We may also be able to read interactional patterns in dialect use, as speaking partners respond dynamically to each other's dialect behaviour.

A rich and growing literature (largely under the heading of the social psychology of language but including some very significant work in sociolinguistics) has explored these attitudinal, symbolic and motivational processes, sometimes with explicit reference to British dialect usage. Surprisingly, this work has had little impact to date on dialect variation-studies. Therefore, as a background to the further empirical studies of Cardiff English to be reported in chapter 5, this chapter selectively reviews the literature to identify broad categories of social psychological processes which can be drawn on to explain stylistic variation in Cardiff speech. Studies which relate to Welsh English (and sometimes Cardiff English) are given most prominence and, where possible and appropriate, generalized conclusions reached in the literature are supported by formal or informal observations from fieldwork in Cardiff. Four categories of social psychological processes are distinguished below: dialect and *perceived status*; dialect and *group identity*, dialect and *perceived personality*; and *interpersonal accommodation* through dialect.

4.1   *Dialect and perceived status*

Some early studies (cf. Giles and Powesland 1975, Edwards 1982, for reviews) set out to examine general attitudes towards selected British (and other) accents of English to assess their relative prestige. Giles (1970, also reported in Giles and Powesland 1975) investigated the reactions of groups of South Welsh and Somerset children to thirteen different accents using the matched guise technique. That is, the child 'judges' were led to believe they would hear thirteen different speakers, although the tape-recorded voices were different 'guises' produced by the same male speaker, reading a passage of prose. The judges were asked to rate each accent on a number of scales, including the prestige of the speaker. Table 4–1 shows mean ratings for each accent where 'affected RP' is defined as 'a more exaggerated . . . form of the Standard, commonly associated with the aristocracy' (Giles and Powesland 1975:28). RP was rated most positively for prestige (as it

Table 4–1: A generalized accent prestige continuum: mean ratings of thirteen accents (from Giles and Powesland 1975: 28).

1. RP (2.1)	8. Italian (4.7)
2. Affected RP (2.9)	9. Northern English (4.8)
3. N. American and French (3.6)	10. Somerset (5.1)
5. German (4.2)	11. Cockney and Indian (5.2)
6. South Welsh (4.3)	13. Birmingham (5.3)
7. Irish (4.6)	

was in terms of aesthetic quality and communicative content); the two accents in the study which are associated with large urban areas of Britain, Cockney and Birmingham, were rated least positively; South Welsh English occupied an intermediate position. Accent-loyalty was revealed in that the (regionally delimited) groups of judges rated their own area's accent more positively than the other group did, but still not as positively as RP. Giles obtained corroborative evidence in support of these findings in a subsequent study (reported in Giles 1971b) using thirteen genuine accents (produced by thirteen different speakers) and a group of judges of mixed regional origin. A rank-order correlation for status across the two studies of $+ 0.94$ was obtained. As a further refinement (Giles 1972), the effect of degrees of mildness-broadness on the perceived pleasantness and prestige of different accents (again including South Wales English) was invest-igated, once again using matched guises. Less broad accents were generally rated more positively in terms of both pleasantness and status, even in the case of Welsh judges rating South Welsh accents.

These comparative studies make little direct contribution to our understanding of the social psychological processes operative in the encoding or decoding of speech within encounters between members of the same speech community. They do lead, however, to the question of how speech community members (in this case, Cardiffians) generally perceive the status of *their own* speech varieties, and this clearly *is* relevant to everyday speech within the community. If we accept that speakers' views of their own dialects do not differ very markedly from the generalized (national) evaluations, it might seem from Giles' early work that Cardiffians will have only moderately negative views of Cardiff speech, since it seems to fall inside Giles' category of 'South Wales' English. What Edwards (1979:87) has referred to as 'the general tendency for non-standard speakers to accept the larger, and negative, stereotypes of their own speech' might seem to be less significant if 'South Wales English' is itself a moderately statusful variety. In fact, there are reasons to suppose that Cardiff English instead falls within the group of heavily stigmatized, urban British dialects represented by Cockney and Birmingham speech in Giles' studies.

Firstly, there is the descriptive linguistic evidence (see section 2.4, above) that Cardiff English is in many respects untypical of the varieties often labelled 'Welsh English' and even 'South Wales English'. If Cardiff English is, at most, representative of urban South-East Welsh English, we might reasonably expect it to enter a different pattern of social evaluations from the predominantly rural varieties more closely influenced by the Welsh language. Secondly, Cardiff English has been vociferously criticized by sections of the community in recent years. These extreme views have surfaced in the local and national press on occasions, where reference has been made variously to 'Cardiff's uniquely strangled vowels' and 'the quirkiness of the voice' (Radio Times, 25 August 1984) and to 'the notorious Cardiff accent – said by some to be the worst in the world' (Western Mail, 21 January 1982). This last source also referred to views expressed at a shareholders' meeting of the local radio-station – that the Cardiff voice was alienating listeners from the station and leading to a loss of revenue.[1] Thirdly, many of the Cardiff informants who took part in the various studies reported in this volume expressed their own views on Cardiff English when the general objectives of the work were made known to them. These views included many extreme critical responses, labelling the non-standard local variety as 'common', 'ugly', 'rasping', 'dreadful' and so on – in fact using the same range of evaluative terms as in many other studies of urban British speech (again, see Edwards 1979 for a review). The terms 'negative prestige' and 'linguistic insecurity' (cf. Macaulay 1975) are generally as appropriate in Cardiff, it seems, as they are in Glasgow, Norwich or New York to characterize the publicly expressed responses of certain sections of the speech community to non-standard speech. In addition, it is interesting that some Cardiff informants tended to group Cardiff English more with certain Midlands or North-Western (English) dialects than with Welsh varieties. Asked to characterize Cardiff speech, these informants chose to label it *a Scouser like* (i.e. Liverpudlian) or *more of a Brummy twang* (i.e. a Birmingham dialect).

For these reasons, we must see Giles' category of 'South Wales' speech as dialectally too imprecise to relate to the social evaluation of Cardiff English. Moreover, the flood of research activity in the social psychology of language in recent years (much of it inspired and led by Giles himself) has clearly shown that the general notion of 'the perceived status' of a speech variety is itself too imprecise from a social psychological perspective. It has become clear that social evaluations of speech are multidimensional processes which relate simultaneously to the sociostructural, personal and interpersonal identities and affinities of interactants, and which are negotiated and manipulated during interaction. Focusing on one part of this complex of processes, the following section briefly reviews relevant studies of dialect and group identity.

4.2   *Dialect and group-identity*

If one pervasive and dominant theme emerges from attempts to explain linguistic variation it is the potential linguistic varieties have for marking group-identity. The choice of individual pronunciation features, lexical, grammatical and discoursal styles and even languages themselves have variously been related to the signalling of ethnic and national identity (Giles, 1977a, Gumperz 1982), socioeconomic status group membership (Robinson 1979, A. D. Edwards, 1976) and even age-group (Helfrich 1979) and sex-group (Smith 1979, Kramarae 1982) membership. As Ryan (1979:147) points out, 'the value of language as a chief symbol of group-identity is one of the major forces for the preservation of non-standard speech styles or dialects'. Moreover, the emergence or redefinition of ethnic, cultural or subcultural groups tends to draw heavily on the symbolic function of language to establish or confirm intergroup distinction (Fishman 1978, Hebdige 1979). As we saw in section 3.5, it is commonplace in sociolinguistic studies to invoke general notions of 'solidarity' or 'covert prestige' in interpreting variation findings, though such studies rarely address subjective matters of attitude and allegiance directly. But a large corpus of social psychological research has explored these areas and can profitably serve as a background against which linguistic variation can be charted.

In particular, a number of studies have examined the symbolic function of dialect in Wales. Bourhis, Giles and Tajfel (1973) established that what they called 'the Welsh accent' of English can, like the national language itself, serve to mark national identity. They found that Welsh people enrolled on Welsh language evening-classes did not regard themselves to be any less Welsh than fully bilingual speakers. In a matched-guise evaluative session, different groups of Welsh individuals, including some who spoke no Welsh, all downgraded speakers who adopted a more standard English accent. Again, Bourhis and Giles (1977) found they could elicit broader 'Welsh accents' from a group of 'integrative' Welsh-language learners (i.e. those committed to learning the language on ideological grounds) when the researchers consciously manipulated conversation-content to make Welsh v. English national categorization more salient. When these learners were asked for their views about the survival and status of the Welsh language in Wales by a researcher who introduced himself as working at an English university and had given his own view that 'the future of Welsh appears pretty dismal', many encoded their responses in broader Welsh accents. Three subjects introduced Welsh words and phrases into their answers and 'one of these actually conjugated Welsh verbs into the microphone instead of replying directly to the question' (:129).

The results of these studies are consistent with the view that the rise of ethnicity in Wales (Khleif 1978, Morgan 1981, Thomas and Williams 1978) has changed or is changing the 'normal' pattern of evaluative responses to standard and non-standard dialect varieties in the area. The suggestion is that, in terms of pronunciation, RP in Wales does not attract the high levels of overt prestige that it does in most other areas of Britain. This is the conclusion drawn, for example, by Chapman, Smith and Foot (1977:143):

> '. . . the vast majority of Welsh people do not aspire to the Standard English mode of speech. Indeed, many appear to reject it for themselves. Whereas only a short time ago there seemed to be a social stigma attached to pronouncing English words with a broad Welsh accent, especially in anglicized communities, the same accent seems now to be exhibited proudly, and it is sometimes noticeably exaggerated. This is presumably because 'Welshness' is now seen as more attractive and the accent today constitutes an overt symbol of group membership, loyalty and solidarity.'

In fact, there are many reasons for seeing this view as seriously overgeneralized. Firstly, as in the case of the studies reviewed in section 4.1, there is no recognition here of the considerable range and diversity of varieties of Welsh English. Secondly, there are many mediating social psychological variables (still to be considered in this chapter) between ethnicity and dialect-production in a given context. Perhaps most significantly, Chapman *et al.* do not recognize that the new ethnicity in Wales is a movement instigated and still essentially represented by a well-defined, influential sub-set of the Welsh population. The following passage from Khleif (1978:107/8) characterizes 'a rising middle class as an agent of ethnic revitalization':

> 'The new middle class in Wales is a middle class mostly appearing after 1945 . . . The current leaders of Welsh opinion are overwhelmingly sons and daughters of coal miners, agricultural workers, steel workers, shopkeepers, and minor civil servants, but especially of coal miners. These leaders are mostly schoolmasters, clergymen and university lecturers, occupational categories highly prized in a country like Wales with its traditional emphasis on education. They come, for the most part, from rural areas both north and south but not typically from Cardiff or Swansea, although they may live there

now . . . Their Welshness sets them apart, for to have spoken Welsh at home, a generation ago, meant that the person by definition was working class. They are very proud of their Welshness, of their ability to speak Welsh, of their ability to "live a full Welsh life". They consider their knowledge of Welsh a badge of achievement, for it differentiates them from other middle-class men as well as working-class men who are English monoglots.'

While it is quite plausible that the attitudes and values promulgated by this focal group will have influence outside the group, it is also predictable (from Khleif's specification) that some groups of Welsh people, working class people living in long established, monolingual, urban communities like Cardiff, will be *least* influenced by, even alienated from, the new Welsh ethnicity.

The polarization emerges quantitatively in a study conducted in Cardiff by Bourhis and Giles (1976). The researchers set out to identify the behavioural consequences of language- and dialect-choice. They made tape-recordings of an announcement – a request for members of the public to collect, fill in and return a questionnaire – to be relayed over the public-address system in the foyer of a Cardiff theatre. The same male bilingual speaker was tape-recorded reading four versions of this message: one in standard Welsh and three in English – RP, 'broad South Welsh accented English' and 'mild South Welsh accented English'. The three English varieties were broadcast on different evenings to Anglo-Welsh audiences who had come to watch English films at the theatre. Later, all four versions, including the Welsh-language recording, were broadcast on different evenings to bilingual Welsh audiences who had come to see a Welsh-language play. The percentage of questionnaires completed and returned by each group in response to the various versions of the broadcast announcement were taken as behavioural indices of co-operation. Bourhis and Giles found very different patterns of response across the two groups of theatre-goers, reflecting different evaluations of the (English) dialectal varieties. The bilingual Welsh audiences responded most favourably by far (26%) to the Welsh-language request. The 'mild-accented Welsh English' version elicited moderate responses (9.2%), with the broader variety marginally in third place (8.1%). The RP version was clearly least well received (2.5%). For bilingual audiences, then, 'Welsh-accented English' elicited significantly more co-operation than RP, a finding broadly in line with Chapman *et al.*'s remarks, above. Even here, though, there are clearly complicating attitudinal factors at work, since the *less* broad voice elicits *more* co-operation than the more broad voice. On the other hand, the monolingual audiences who were by far the more representative group in a Cardiff context, showed quite positive responses to both the mild-accented voice (25%) and the RP voice (22.5%). The broad-accented voice once again elicited only a moderate response (8.1%). This pattern of responses again suggests a complex set of interpretive factors at work in Cardiff. Certainly, there is no simple correlation between degree of non-standardness (and perhaps therefore, degree of ethnicity-marking) and degree of co-operative response. The authors explore possible complicating factors to do with the perceived appropriateness/inappropriateness of using the different varieties in the context of a public announcement; for example, a broad regional voice may be judged inappropriate in this context even if valued elsewhere. In general, though, the study clearly demonstrates the danger in assuming uniform evaluative responses to dialectal variation across different social groups in Wales. It also shows that there need not be a simple dimension of social prestige attaching to dialectal standardness (more standard more prestigious), since RP, mild and broad varieties are *not* associated with a linear scale of co-operative responses from either group of theatre-goers. The finding that monolingual Cardiffians react more positively to mild than to broad varieties of 'Welsh English' is generally consistent with the descriptive evidence of social and stylistic stratification presented in sections 3.3 and 3.4. But the finding that they respond *less* well to RP than to the mild variety forces us to consider other social psychological factors, some still to do with group-identity marking.

The question of socioeconomic class receives little consideration in Bourhis and Giles' study, even though they point out (:14) that the population of theatre-goers were presumably 'middle class'. Yet the assumption made in sociolinguistic survey research is that non-standard dialect forms principally mark low socioeconomic status (SES) groups rather than nationally-based ethnicity. In many instances, of course, these processes are fused, in that minority ethnic groups (e.g. West Indians in Britain, Chicanos in the USA) are often also low SES groups within majority communities. Given Khleif's analysis (above) of the new Welsh ethnicity as essentially a middle-class inspired phenomenon, we find competing hypotheses about language and group-identity in Wales. For some Welsh people in some contexts, some non-standard Welsh English varieties may be positively evaluated as symbols of ethnicity; for others, some non-standard forms (perhaps even *the same* forms) may be negatively evaluated for their low SES associations. The relatively low levels of co-operative response to 'broad South Wales accented English' in the theatre study may well be the familiar negative reaction by middle class community members to socially stigmatized non-standard speech in formal settings. Cardiffians' (and particularly, it seems, working class Cardiffians') likely alienation from the Welsh ethnic revival strongly suggests that it is the SES-related dimension of group identity that will be most salient in the encoding and decoding of Cardiff English, as with most other non-standard varieties of British English.

Sociolinguistic studies of language and SES have revealed some characteristic patterns of subjective responses to standard and non-standard dialect varieties. Labov (1966) found that listeners were able to make quite consistent judgements about suitable occupations for individuals whose speech differed in respect of SES-related phonological variables. Similarly, Shuy, Baratz and Wolfram (1969; cf. also Robinson 1979) found that listeners could identify speakers' SES very accurately on the basis of brief samples of speech. A study conducted in Cardiff (Bates 1983) confirmed that different levels of dialectal standardness are associated with different occupation types. Using a simple matched guise technique, Bates obtained two groups of children's ratings of suitable occupations for two speakers – a male and a female, each in the guise of two speakers, an 'educated regional' speaker and a 'Cardiff' speaker. The female speaker was most frequently assessed to be a bank clerk in her 'educated regional' guise and a shop assistant in her 'Cardiff' guise. The male speaker was typically assessed to be a teacher in his 'educated regional' guise and a factory worker in his 'Cardiff' guise. If occupational class membership is taken to be one criterion for determining an individual's social status and advantage, these studies show a consistent symbolic association between dialectal standardness and general standing in the community at large. But a complementary pattern of associations has emerged from certain well-known sociolinguistic studies, suggesting that non-standard dialect forms can carry their own form of prestige – so called 'covert' prestive (cf. Section 3.5 above), which operates at a more local level. For example, Labov (1972a) proposes that non-standard New York speakers do not necessarily want to adopt the speaking norms of the dominant middle-class group, even though they tend to endorse those norms in formal test situations. Trudgill (1974a) in fact found that both working-class and middle-class males *claimed* to use non-standard forms even when they did *not* regularly do so in speaking, pointing to the potentially positive subjective associations of non-standard speech. In this way, the marking of (SES) group-identity through dialect is clearly a double-edged sword, and the encoding of *any* level of dialectal standardness inevitably involves a speaker in trading off profits and losses in the marking of degrees of nationally based 'power' and local 'solidarity'.

The studies referred to so far in this section focus on the *de*coding of identities (or likely identities) from speech. But it is important to see the *en*coding potential of the associative patterns discussed above. That is, speakers are in a position to make (indeed, cannot avoid making) acts of group-identity through dialect selection. While there is a sense in which group-identities relating to ethnic, national or SES categories are 'given' or at least predictable by virtue of speakers' actual provenances, it is also true that we have some latitude in identifying ourselves, in presenting ourselves to others, as we wish. It follows that our identities need not be enduring or even consistent, and that we can signal *varying* identities in an essentially dynamic way, either across or within speaking situations. This view is consistent with Fishman's recognition (1977:33) of 'man's (and particularly modern man's) peculiar capacity for multiple loyalties, multiple identities and multiple memberships.' Following from our experiences of the association of dialect forms with social groups, we are able to *use* these associations productively as a communicative resource, marking degrees of affiliation to ingroups/outgroups as these suit our momentary wishes and needs. Within sociolinguistics, this 'acts of identity' approach has been promoted by Robert LePage (e.g. 1972, 1977, 1980; LePage *et al.* 1977), who has developed the notions of 'projection' and 'focusing' to characterize some central aspects of dynamic group-identity marking:

> 'We engage in language activities I call projection and focusing: we project on to the social screen the concepts we have formed, by talking about them, so as to furnish our universe and try to get others to acknowledge the shape of the furniture; we in turn try to bring our concepts into focus with those of others, so that there is feedback from the social screen through language.' (1980:15,16)

Le Page's work in multilingual settings fits well with the conceptual orientation adopted by Gumperz in his investigations of language and social identity in interethnic encounters (1982). It is Gumperz' assumption that social categories, including ethnicity, which we take to be given parameters and boundaries delimiting our social identities are in fact 'not constants that can be taken for granted but are communicatively produced' (1982:1). Together, these interdisciplinary efforts towards explaining sociolinguistic behaviour amount to a powerful case for a dynamic, motivational and interpretive account of linguistic variation, including monolingual variation in dialect-use.

4.3   *Dialect and perceived personality*

Another broad pattern of association between dialect and identity has emerged from social psychological studies, relating to the perceived *personal* identity of a speaker. Aspects of a speaker's perceived personality have been shown to be associated with that speaker's dialectal standardness/non-standardness in many different research contexts. For instance, Strongman and Woosely (1967) and Cheyne (1970), reviewed by Giles and

Powesland (1975:66ff.) found that speakers with RP-type accents (rated by 'Southern' and 'Northern' listeners and 'Scottish' and 'English' listeners in the respective studies) attract stereotyped personality impressions of greater *competence* than speakers of non-standard regional accents. In this characterization, competence relates to individual personality traits which include self-confidence, intelligence, ambition, leadership, and so on, even good looks and height. On the other hand, these studies also showed that '*non*-standard speakers' (here referring to speakers with Yorkshire and Scottish accents) attract judgements of greater *personal integrity* and *social attractiveness*, including the traits honesty, reliability, generosity, good-naturedness, and so on. The tripartite classification of personality traits as relating to competence, personal integrity or social attractiveness derives from Lambert (1967), although many studies suggest that the last two categories can be further resolved into single factor. For example, Edwards' general conclusion after a review of British work done in this area (1982:25) is that 'standard accents usually connote high status and competence; regional accents may be seen to reflect greater integrity and attractiveness.'

Giles (1971a) ran a matched-guise study to assess the personality-traits associated with South Welsh and Somerset accented English as opposed to RP. Representative groups of South Welsh and Somerset listeners produced the familiar pattern of evaluative responses. Both groups perceived the RP speakers as relatively more ambitious, intelligent, self-confident, determined and industrious (i.e. 'competence'-related traits) and the non-standard speakers as relatively less serious, more talkative, good-natured and humorous (i.e. 'personal integrity' and 'social attractiveness'-related traits). As part of a follow-up study, Bourhis, Giles and Lambert (1975) demonstrated that the same general pattern of personality evaluation can accompany dynamic rather than static dialect behaviour. An elaborate array of stimulus tape-recordings were constructed which purported to be interviews between a Welsh athlete and two different interviewers after a diving competition. The two interviewers differed in respect of their accents (RP and 'mild South Welsh'). The athlete was recorded in three so-called accent-conditions, firstly maintaining his own 'mild South Welsh' accent, secondly shifting towards RP, thirdly shifting towards a broader accent. Matched groups of South Welsh judges evaluated the six recordings. In the cases where significant effects between accent-condition and evaluations were found, the generally predicted associative patterns again emerged. That is, the athlete was perceived as more intelligent, but less trustworthy and kindhearted when he shifted towards RP (than when he did not shift). Also, he was assessed as more intelligent when he did not shift (than when he broadened his accent), but as more trustworthy and kindhearted when he did broaden his accent.

Studies of personality-perception from dialect in Wales have not produced entirely consistent findings. Bourhis, Giles and Tajfel (1973) extended the matched-guise research paradigm to include Welsh people's evaluative responses to the Welsh language itself, as well as RP and 'Welsh-accented English'. They asked three groups of listener-judges – Welsh/English bilinguals, Welsh language learners and monolingual Welsh people – to evaluate personality-dimensions on the basis of each of these linguistic varieties which, as usual, were actually produced by the same speakers in different guises. Surprisingly, there were no significant differences between the evaluative patterns emerging from the three groups of judges. All judges upgraded the Welsh language speaker on most personality traits. What is most relevant to the present discussion is that all judges *also* upgraded the Welsh-accented (English) speaker *to the same level* on some traits – for example, trustworthiness, friendliness and sociability. Also, the RP speaker was rated highest mainly on quite negative traits like conservatism, snobbishness and arrogance, but including self-confidence. Interestingly, judges perceived no significant differences between speakers in respect of intelligence. These findings show a more positive evaluation of Welsh-accented English than in the studies by Giles and by Bourhis *et al.* reviewed earlier. Giles and Powesland (1975:77 ff.) suggest this discrepancy might stem from the different populations used as judges (adults in the 1973 study, adolescents in the other studies). Alternatively they note that data for the various studies were gathered at different times (the 1973 data were collected more than a year later than data for the other studies) and that attitudes in Wales as a whole might have changed dramatically in that short period. But interpretations of these findings are limited by a pervasive weakness of social psychological research in this paradigm that has already been commented on above – the imprecise characterization of the linguistic varieties used as stimulus material. It is to be expected that quite small variations in phonetic/phonological/other features may be associated with different personality stereotypes. Also, there is likely to be systematic perceptual as well as sociolinguistic variation within a dialectally diverse community such as South Wales (cf. section 2.4, above). Unfortunately, no information on these matters is recoverable from Bourhis *et al.*'s study where the labels 'Welsh English' and 'Welsh-accented English' are left unexplicated.

Bates (1983) set out to replicate aspects of Giles and others' South Wales studies using data from the Cardiff speech-community. Two groups of Cardiff-accented children evaluated four voices (two 'Educated Regional' and two 'Cardiff' voices) on ten bi-polar, seven-point adjective-scales. The groups of judges were matched for age, SES and accent, differing only in respect of what school-classes they belonged to ('examination' and 'non-examination' classes). Personality traits investigated were 'intelligence', 'sincerity', 'good-naturedness', 'sympathy', 'fair-mindedness', 'enthus-iasm', 'sense of humour', 'friendliness', 'helpfulness' and 'interesting'. Overall, the Educated Regional speakers were perceived significantly more favourably in terms of 'intelligence', and the Cardiff speakers significantly more favourably in terms of 'sense of humour', 'enthusiasm' and 'interesting'. Some intergroup differences emerged, as the non-examina-tion group rated the Cardiff speakers significantly more favourably only on the 'sense of humour' trait. On the other hand, the examination group produced a significant association between Cardiff speech and 'sympathy' in addition to 'sense of humour', 'enthusiasm' and 'interesting'. These findings broadly support the anticipated pattern of more standard dialect-use being associated with competence and less standard with social attractiveness, though they do not confirm the association of less standard dialect with personal integrity traits (e.g. 'sincerity', 'fair-mindedness'). Bates went on to explore the particular patterns of evaluation of male and female speech by sub-groups of male and female listeners. As earlier studies had suggested (Kramer 1977; Elyan, Smith, Giles and Bourhis 1978), Bates found that there was considerable sex-based variation in personality-assessment from speech. Overall, the female Cardiff judges assessed Cardiff speakers (both male and female) more favourably than did the male judges, seeming to possess more accent-loyalty – loyalty to non-standard Cardiff speech – than the male sub-groups. For instance, male judges rated the female Cardiff speaker significantly more favourably (than the female Educated Regional speaker) on the traits of 'sense of humour' and 'enthusiasm', while the female judges also produced significant favourable scores for the trait 'interesting'.

It is worth emphasizing that, on balance, studies of dialect and perceived personality in Wales show interpretive patterns which do not differ substantially from those found in other British studies. In the light of the findings and conclusions of Bourhis *et al.* and Chapman *et al.* discussed in section 4.2, we might have expected more positive reactions to *non*-standard South Wales speech in terms of speakers' perceived levels of competence, following from observations about the revitalization of Welsh ethnic identity. Even if Bourhis, Giles and Tajfel's 1973 study is in some ways inconsistent with the general pattern, it does not break the mould. Even there, RP speakers were seen as more self-confident than less standard speakers and intelligence was simply not a trait differentiating speakers. The usual inverse correlations between perceived competence and non-standard speech are found in Cardiff and elsewhere in South Wales, providing further evidence of the new ethnicity's restricted role in contemporary Wales. If there is an on-going reappraisal of the symbolic values associated with non-standard Welsh English it applies only to certain sub-groups of Welsh listeners and perhaps only to certain varieties of Welsh English. Although no comparative evaluative studies have yet been conducted, issues of language and identity in Wales would be significantly clarified by investigations of different groups of listeners' (differing in regional provenance, SES, sex and ethnocentrism) evaluations of qualitatively different Welsh English varieties. For instance, the variety tentatively labelled 'standard Welsh English' in section 2.4 above might be hypothesized to elicit favourable assessments of speakers' perceived competence levels from groups of middle class, highly ethnocentric Welsh listeners of the sort identified by Khleif (1978). For Cardiff and contemporary Cardiffians, the evidence suggests that non-standard dialect-forms attract positive evaluations only in terms of a speaker's perceived social attractiveness, with perceptions of competence confined to more standard speech.

Once again, there is no reason to believe that these interpretive patterns are fixed and durable rather than subject to modification over time, across and even within interpersonal encounters. Indeed, we could argue that impression-formation through speech is *essentially* a dynamic *process*, wherein interactants seek to gain knowledge about each other or reduce their individual levels of uncertainty about each other (Berger and Bradac 1982). Uncertainty reduction is most obviously a need in first encounters between strangers, where dialect-cues are evidently relevant sources of stereotypical information. But *any* encounter is a potential locus for variable, shifting identities and their interpretation. That is, speakers are routinely in the business of stageing desirable self-identities for inspection and acceptance by others (Goffman 1959, 1971; Scherer 1979) and may attempt to convey varying personas from moment to moment during interaction. The predominantly static studies reviewed in this section do not demonstrate, but certainly imply the possibility of dialectal shifting or switching being employed as encoding strategies in the managing of variable personas. In the Cardiff context, for example, speakers may be motivated to shift fleetingly between more standard and less standard pronunciation, as 'competent' and 'socially attractive' projected personas become variously salient, appropriate or desirable while speaking. Since most speaking situations allow for speakers to fill varying social and communicative roles – more or less authoritarian, more or less intimate, more or less serious, and so on – we may expect dialect to function as a fund of potential personal images which speakers can, as LePage puts it, project upon the social screen.

4.4   *Interpersonal accommodation through dialect*

In sections 4.1, 4.2 and 4.3 we have considered some of the cognitive factors and processes which affect the decoding of dialect behaviour and suggested that parallel factors and process also impinge on dialect users' encoding strategies. At the encoding stage, the principal claim has been that speakers seek to manipulate aspects of their individual or group-identities in accordance with what they perceive to be patterns of association between dialectal behaviour and generalized or stereotypical evaluative responses. That is, the emphasis so far has been on the individual, or at least the individual's perceptions of social stereotypes and his/her responses to these perceptions. Another set of considerations relates specifically to *inter*-personally based communicative strategies which have regularly been shown to influence dialect-use. From this perspective, aspects of a speaker's dialectal and other linguistic behaviours can be explained as *adaptive* behaviours, originating in the perception of interactants' communication characteristics.

The central research-paradigm in this area is so-called speech-accommodation theory (SAT) developed by Giles and others (1973, 1980, 1984; Giles and Powesland 1975; Thakerar, Giles and Cheshire 1982) as a set of propositions able to account for some of the motives and effects of style - or code-shifts or switches in interpersonal encounters. Central concepts in SAT are speech *convergence* and *divergence*. Convergence is a linguistic strategy whereby individuals adapt to each other's speech in terms of a wide range of speech characteristics, including dialect, speech-rates, pause and utterance lengths, language-choices, and so on. Divergence refers to the linguistic process by which speakers may accentuate linguistic differences between themselves and others. Convergence and divergence are motivated by speakers' varying wishes to *accommodate* to their interlocutors. Specific motivations for accommodation are to evoke listeners' social approval and/or to make interpersonal communication more efficient and/or to maintain positive social identities. The central propositional statements of SAT have recently been outlined as follows (derived from Beebe and Giles 1984:89; cf. also Street and Giles 1982; Thakerar *et al.* 1982):

1. People will attempt to converge linguistically toward the speech patterns believed to be characteristic of their recipients when they (a) desire their social approval and the perceived costs of so acting are proportionally lower than the rewards anticipated; and/or (b) desire a high level of communicational efficiency, and (c) social norms are not perceived to dictate alternative speech strategies.

2. The magnitude of such linguistic convergence will be a function of (a) the extent of the speakers' repertoires, and (b) factors (individual difference and environmental) that may increase the need for social approval and/or high communicational efficiency.

3. Speech convergence will be positively evaluated by recipients when the resultant behaviour is (a) perceived as such psychologically (i.e. as integrative); (b) perceived to be at an optimal sociolinguistic distance from them; and (c) attributed with positive intent.

4. People will attempt to maintain their speech patterns or even diverge linguistically away from those believed characteristic of their recipients when they (a) define the encounter in intergroup terms and desire a positive ingroup identity, or (b) wish to dissociate personally from another in an interindividual encounter, or (c) wish to bring another's speech behaviors to a personally acceptable level.

5. The magnitude of such divergence will be a function of (a) the extent of speakers' repertoires, and (b) individual differences and contextual factors increasing the salience of the cognitive or affective functions in (4).

6. Speech maintenance and divergence will be negatively evaluated by recipients when the acts are perceived as psychologically diverging (i.e. dissociative), but favorably reacted to by observers of the encounter who define the interaction in intergroup terms and who share a common, positively valued group membership with the speaker.

The six propositional statements relate to a vast range of interpersonal linguistic phenomena, and are relevant to many levels of language and many situations. Giles and Powesland (1975:158) in fact suggest that accommodation is the norm in interpersonal encounters, since 'it would not seem unreasonable to suppose that there may be a general set to accommodate to others in most social situations'. In this section, it will only be possible to refer to a few studies in the SAT paradigm which relate to dialectal variation as examples of accommodative strategies in action.

In his 1973 study, Giles set up one-to-one interviews between nine working-class Bristol-accented schoolboys (of around seventeen years) and each of two interviewers. The first interviewer, Giles says, would have been perceived by the interviewees as higher in prestige than themselves in terms of age, educational level and accent (he adopted an RP voice). The second interviewer was another seventeen year-old schoolboy with a marked Bristol accent, he would have been perceived as an equal, given his age, voice and appearance (he wore school uniform). Each interviewee was interviewed on separate occasions by each of the two interviewers, on the subject of attitudes towards crime and capital punishment. All interviews were surreptitiously tape-recorded. Subsequently, edited versions of all eighteen tape-recordings were evaluted by two groups of college students from Bristol and south Wales. Paired speech-samples – excerpts from each interviewee's speech to each of the two interviewers – were played, in random order, to judges who were asked, among other questions, to record which of each pair of fragments was broader in accent and to rate the difference on a seven-point scale. Giles found that the Bristol judges rated speech to the high status interviewer as less broad more than twice as often overall as speech to the equal status interviewer. The Welsh judges rated speech to the high status interviewer as less broad about five times as often overall as speech to the equal status interviewer. These findings are evidence of quite regular perceived accent-convergence by schoolboy interviewees to a higher status interviewer, which Giles interpreted as attempts to be viewed in a more favourable light by a listener.

Bourhis and Giles' language laboratory study (1977) referred to in section 4.2 is a particularly striking example of linguistic divergence. Within SAT, divergence has been seen primarily as a sociolinguistic strategy available to ethnic *groups* as a symbolic tactic for maintaining their identity and cultural distinctiveness. When the group of Welsh language learners in the language laboratory felt threatened by the English-sounding 'outsider's' remarks about the dismal future of Welsh, their broadening of their Welsh accents was an instance of accent divergence. In terms of the propositional predictions of SAT, these learners were 'attempting to diverge linguistically' (proposition 4) because they 'defined the encounter in intergroup terms and derived a positive ingroup identity' (4a), *and* 'wished to dissociate personally from another in an interindividual encounter' (4b). Giles (1980) discusses a rather different incentive to diverge in the case of what he calls 'cross-over divergence'. He suggests that divergence may occur not only by simple dissociation away from the interlocutor towards an opposing reference group, but also by expressing sociolinguistically a greater identification with that other's reference group than the other can display him/herself:

> 'For example, when talking to a shop assistant who is using a higher prestige language variety than one's own in a seemingly aloof manner, one might adopt an even more prestigious speech style than he in order to display one's greater qualifications to appeal in this direction.' (:119)

The examples of accommodation through dialect discussed above, and indeed all examples discussed so far in this chapter, have been of 'normal' dialectal variation, in the sense of variation within speakers' habitual stylistic repertoires. However, some studies have examined instances where speakers transcend their normal community-bound speech-repertoires and accommodate linguistically to the speech-patterns associated with other communities. For example, Trudgill (1981) offers an analysis of long-term accommodation in his own speech during a year's stay in the United States. He comments on his inconsistent but considerable adoption of voiced, flapped realizations of intervocalic /t/ (a regular feature of General American English) as well as possible explanations for his failure to adopt other American features such as non-prevocalic /r/ and [ɒ] for English [ɑ]. Interestingly, Shockey (1984) documents the reverse process with intervocalic flaps – the *decrease* in the percentages of flapped realizations of /t/ and /d/ produced by four originally Midwest or Californian American speakers living in England. Like Trudgill, Shockey also comments on her own speech, which shows progressive lowering of the frequencies of /t/ and /d/-flapping over time. Both researchers acknowledge pressures to conform linguistically to the non-native pronunciation norms, but also explore linguistic constraints on the accommodative phonetic and phonological shifts.

Within the more usual SAT experimental paradigm, Giles and Smith (1979) investigated the likely evaluative consequences of accommodating (and failing to accommodate) pronunciation-style towards a non-native norm. They asked twenty-eight qualified British teachers to rate (on five scales) eight different spoken texts, purported to be recordings of a Canadian speaker trying out different styles of presentation for an English audience (in England). One dimension along which the stimulus tape-recordings varied was pronunciation, where the speaker variously used a 'mild RP accent' and his native Canadian English variety. The results suggested that accent-convergence in this case had a very limited positive effect on subjects, the most favourable reaction being to convergence in rate of speaking. Giles and Smith speculate that the cumulative effect of simultaneous convergence at three linguistic levels (content, speech-rate and pronunciation) may have been seen as *overly* accommodative, and that the English listeners may have felt that the cross-national accommodation was 'stripping them of the veil of their own group distinctiveness' (:62). In any event, these findings are a salutary reminder of the dangers in overgeneralizing on the basis of any one of the propositional predictions of SAT to all speaking situations and all linguistic levels. With accent-mobility, it seems wise to recognize a distinction introduced in Giles' early work (1973:90) between a primary and a secondary level of accent repertoire, where the primary level designates a habitual, community-bound repertoire and the secondary level 'consists largely of those accents which an individual can effectively mimic, but commonly uses only for entertainment and amusement'. Even if speakers are motivated, as predicted by SAT, to accommodate in the uncharted waters of their secondary dialectal repertoires, the evaluative responses and communicative effects may be quite unexpected – to speakers as to researchers.

Some recent developments in SAT have both increased the explanatory power of the theory and raised novel questions and problems, though it is appropriate to refer to them only briefly here. One significant advance is the separation of psychological and linguistic aspects of accommodation, which early statements of SAT assumed to be isomorphic. So, Giles (1980) considers cases of 'speech complementarity' where what is speech divergence in a 'simple descriptive linguistic sense' psychologically involves acceptance of the situation rather than dissociation. Speech complementarity is likely to arise where interactants share perceptions of strong sociolinguistic norms governing role-relationships in a particular situation. Where this is the case (i.e. where social norms are perceived to dictate particular speech strategies – cf. proposition 1 (c), above), the familiar patterns of accommodative motives and effects are overridden. Giles gives the example of a job applicant being interviewed by a prospective employer:

> 'Although the former [the applicant] is likely to be perceived favourably because of his convergent strategies, had he failed simultaneously to maintain his inferior role position by means of other verbal and non-verbal cues, his overall performance may have been evaluated very poorly.' (:123)

Thakerer et al. (1982) introduce another distinction – between subjective and objective convergence/divergence. They demonstrate that the objective linguistic characteristics of interactants' speech may not be as significant as individuals' perceptions of these phenomena. A study of speech-style variation between low-status and high-status interlocutors showed that participants were inaccurate in assessing partners' dialectal standardness and speech-rate but still converged to their *perceived* speech-levels. For instance, low status speakers *thought* their higher status partners used more standard accents than they actually did, and converged to these perceived standard voices. SAT is undoubtedly enriched by these observations, but they also have a disorienting effect. It seems that the 'objective linguistic' dimension which once lay at the heart of SAT has become peripheral. It is no longer appropriate to talk of a speaker sampling the speech of an interlocutor and subsequently selecting specific speech-patterns from his/ her own repertoire, as earlier discussions of the theory have done (cf. Giles and Powesland 1975:158). It is even doubtful whether the theory can still be appropriately labelled a theory of *speech* accommodation in the strictest sense, having outgrown its linguistic origins in some significant respects.

4.5   Overview: a model of dialect in use

There is no suggestion that the theories, findings and suggestions reviewed in this chapter constitute a single coherent, explanatory framework for understanding dialect in use. It is more realistic to see the foregoing sections as offering a battery of explanatory propositions and hypotheses which sociolinguists can both draw on and elaborate on in their own work. Nevertheless, in the longer term, the aim must be to integrate individual approaches – social psychological, dialectological and sociolinguistic. And it is with this intention that the model of dialect in use is offered below, on the assumption that models in general are heuristic, exploratory conceptual aids to hypothesis-formation rather than (even attempts at) definitive statements. Any move to synthesize explanations of dialect-use will be hampered by inconsistency and omission, and there is one clear instance of each of these problems in the earlier sections of this chapter which can be aired at this point.

Accommodation theorists are beginning to recognize that SAT tenets (section 4.4) may, on certain occasions, predict different patterns of linguistic behaviour and interpretation from those deriving from studies of dialect and perceived personality (section 4.3). Particularly, the stereo-typical associations of standard dialects with competence (and less standard with social attractiveness) may well suggest quite different encoding and decoding strategies from those implied by SAT. If a speaker converges 'upwards' along a dimension of dialect towards a more standard interlocutor, SAT implies this may be to gain social approval (proposition 1(a)) and predicts that the strategy will be positively evaluted (proposition 3). However, personality studies suggest that, in this case, it is only *one* aspect of 'social approval' – that relating to perceived competence – that will be obtained. The converse case is even more problematical (cf. Putnam and Street 1984). What if the interlocutor has a *less* prestigious dialect? Where SAT predicts 'downward' convergence as the strategy for gaining social approval, personality studies suggest that to 'lower' one's dialectal standardness will be to be perceived as less competent. It is quite possible that these conflicts are 'real' in the sense that they are conflicts as much for speakers and listeners as they are for analysts. Nevertheless, they suggest that one (or both) of the sets of explanatory propositions is, as yet, oversimplified. Putnam and Street's work in fact suggests two different resolutions to the conflict; firstly that convergence 'is typically more a determinant of social attractiveness than of competence impressions' (:108), so that perceptions of competence are likely to stem more directly from independent, non-interpersonally based stylistic selections of, for example, standard dialect; secondly, the multiple dimensions of intention and evaluation (:110) may be realized simultaneously in multiple socio-linguistic behaviours in respect of different linguistic levels and/or features. These remain questions for future empirical work.

A more general problem relates to the role of the situation in explaining dialect variation. We began this chapter arguing the case for a less deterministic, more motivational approach to dialect-use, hostile to the assumption that speech-style could be adequately explained as determined by the situation. Certainly, the studies reviewed in this chapter show that dialect-use and dialect variation are most often best characterized (in the terms of Blom and Gumperz 1972) as 'metaphorical' rather than 'situational' choices. Although metaphorical switching between codes is presented as a minority occurrence, we have seen that *most* and arguably *all* instances of dialect encoding are mediated by symbolic or metaphorical associations 'borrowed' from outside the particular speaking-situation. But recent social psychological work has suggested – though not for the first time, (cf. Goffman 1964) – that the contribution of the situation has been underestimated (cf. Ball, Giles, Byrne and Berechree 1984; Beebe and Giles 1984; Giles and Ryan 1982). To say this is not to support a return to correlational non-explanations, but to stress that speakers themselves may feel more or less constrained by implicit social norms operating within different situations. And these norms, as Giles argues in the case of 'speech complementarity', may inhibit attitudes, perceptions or strategies predictable elsewhere. That is, *as part of* a motivational account of dialect variation, we need to begin to appreciate the variable subjective dimensions of speaking-situations. For instance, Ball *et al.* conclude that interview speech is valued primarily for its adherence to sociolinguistic norms, and that interpersonal accommodation shifts in accent have little judgemental significance in their data (:125).

With such provisos in mind, we can turn to figure 4-1, a detailed but preliminary model of dialect in use. It is organized as a simple, dyadic communication model incorporating the various linguistic, social and psychological factors and processes whose relations to dialect-use have been discussed earlier in this chapter. Contextual variables – the major input components to the communication chain, shown at the top and bottom of the model – are distinguished somewhat arbitrarily as either 'social' or 'individual' contextual variables. Social contextual variables are further divided: into 'macro-level' and 'micro-level' variables. The former relate to community-wide consensual views of dialect-varieties themselves – how standard are they?; how much vitality do they show? (cf. Ryan, Giles and Sebastian 1982); what generalized levels of status do they attract?; how central are they to perceptions of ethnicity? (cf. section 4.1 above). Micro-level variables are those relating to particular speaking-situations. Giles and Ryan (1982 and cf. section 5.2, below) have argued that the situational dimensions listed here – group-centered/person-centered, status-stressing/solidarity-stressing – have a systematic influence on participants' attitudes to language-varieties. More generally, we may expect these dimensions also to influence *en*coding processes through the operation of situational norms. It is through recognizing that situations vary along multiple

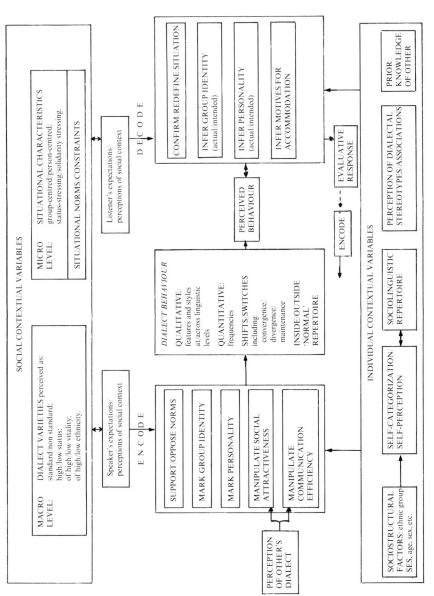

Figure 4–1 A dyadic model of dialect in use

dimensions of this sort that we can begin to clarify obscure notions such as 'formality' which, as we saw in discussing Labov's concept of stylistic stratification, are often adduced as explaining dialectal behaviour. Individual contextual variables are those more clearly relating to individual participants' backgrounds, attitudes, abilities, and so on, though it is clear that the 'social' variables outlined above can only operate, as the model shows, when mediated by individuals' expectations and perceptions. The model further shows that sociostructural factors have less explanatory value for dialect-research than individuals' self-images concerning their own ('actual' and desired) SES, age, sex and other identities.

All of these contextual influences are shown to impinge upon the encoding and decoding of dialect. The encoding processes shown relate broadly to foregoing sections of this chapter: group-identity-marking, personality-marking and interpersonal accommodation. The process 'support/oppose norms' follows from the discussion of situational norms earlier in this section, and allows for perceived norms to be (subconsciously or consciously) violated. The listing of encoding processes does not distinguish degrees of intentionality. If the accommodation strategies are activated ('manipulate social attractiveness', 'manipulate communication efficiency'), they must be classified as intentional, though not necessarily conscious processes. On the other hand, the identity-marking processes may or may not be intentional in this sense. They may reflect motivated self-presentational strategies in specific contexts (where the term 'manipulation' would again be appropriate) or they may stem 'automatically' from individuals' regular perceptions of their own group- or individual identities.[2] Note that the accommodative strategies cannot be implemented unless there is a means of perceiving the other's dialect characteristics. If this information is not available, as would be the case at the beginning of an encounter with a stranger, a speaker can only work from his/her own perceptions of non-dialectal cues (e.g. appearance) or his/her own expectations and the dialect-stereotypes associated with these. In such cases, we could find either accommodation to a stereotype or encoding based entirely on personally-based processes.

The dialect behaviours referred to in the model relate to all linguistic levels – phonetic, phonological, morphological, syntactic, lexical, and discoursal – and to qualitative as well as quantitative variation (cf. section 3.5). While it is often most convenient to 'freeze' descriptions of dialect-use into apparently static patterns of behaviour, the model also allows for the dynamics of dialect-use. Indeed, the interpersonally-based (accommodative) encoding processes lead naturally to variable patterns of dialect behaviour as interactants progressively modify their speech under the pressures of momentary situational and motivational changes. Dialect behaviour is clearly differentiated from 'perceived behaviour' in the model. This is in recognition of the range of potential perceptual biases which may influence what listeners hear (cf. Street and Hopper 1982). The two-way arrow between 'perceived behaviour' and the decoding component represents the likelihood of a range of contextual factors predisposing listeners to focus on expected elements of actual dialect behaviour (perhaps those dialect features consistent with an existing stereotype) and to retain and process selective or even non-existent elements of actual behaviours. Robinson (1979: 215ff.) has emphasized these possibilities in his distinction between 'etic' markers – those features *available* for conveying social meanings – and 'emic' markers – those which actually *serve for* discriminating social meanings, even if on occasions they are no more than imagined characteristics of the linguistic behaviour.

The model is unable to predict particular evaluative responses from the various decoding processes which it taxonomizes. Once again, it emphasizes that a host of contextual variables may impinge on evaluative responses made, to the extent that judgements of situational appropriateness, for instance, may totally dominate or be totally dominated by the perception of personally- and interpersonally-based encoding strategies. The general aim of future empirical studies of dialect in use should be to examine the interaction of the variables listed in the model in particular instances, and the case-studies reported in chapter 5 are to be seen as contributions to this general activity.

5

Dialect in Use: Two Case-Studies

The case-studies to be reported in this chapter are attempts to understand phonological style-shifting in two naturally occurring speaking situations in terms of some of the sociolinguistic and social psychological processes outlined in figure 4-1. The first study (section 5.1) extends the analysis of stylistic variation in the travel agency (cf. section 3.4). The second study (section 5.2) introduces and examines data from a broadcast local radio request-show.

The use of case-studies as a research method in this area merits some comment, especially since the studies to follow are presented against a background of Labov-inspired large-scale sociolinguistic surveys of speech communities involving quite large samples of informants. One of the criticisms of correlational, stratificational studies discussed in section 3.5 was the way aggregated scores across groups of individual speakers may disguise variable intragroup behaviours and processes. Although statistical analyses of variance can identify extents of inter group variation, they cannot demystify the different motivational factors which lead to variance and which may even, on occasions, lead individuals to produce similar sociolinguistic behaviours by quite different communicative means. In research-designs directed at discovering generalizations about the patterned behaviours of social groups, these considerations are not seen as problems if intragroup variation can be shown to be within acceptable limits. However, when the focus of attention is stylistic variation, when we need to account for situated instances of dialect in use, generalizations across aggregates of speakers are at best premature. Figure 4–1 hypothesized that, in any one speech-event, there will be an array of macro-level and micro-level social contextual factors impinging on the section of speech-forms and styles, mediated by individuals' perceptions, beliefs and experiences. An attempt to generalize to groups of individuals' stylistic selections in ostensibly 'the same' or 'similar' speaking situations will further underestimate the contribution of the individual, as social psychologists have already accused sociolinguistics of doing. For the moment, at least, there is more than enough to be learnt about the interaction between context and idiolect.

The case for case-studies can be further supported by epistemological arguments in favour of an 'interpretive' as opposed to a 'positivist' orientation to social science research[1] (cf. Worsely 1978:88). The positivist orientation regards the procedures used in social science as fundamentally of the same kind as those used by natural scientists: assuming, that is, that social phenomena constitute a reality which exists in its own right. The interpretive approach is less dogmatic about this and accepts that social phenomena have largely to be deduced, often intuitively and subjectively, by the researcher, who therefore (as Worsely puts it :74) '. . . is . . . said to "construct" social reality by the way in which he interprets what he learns about it'. The two methodologies represent conflicting ideologies, but can also be seen to stem quite naturally from different particular research objectives. Figure 5–1 suggests that research aimed at generalizing about broad patterns of sociolinguistic differentiation will appropriately adopt a positivist orientation, involving large numbers of informants and some form of survey technique, probably involving random sampling. Here, the gains in generalizability and control over data are likely to outweigh losses in terms of scope for analysis and explanation. The study of

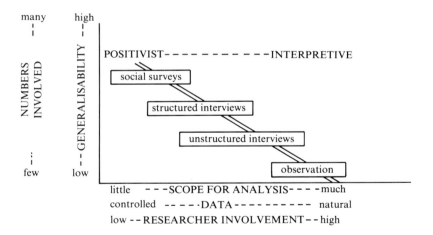

Fig. 5–1: Research designs in sociolinguistics (adapted from Worsely 1978:88).

stylistic dialectal variation in context, on the other hand, *requires* a more interpretive orientation. Here, the losses in terms of generalizability and control will be offset by the richness of contextual understanding available through the detailed observation of a small number of particular, naturally situated instances.

5.1   *Dialect at work*

The correlational study of style-shifting in a Cardiff travel agency (section 3.4) was able to show that broadly characterized dimensions of a speaking-situation can be systematically associated with patterns of phonological selection. The numerical findings (table 3–11) suggested that Labov's concept of stylistic stratification is broadly applicable to a speaker's phonological output *within* a single speaking-situation. The study was methodologically and theoretically deterministic in that it correlated frequencies of occurrence of speech-variants with pre-existing situation categories, and implied that these categories 'caused' and 'explained' the 'resulting' phonological behaviours. In other words, no detailed consideration was given to many of the processes said to underline dialect in use as summarized in the model in figure 4–1. Participants in the speech-events analysed were treated merely as a factor in establishing the independent variable 'contextual type' and not as interacting communicators. The two following sub-sections extend and clarify the analysis of style-shifting in the travel agency, firstly in terms of the *de*coding of the assistant's style-shifting, secondly by exploring the accommodative *en*coding potential of her shifts.

5.1.1   *Stylistic stratification revisited*

Given that table 3–11 reported frequency-scores for arbitrarily selected phonological varibles and that different variables produced somewhat different stratification patterns, it is appropriate to ask what perceptual significance, if any, the assistant's style-shifting is likely to have had for her interlocutors. The actual recipients' views are, of course, not recoverable; they were groups of friends and other colleagues in the travel agency and certain other travel agents and tour operators Sue spoke to over the telephone. It is possible, though, to follow the established practice of researchers in the social psychological paradigm and gather evaluative data from relatively large groups of judges who have listened to edited extracts of the tape-recorded data. By this means we can reach conclusions about the 'emic' status of the variables (cf. Robinson 1979 and section 4.5 above), seek support for the perceptual significance of the four contextual types identified in the earlier study (figure 3–8) and possibly advance our understanding of how phonological styles are perceived to vary.

Two groups of university students were asked to evaluate nine of the original fifteen extracts used in the earlier study on the basis of accent mildness-broadness. They first listened to the extracts to 'tune in' to Sue's accent repertoire across the extracts, and then were asked to use a five-point scale to cover Sue's range of accent usage, where 1 represented her most standard style, 5 her least standard style. Subjects were given transcripts in conventional orthography of Sue's speaking turns, and were asked to mark every point where they were conscious of a shift in accent mildness-broadness together with the direction of shift, and to rate each half-line of text with a figure from the five-point scale. The first group of subjects consisted of eighteen first-year students who had very little experience of Cardiff speech, while the second consisted of twenty third-year students, all of whom were familiar with Cardiff speech. Although there was a slight tendency for the less experienced group to use the extremes of the scale more often, pointing to rather less sensitivity to degrees of shift compared with the more experienced group, there were no significant intergroup differences in judgements of points and directions of shift.

Overall, there was a remarkable degree of consistency over the thirty-eight sets of evaluations, often with thirty or more subjects agreeing as to point and direction of shaft. It was clear that these subjective responses correlated well with the classification of extracts into the four contextual types. In *all* cases where there was a change in one or more of these situational components, a shift in style was responded to by at least sixty per cent of subjects. Interestingly, the most regularly perceived of these shifts involved *simultaneous* changes of channel, participants and topic. To allow a more precise assessment of the correlation between objective and subjective measures, scores were calculated for the original five phonological variables across the subset of nine extracts, as shown in table 5–1.

Table 5–1: Mean values of 38 subjects' ratings of four contextual types compared with mean values of five linguistic variables across nine extracts.

Contextual type	Means of subjective evaluations	Means of 5 linguistic variables (for 9 extracts)
I 'casual'	4.3 (85%)	76%
II 'informal work-related'	3.5 (70%)	53%
III 'client'	2.4 (48%)	33%
IV 'telephone'	1.6 (32%)	28%

(Interestingly, the means obtained were almost identical to those obtained from the larger sample). By taking the mean value of the thirty-eight subjects' ratings of each contextual type, a rank-ordering of evaluated styles was produced. This directly matched the rank-ordering of the composite indices for all linguistic variables, also shown in table 5–1.

These findings offer some support for the intuitive selection of the variables 'participants', 'channel' and 'topic' as common correlates of (perceived) phonological style. Each of these variable situational dimensions, and particularly the co-variation of two or more of them, was associated with a perceived shift in phonological style. At this stage, however, we can still only speculate about how and why this is the case. It may be that Sue sees herself occupying different social roles on as opposed to off the telephone, when addressing clients as opposed to addressing colleagues, and when talking about work as opposed to other topics – the narrowly defined travel-company-representative role versus the less clearly specified individual role. That is, there may be a single social psychological dimension underpinning Sue's phonological variation, relating to her perception of her various routine speech-events at work as more or less 'transactional' or 'personal' in the senses intended by Gumperz (cf. also section 1.6, above):

> 'One type of interaction, which we will call TRANSACTIONAL, centers largely around certain limited goals such as purchasing such items as groceries or clothing, cashed a check at the bank, getting the telephone operator to put a call through, going to the doctor. Participants in such interactions in a sense suspend their individuality and act by virtue of their status, in the sense in which this word is used in anthropology . . . They act as salesmen, customers, bank tellers, physicians, rather than as Tom Hansen or Inger Stensen. Each society has definite norms of behavioral and linguistic etiquette which attach to these statuses. Regardless of their individual personalities, occupants of such statuses are expected to conform to these norms'. (Gumperz 1975:35).

Alternative or complementary processes might be the variable need to mark group-identity (e.g. more recognizably Cardiff dialect-features in speaking to friends and other in-group members), the projection of variably salient personality-traits (e.g. perceived competence in transactional speech-events), a complex array of interpersonally-based accommodative strategies (e.g. manipulation of communication efficiency in conversation with clients) or the perception of overriding situational constraints (e.g. recognition of telephone-talk as a register requiring, among other stylistic features, quite standard pronunciation). As we shall see, some of these processes can be clarified by a more detailed analysis of particular instances. Table 5–1 at least offers support for the 'emic' status of the sociolinguistic variables quantified in the earlier study. These five variables are of course only a small part of the total set of features available for 'etic' phonological variation. But the close matching of values of objective and subjective analyses shown in the table strongly suggests a casual link behind the correlational pattern – that values of variables (h), (r), (C cluster), (intervoc.t) and (ɔu) are perceptually stylistically diagnostic of at least one Cardiff speaker's speech, as perceived by listeners.

The thirty-eight judges' evaluations were a rich source of information about style-shifting beyond their ability to confirm aspects of the original study. The shifts predicted by the classification of contextual types were all perceived to exist, but judges were able regularly to identify more than these in the data, including some shifts which were perceived to be progressive rather than categorical. An example is seen in extract 5–1, below:

Extract 5–1   (Sue in conversation with client 64)

line

1.	Sue:	Whitsun is quite full I know at the moment they've got something about the twenty-first of May from <u>Bris</u>tol for a <u>week</u>
	Client:	only for a week?
5.	Sue:	I'm sure they'll get a <u>for</u>tnight on the same date though mm I think you'll get <u>some</u>thing
	Client:	it'd have to be from <u>Bris</u>tol there's nothing from <u>Cardiff</u>?
10.	Sue:	yes I'm sure you'd get <u>some</u>thing from <u>Cardiff</u>

Over Sue's last two speaking-turns in the extract (i.e. over lines 5–7 and 10–11), more than seventy per cent of subjects noted that Sue shifted towards a less standard style, though no clear point or points of shift emerged when the marked transcripts were collated. This is interesting because there is no obvious situational change here, although a possible motivation for this shift is discussed below. The immediate point is that a progressive (perceived) style-shift of this sort, whereby a speaker is heard to move gradually from one stylistic 'level' to another, is by definition not detectable by a deterministic methodology which establishes situational categories before examining linguistic behaviours.

A similar example is provided in extract 3–3 (in section 3.4). Here we have a major situational change, according to our earlier classification, involving changes in channel and addressee before the words *computers are down* (line 7) which is perceived by more than seventy-five per cent of subjects. What is interesting is that most of these subjects noted a second shift towards a less standard style after the uttering of these words. This 'step-ladder' effect again suggests that Sue moves out of her 'telephone style' only gradually, with a sort of sandhi effect operating at the style-boundary, one style assimilating towards the level of the other, resulting in a finely graduated transition between styles. Again, in extract 5–2, below, the change of topic (non-work to work-related) and presumed though not actual addressee (from colleague to client) after the pause (beginning at line 4) corresponds with a major perceived shift towards more standard speech – more than seventy per cent of subjects marked this shift on their transcripts. But half the subjects noted a second 'upward' shift a line later (line 5). Again, Sue finds it appropriate to move into the 'letter-composing style' gradually, after her 'casual' discussion of eggs, mayonnaise and coffee.

Extract 5–2 (Sue is chatting to another assistant who, during the pause, asks Sue how she should start a letter)

line
1. I don't <u>like</u> egg   I don't <u>like</u> er mayonnaise
    I was going to make a <u>coffee</u> about an hour ago
    (pause)
    dear Sir with reference to your forthcoming
5. holiday with us to Os<u>tend</u> an explanatory letter
    that we have today received from H. Limited we
    sincerely apologize for the inconvenience this
    may cause.

The finer detail of the judgemental analysis clearly demonstrates the inadequacy of one of the supposed 'determinants' of style – topic. For instance, the whole of extract 5–1 is seemingly topically homogeneous. It deals exclusively with the availability of flights in May from Bristol and Cardiff. It is Sue's attitude towards the subject matter and her conversational role that seem to change towards the end of the extract; Sue's first statement to her client is unhelpful and off-putting, but she later becomes more encouraging. This change of role and communicative function may be seen to activate social psychological processes which result in the selection of less standard dialect forms, as discussed above. Some contextual detail is needed to appreciate how these processes might apply in extract 5–1. The fragment is from the middle of an encounter. Previously the client has made two requests for services which Sue has not been able to comply with, and Sue is likely to feel she (herself) is being unhelpful. The client is female, in her fifties, a secretary, married, and a fairly broadly-accented speaker – a number of features in her speech resemble Sue's less standard forms. Arguably, then, at the end of extract 5–1, Sue is repairing the cold, rather hostile situation she was forced into creating earlier in the encounter, partly by the propositional meaning of her utterance *(I'm sure you'd get something from Cardiff)*, partly by stylistic meaning. Through the 'downward' phonological shift, Sue simultaneously emphasizes her affinity with her client (marks solidarity and shared group identity), is perceived as socially attractive (marks personality) and converges linguistically towards her interlocutor, (heightens social approval and communication efficiency).

The possibilities and suggestions thrown up by the evaluative study clearly need to be examined more systematically over larger corpora than the fragments discussed above. Two sets of encoding strategies are obvious candidates for further study – identity-marking processes and inter-personal accommodation processes. The variable marking of group- and individual-identity through dialect will be examined in the radio-show context in section 5.2. Section 5.1.2 continues the analysis of Sue's stylistic variation from the perspective of speech accommodation theory.

5.1.2   *Accommodation at work*

One of the limitations of the correlational study of Sue's stylistic variation was its failure to recognize systematic variation within the population of fifty-one travel agency clients. Yet, we have already seen (i) that Sue does appear to vary her pronunciation in response to interpersonal factors (section 5.1.1); and (ii) that the population of clients is linguistically stratified (section 3.3) according to SES-linked variables such as occupation (table 3–8) and educational background (table 3–9). Because of this pattern of differentiation, SAT predicts that Sue's phonological behaviour will, within limits and provided she does not perceive social norms for speech in the travel agency to override the accommodative strategies, vary in relation to that of her interlocutors, if (a) she desires their social approval (provided she perceives the rewards of so doing as greater than the costs); and/or (b) desires a high level of communicational efficiency (cf. the propositional statements of SAT in section 4.4). The fifty-one travel agency encounters, therefore, offer an opportunity to study phonological accommodation within a large corpus of naturally occurring data. Given Giles and Powesland's observation that there may be a general set to accommodate to others, and particularly Sue's own observations (in informal discussion at the end of the data-collection period) that she sees the function of a travel agency assistant as 'to be liked' ('desires social approval') and 'to get on with clients' ('desires communicational efficiency'), SAT predicts that Sue's phonology will show convergence to that of her interlocutors.

To characterize Sue's speech to the clients, scores for four sociolinguistic variables – (h), (ng),[2] (C cluster) and (intervoc.t) – were calculated over the whole of Sue's speech to all fifty-one addressees. Variables were defined in the same way as they had been in the social stratification travel agency study in chapter 3. Across Sue's speech to all clients, the mean scores shown in table 5–2 were obtained. The table also reproduces from table 3–8 mean values of the 'skilled non-manual' clients' scores for the same phonological variables. Overall, Sue's scores are not too dissimilar from the means for

Table 5–2: Mean variable-scores for four phonological variables in Sue's speech to clients (bracketed figures are numbers of tokens) compared with mean values of 'skilled non-manual' clients' use of the same variables.

| | (h) | (ng) | (C cluster) | | | | (intervoc.t) |
			(i)	(ii)	(iii)	All	
SUE	21.3 (320)	67.4 (172)	44.7 (132)	56.0 (166)	37.0 (254)	45.9	31.4 (172)
'Skilled Non-Manual' clients (mean)	16.3	41.8	59.1	68.1	52.3	59.8	42.1

the socioeconomic class to which she would be assigned on the basis of her occupation.[3] Still, she produces more standard variants than the mean with variables (intervoc.t) and (C cluster) and more non-standard variants with (h) and particularly with (ng). The table is a useful reminder of the need to recognize idiolectal or interpersonal factors within aggregated scores.

The immediate question is whether Sue's speech, as indexed by the four variables, reflects the variation apparent in the clients' speech in the manner predicted by accommodation theory. Individual encounters suggest that this covariation does occur. Extract 5–3 shows Sue in conversation with client 34 – a female staff nurse from Llanishen (which is held to be a relatively prestigious area of the city). Client 34 is a relatively standard speaker, at least in this context, as shown by the high frequency of more

Extract 5–3   (Sue in conversation with Client 34)

line

          (Cii)
1. S. I don't know of another one in March for <u>three</u> nights actually
          0

    C. oh or perhaps I // made a mistake last

          (Cii)
    S. wasn't Maj<u>or</u>ca was it?
          1
                    (t)   (Cii)
    C. no no it was <u>Benidorm</u> but I couldn't book then // they were
                           0   1
          (Ciii)
5.   fully <u>booked</u> so it's//back on Tuesday
             0
              (Ciii)   (t)
    S. /mm/ this is Tuesday it's three nights at fifteen <u>thirty</u>
                           1   0

    C.   that leaves

          (ri)
    S. you ar//rive <u>back</u>   yes
                 1
        (ri)   (ri)   (h)
    C. arrive <u>back</u>   oh I you   //arrive back here
         0   0   0
          (ri)   (t)
10. S. you arrive back into <u>Cardiff</u> at fifteen <u>thirty</u>
            0   0
          (Ciii)
    C. and it's fifty // seven
             0

    S. fifty   fifty <u>nine</u>

    C. fifty nine plus

          (ri)   (Ci)
    S. <u>in</u>surance and <u>air</u>port taxes
           0   1
          (h)
15. C. and how much does it normally come in // to?
          0

S.   about six <u>pound</u>

C.   and the airport // taxes

S.   no approximately al<u>toge</u>ther

C.   oh al<u>toge</u>ther

20.   S.   yes

        (rii)
C.   <u>right</u>   sixty five pound
       0

(S.   speaks briefly aside)

        (Ciii)   (rii) (ri)
C.   and it's the Riviera
        0   0   0
     (Ciii) (rii)
S.   that's right yes
     0 0

standard variants (marked with a figure 1 below the line of transcript at the point where the particular variable occurs) of the variables shown.[4] In this extract, Sue's speech, too, is relatively standard. We get an impression of her phonological range when speaking to clients by comparing her speech in extract 5–3 with that in extract 5–4, below. In extract 5–4, Sue's principal interlocutor (client 25) is a factory girl from Adamsdown. Both client and assistant show a high frequency of non-standard variants of the four phonological variables. These two extracts (to which we return below) can be said to suggest a convergent accommodative pattern; Sue seems to be accommodating her phonology to that of her interlocutors.

Extract 5–4   (Sue in conversation with Client 25)

line

           (h)
1.   C.   where do you have to get the <u>plane</u> then?
           1

```
                    (rii)
     S.   Cardiff Rhoose
                     0
                          (Ci)
     C.      twenty past three is it?
                            1
                (h)                  (r)
     S.   so you'd have to be there at least     um
                 0                    0
          (Cii)
 5.  C.   I can't think
           0
                     (Ci)
     S.   twenty past did I say?
                        1


     C.   I think // so yeah



                     (Ci)
     S.   twenty past three
                      1


     C.   yeah


                (h)              (ri)           (t) (t)
10.  S.   so you'd have to be there about quarter to three
                 0                 1              0  1
                          (ri)            (Cii)
     C.   (to C1) get there on time wouldn't we?
                          1                1
                          (h)        (t)
    *C1   (to C) yeah but we'd have to get our wages first
                           1          1
          (t)
     C.   get em there // (( ))
           1


     S.   what time do you get paid?


          (Cii)                      (h)    (Ci)
15.  C.   don't know usually about half past three
           1                          0      1
                (Cii)                      (h)    (t)
     S.    mm can't you ask them if you can have it earlier?
            1                                1     1
                     (Ci)  (ng)
          you're just going to go then // are you?
                      1     1


     C.   yeah
```

             (ng)
S.   you're not going to tell them are you? (laughs)
          1

20. C.

     and C1 no.

       (Cii)   (ri)   (ng)
C.   we won't lose our job or anything you know
        1   0   1
    (Ci) (ng)
C1 just going for the weekend like
     1   1
    (Cii)
C. isn't there one earlier than that?   (t)
     1   // or later
                                      υ
       (Ciii)
S. /no/ no that's there's only one flight Monday Wednesday Friday
      1

25.   and Sunday (pause)

             (t) (t)   (Ci)
    well think about it anyway and then if you want to call back . . .
           0 0   0

(*C1's two speaking turns are transcribed and her variants are noted along with S and C's; C1's speech is not, of course, included in the variable-counts).

We need to find a means of assessing whether this sort of convergent phonological shifting is repeated across Sue's speech to the population of clients as a whole. One way of achieving this is to tabulate variable-scores for her speech to sub-groups of the client population. Table 5–3 shows values for the four phonological variables in Sue's speech when in conversation with six sub-groups of clients, identified on the basis of their occupational class. This table can be compared with Table 3–8 which showed these sub-groups' *own* scores for the same (and other) variables. Sue's speech shows a general pattern of differentiation according to the occupational class of her interlocutor, as variable-scores generally rise (speech becomes less standard) with the progression from more prestigious to less prestigious occupational class of interlocutor. The numerical progressions for the four variables are, naturally enough, not perfectly linear. We must remember that the quantitative procedures used to arrive at numerical indices are not beyond criticism (cf. section 3.5); that individual clients within each sub-group, and therefore quite possibly Sue's accommodative behaviour to individuals, will show interpersonal variation; and that the quantitative indices for variables in the clients' own speech in table 3–8 do not themselves form perfect linear progressions. Notwithstanding these considerations, Sue's pronunciation in respect of the four variables is almost as good a marker of the occupational status of her interlocutors as her interlocutors' *own* speech. The pattern of differentiation in table 5–3 is highly suggestive of regular speech accommodation.[5]

Table 5–3: Phonological variables in the assistant's speech to clients by %; clients are distributed into six occupation groups.

	CLIENTS' OCCUPATION CLASS					
	I	II	IIIN	IIIM	IV	V
(h)	3.7	15.9	13.4	35.3	29.3	28.6
	(27)	(63)	(97)	(85)	(41)	(7)
(ng)	58.3	53.8	55.7	75.0	83.8	85.7
	(12)	(26)	(70)	(20)	(37)	(7)
(C cluster)	42.9	42.9	42.1	40.0	69.2	50.0
(i)	(7)	(21)	(64)	(25)	(13)	(2)
(C cluster)	35.7	55.6	49.3	67.7	75.0	66.7
(ii)	(14)	(27)	(71)	(31)	(20)	(3)
(C cluster)	11.8	35.5	25.7	54.5	57.1	60.0
(iii)	(17)	(31)	(113)	(55)	(28)	(10)
All (C clus.) by %	30.1	44.7	39.0	54.1	67.1	58.9
(intervoc.t)	26.1	12.0	27.1	37.8	50.0	66.7
	(23)	(25)	(59)	(37)	(22)	(6)

However, the relevant propositional predictions of SAT are specifically to do with linguistic similarity/dissimilarity, and it is necessary to adopt a *relational* perspective to the numerical information tabulated above. In the first instance, this may be achieved graphically by plotting the tabulated scores in a series of bar-charts. Figures 5–2 to 5–5 compare the mean values of the client occupation sub-groups' indices for the four variables with Sue's speech in conversation with them. Again, there is a clear suggestion in these figures that Sue's accent behaviour does match that of her interlocutors in a way that conforms to the predictions of SAT. As

Figs. 5–2 – 5–5: Degrees of standardness in clients' use of phonological variables compared with the assistant's use of the same variables in conversation with them.

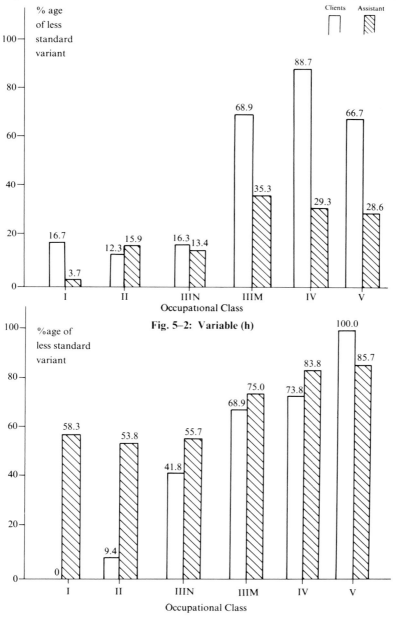

Fig. 5–2: Variable (h)

Fig. 5–3: Variable (ng)

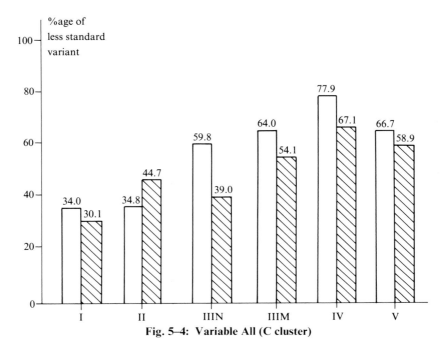

Fig. 5–4: Variable All (C cluster)

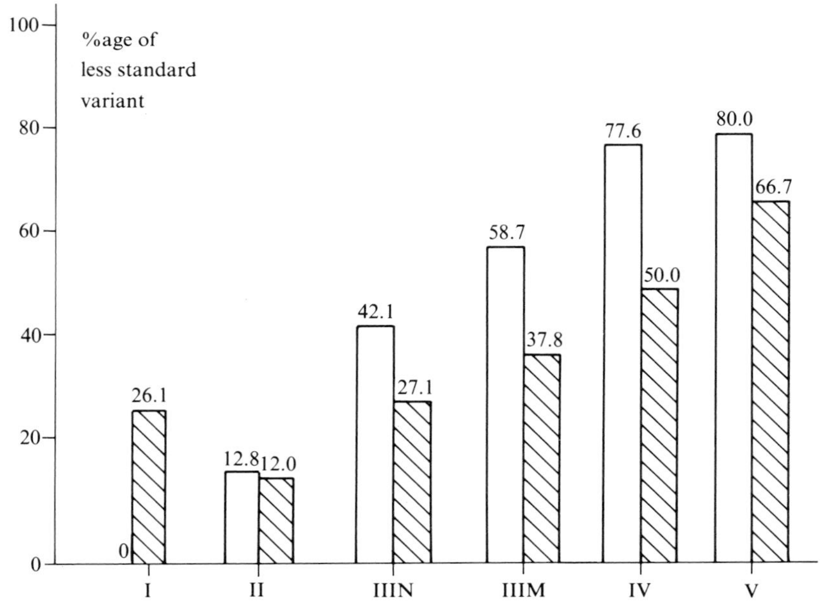

Fig. 5–5: Variable (intervoc.t)

percentages of the less standard variants of each variable generally rise in the clients' speech (as we move from occupation class I to V), so the percentages of these variants in Sue's speech generally rise. Beyond this, the bar-charts show how, on occasions, breaks in this progression from more standard to less standard forms in the clients' speech are replicated in Sue's speech (for example over groups IV and V with variables (h) and (C cluster)).

Figures 5–2 to 5–5 still partly disguise the true extent of the inter-correlation between the clients' and the assistant's scores, since the figures force us to compare absolute levels of standardness. There is no reason to expect the assistant to show the same phonological range as her clients, so it is more meaningful to compare participants' phonological behaviour in terms of *their own* repertoires. Figure 5–6 allows us to do this by plotting

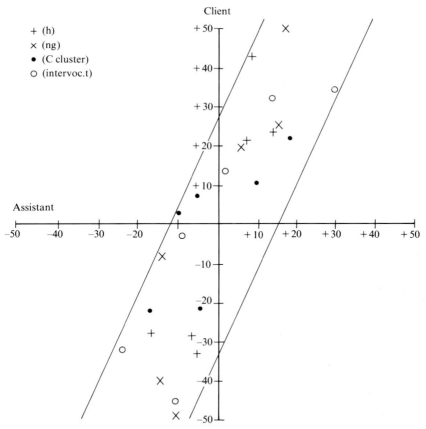

Fig. 5–6: A comparison of deviations from means of assistant's and occupation sub-groups' values for all variables.

deviations from the mean for each variable in Sue's speech against those in the speech of the client sub-groups. The spread of points about the means in this figure confirms the high degree of correlation between clients' and assistant's accent patterns suggested by the earlier bar-charts. In figure 5–6, a perfect correlation would be represented by all plotted points lying on a straight line (of any gradient) through the point at which all the axes cross. Here, the plotted points are distributed within a relatively narrow band, to either side of such a straight line. Further statistical support for this interpretation may be obtained by calculating intercorrelation coefficients between the values shown in figures 5–2 to 5–5. The following coefficients, each deriving from six pairs of indices, were obtained between the clients' and the occupation sub-groups' values of the four variables:

(h)	+ .87
(ng)	+ .90
(C cluster)	+ .76
(intervoc.t)	+ .86

From these statistics and figures 5–2 to 5–6, it is clear that, in an objective linguistic sense, phonological convergence is a speech strategy that the assistant uses in her daily association with clients. The fact that it is produced spontaneously in a natural setting must constitute a small but powerful piece of evidence to support the first proposition of SAT.

The relational perspective adopted above is based on analyses of covariation – participants arriving at similar phonological output in terms of their own speech-repertoires. Although it is reasonable to interpret the findings as evidence of convergence, the term 'convergence' suggests a rather different relational perspective – seeing one (or more)[6] speaker(s) shifting from a defined start-point towards an interlocutor. It is possible to conceptualize Sue's style-shifting accordingly if we take her speech to clients of her own occupational class as a set of base-values for the different variables – that is, as a start-point. On this assumption,[7] we can say that, in speech to the five occupation classes other than her own, Sue converges to her interlocutors in twelve cases, diverges in four, and in the remaining four actually shifts beyond the interlocutors (cf. Bell 1984:165). Figure 5–7 charts these patterns for one sociolinguistic variable (intervoc.t). Bell goes on to point out that Sue's convergence is most marked in her speech to the 'lower' occupational classes; that is, when it is 'downward convergence':

> 'The assistant's degree of shift differs depending on whether the client's class is higher or lower than her own. To the two higher classes, her shifts are slight and inconsistent, half of them divergent.

To the three lower classes, she converges consistently and often massively on all four variables. She shifts on average some 55% of the distance from her own 'input' level to the 'target' level of the client's speech. The travel assistant thus goes – quite literally – more than halfway to meet her clients'.(ibid.)

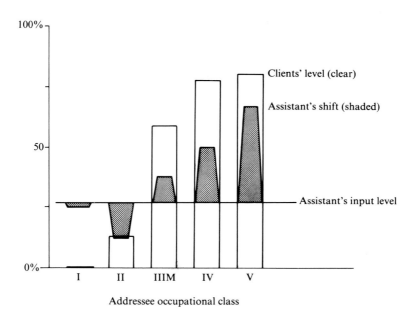

Fig. 5–7: Sue's convergence in respect of variable (intervoc.t) to five occupational classes of clients. 'Input level' is taken as the assistant's speech to her own occupational class (from Bell 1984: 165).

These findings show the value of detailed sociolinguistic methods in providing clear descriptive evidence in support of a social psychological explanatory theory. However, the data also invite a reappraisal of the theoretical propositions themselves – of the precise mechanisms of phonological accommodation. We have been assuming that Sue's accommodative shifting is motivated by the two central factors specified by SAT – gaining interlocutors' approval and making communication more efficient. This is a reasonable assumption since travel agency assistants are employed partly to ensure that these aims are met. But the findings have been presented as if these accommodative processes operate in isolation from the other social psychological considerations summarized in figure 4–1. As we have seen (cf. section 4.5), SAT is beginning to consider the interaction between accommodative and other processes and strategies, and there is evidence of such interaction in the travel agency data. A 'purely' accommodative interpretation of the quantitative findings reported in this section would posit that Sue is attempting to match aspects of her interlocutors' speech in her own phonological output. That is, we could argue that Sue becomes aware of the degree of standardness/non-standardness in her interlocutors' use of particular linguistic variables and, consciously or unconsciously, shifts her own speech in an attempt to reproduce that degree of standardness. Moreover, it would appear she is successful in doing this, particularly with lower occupational classes. But an alternative interpretation is that the well-attested linguistic matching that we find here and in other interactive settings is, in a sense, only incidental. In the travel-agency investigation, for example, we could argue that Sue is *not* attempting to reproduce the actual levels of standardness for particular variables that she detects in the speech of her interlocutors; rather, she is attempting to convey via her pronunciation and presumably other behaviours, verbal and nonverbal, a persona which is similar to that conveyed by her interlocutors. If the participants' pronunciation characteristics converge, it is only as a result of attempts to reduce dissimilarities in social images.[8] By this reading, Sue's accommodation subsumes and is mediated by a set of interpretive, self-presentational strategies to do with personal and group-identity marking (cf., again, figure 4–1). To model her behaviour, we need to include a mediating component where *(inter alia)* phonological features in her clients' speech are processed for intended and actual social meaning (e.g. evaluation of socioeconomic status) and Sue formulates a persona of her own to be projected in return. Sue's accommodative behaviour might therefore be motivated by a desire to be variously perceived as competent (e.g. intelligent, efficient) and socially attractive (friendly, trustworthy, etc.) by and in relation to her interlocutor. The fact that Sue's most frequent and most significant convergent shifts are 'downwards' would suggest she is generally most concerned to be perceived as socially attractive, and concerned not to alienate herself from her lower status clients through 'accent superiority'.

A clear example of the dynamic implementation of such 'interpretive' or 'mediated' accommodation can be found in extract 5–4 above. Over the extract, Sue's speech shows a normal (for her) mixture of standard and non-standard variants. At one point, however, she produces a sequence of seven non-standard forms (lines 16 to 25) before reverting to a more standard style in line 26. A simple matching model cannot explain the motives and effects of this downward shift over the assistant's three speaking turns. There is no comparable shift in the interlocutors' pronunciation. There is no sudden need, it would appear, to gain social approval or increase communicative efficiency; these are unchanged objectives for a travel-agency assistant. Rather, the downward shift is the result of a change in projected social role and persona. Over lines 16 to 25, Sue adopts the role of sympathetic co-conspirator: the clients are planning to leave work early and Sue is an accessory before the fact. Later, as the extract ends, she reverts to her more formal persona of business-transacting travel-agency assistant. This sociolinguistically encoded self-presentational shift has simultaneously enabled Sue to emphasize successively the traits competence, social attractiveness and competence again.

When simple ('non-interpretive') matching on a feature-for-feature basis *does* occur in phonological selection, it is likely to operate over a small portion of text and to relate to particular phonological sequences. In conversation, it is inevitable that words or phrases will be repeated in close proximity, and there may be cohesive effects across the pronunciation of these items as well as across the lexical or grammatical items themselves. An example, again from extract 5–4, is the pronunciation of *twenty past three* in lines 3 to 8. The client, a relatively non-standard speaker, produces a simplified consonant cluster in *past three*; Sue is producing a number of standard variants (in lines 2 and 4) but produces two non-standard (C cluster) variants of the same sequence *past three* under the influence, perhaps, of the client's own earlier pronunciation. Sue's motives for this 'downward convergence' may be to avoid distinguishing herself as a more standard and so a higher-status speaker in respect of this particular phonological sequence. Another example of cohesive matching is the repetition of *arrive back* in lines 8, 9 and 10 of extract 5–3, above. Sue's first realization is with a (non-standard) flapped intervocalic (r) variant; the client – a relatively standard-accented speaker overall – follows with a standard continuant variant of (r); Sue's second realization (line 10) is the standard form, perhaps influenced by her interlocutor's pronunciation. Although the usual quantitative approach would treat these specific selections of variants as the product of random variation, it is not unreasonable to see Sue's standard (r) variant in line 10 as in itself a particular instance of 'upward accent convergence' – in this case a phonological matching process whereby a speaker seeks to minimize interpersonal linguistic differences which would be made salient by the repetition of a particular phonological sequence.

The distinction between 'interpretive' and 'matching' accommodative strategies needs to be confirmed and clarified by further research designed (unlike the present study) specifically to consider this issue. In the travel agency data, the linguistic implementation and the evaluative consequences of the two types of strategy are indistinguishable: Sue's pronunciation in both cases shifts to resemble more closely that of her interlocutor; we assume that convergence resulting from either strategy is positively evaluated (as predicted by SAT's third proposition – cf. section 4.4). Whether Sue's convergence is of a more global or more local kind is only of academic interest in this instance. But, for example in the case of encounters between speakers from different dialect communities, the interpretive and matching models predict *quite different* dialectal behaviours, each of which might be quite differently evaluated by recipients. Future sociolinguistic studies of instances like these should therefore be able to refine the theoretical propositions of SAT at the same time as lending it descriptive support.

5.2   *Dialect on the air*

The travel agency setting was entirely appropriate for studying inter-personally-based style-shifting processes. The dyadic, transactional encounters between an assistant and her clients required participants to attend to each other's behaviour in a more focused way than is necessary in many other situations. In particular, given that assistants like Sue are to an extent required to be 'accommodating', the assistant's speech to clients was a prime context for speech-accommodation strategies to be implemented. To study more personally-based (rather than interpersonally-based) stylistic processes operating through Cardiff English, a corpus of data is needed where accommodative processes are less directly relevant and where we may expect to find identity-marking and identity-management processes dominating stylistic choice. The speech of a Cardiff local-radio presenter in the course of a three-hour broadcast record-request show seemed to be an appropriate corpus for this purpose and is the basis of the case-study reported in this section.

It is essential to appreciate the uniqueness of this particular speech-event, even within the genre of broadcast record-request shows. Firstly, the speaker (FH)[9] is a broad-accented Cardiff English speaker, well-known in the community not only as a local radio presenter but also as an entertainer, folk-singer/song-writer, social commentator and humorist. His popular image is, as he recognises, built around his affiliation to and promotion of local (Cardiff) culture and folk-lore, in part *through* his dialect. For many, his media persona typifies the non-standard Cardiff voice, perhaps even the stereotypical Cardiff world-view – a nostalgia for dockland streets and pubs, a systematic ambivalence to 'Welshness', a sharp, wry humour and a reverence for the local brew. Overall, the radio-show is no less than a celebration of in-group solidarity, both symbolically (through dialect) and directly, through the show's content and design. So, for example, many correspondents are regular contributors to the show and thereby radio personalities in their own right alongside FH the presenter. Some open their letters with very familiar forms of address – *Hello Franky Boy Hi Hi Frank, How's things Our Kid?* A quiz feature asks listeners to supply the original name of Wimbourne Street in 'lovely old Splott' (a long-established working-class Cardiff city-district) and the names of six paddle-steamers which operated in the Bristol Channel after the Second World War. This unashamed parochialism is not without its detractors and, as FH notes (in a personal communication) early criticisms of the show took the form of violently expressed objections to the presenter's dialect, giving media exposure to the 'ugly', 'harsh', 'uneducated' Cardiff voice (cf. section 4.1). In fact, FH's radio shows are still the only instance of Cardiff English getting regular radio (or television) exposure in Wales. Whereas some Welsh English voices may carry their own prestige (cf. the conclusion reached by Bourhis *et al.* and Chapman *et al.*, referred to in section 4.1, above) and may even be considered standard English varieties, Cardiff English we have seen attracts predominantly negative evaluations in the same way as many other urban British dialects do. Certainly, FH is so far unique in succeeding to build a media image around the heavily stigmatized Cardiff voice.

Cardiff dialect is FH's stock-in-trade and the show is constructed around it; more particularly, around what is clearly Cardiff English's central stereotypical feature – the variable (a:) which was discussed in sections 2.1 and 3.2. The salience of this feature's occurrence in a few focal words such as *half, dark* (e.g. *half a dark,* i.e. half a pint of a well-known local ale), *Arms Park* (the national rugby stadium), and of course *Cardiff,* noted in section 2.1, owes a good deal to FH's popularity and particularly his radio show entitled 'Hark, Hark, the Lark!' The show is introduced and punctuated by a jingle described in the earlier section as a sung fanfare of *Hark, Hark the Lark* dominated by the vowel quality [æ:]. FH perpetuates this phonological theme in his own catch-phrases, such as *it's remarkable, well there we are, that's half tidy.* Correspondents often make their own contribution to the theme, sometimes consciously ending their letters with an opportunity for FH to produce a broad Cardiff variant of (a:) – for example, *yours through a glass darkly . . . signed Prince of Darkness* (oblique references to dark ale), *don't forget Derby day,* or simply the words *ta* ('thank you') or *tarra* ('goodbye'). This single phonological variable, then, is a focus for the symbolic expression of solidarity – of shared provenance, attitudes and allegiances. It is a striking example of the socially and textually cohesive potential of phonological behaviour in a corpus of spoken text. As we would expect, FH's speech shows the full range of Cardiff dialectal features, and all sociolinguistic variables discussed in section 3.2 are used in the following analyses (where they are defined as previously).

The following randomly chosen extract gives an impression of the degree of nonstandardness in FH's encoding of these sociolinguistic variables during the radio show (some personal names have been deleted):

Extract 5–5 (A 152–181)

line

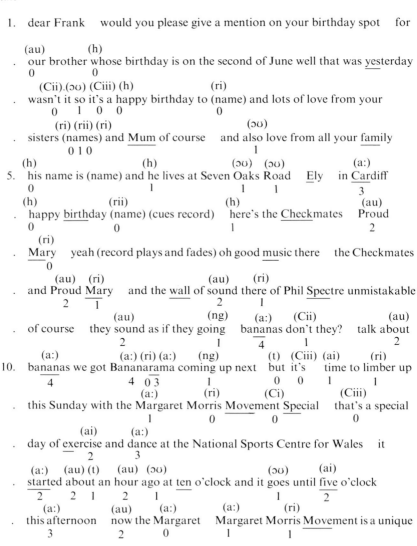

1. dear Frank   would you please give a mention on your birthday spot   for

       (au)   (h)
.   our brother whose birthday is on the second of June well that was <u>yesterday</u>
       0   0

     (Cii).(ɔʊ) (Ciii) (h)   (ri)
.   wasn't it so it's a happy birthday to (name) and lots of love from your
     0   1   0   0   0

    (ri) (rii) (ri)   (ɔʊ)
.   sisters (names) and <u>Mum</u> of course   and also love from all your <u>family</u>
       0 1 0   1

   (h)   (h)   (ɔʊ) (ɔʊ)   (a:)
5. his name is (name) and he lives at Seven Oaks Road   <u>Ely</u>   in <u>Cardiff</u>
   0   1   1   1   3

   (h)   (rii)   (h)   (au)
.   happy <u>birth</u>day (name) (cues record)   here's the <u>Check</u>mates   Proud
   0   0   1   2

  (ri)
.   <u>Mary</u>   yeah (record plays and fades) oh good <u>music</u> there   the Checkmates
   0

     (au) (ri)   (au)   (ri)
.   and Proud <u>Mary</u>   and the <u>wall</u> of sound there of Phil <u>Spectre</u> unmistakable
     2   1   2   1

        (au)   (ng)   (a:)   (Cii)   (au)
.   of course   they sound as if they going   bananas don't they?   talk about
        2   1   4   1   2

 (a:)   (a:) (ri) (a:)   (ng)   (t) (Ciii) (ai)   (ri)
10. bananas we got Bananarama coming up next   but it's   time to limber up
   4   4 0 3   1   0   0   1   1

          (a:)   (ri)   (Ci)   (Ciii)
.   this Sunday with the Margaret Morris <u>Movement</u> Special   that's a special
                             1   0   0   0

      (ai)   (a:)
.   day of <u>exercise</u> and dance at the National Sports Centre for Wales   it
         2   3

  (a:) (au) (t)   (au) (ɔʊ)   (ɔʊ)   (ai)
.   started about an hour ago at <u>ten</u> o'clock and it goes until <u>five</u> o'clock
   2   2 1   2   1   1   2

 (a:)   (au)   (a:)   (a:)   (ri)
.   this afternoon   now the Margaret   Margaret Morris <u>Movement</u> is a unique
   3   2   0   1   1

```
              (rii)                    (Ciii)        (Ciii)
15.  form of recreative movement    and it's um    well it's a system of
              0                              0              0
          (ai)                                  (t)  (Ciii) (ɔʊ)
  .  exercise    which achieves physical fitness but  it's    also capable of
          2                                         0    1          (reduced)
          (ng)   (t)              (t)                      (t)
  .  developing creative and aesthetic qualities which make it exceptional    in
          1      0               0     0                  0
                       (ng)  (a:)                            (ai)
  .  physical education and training    are you with me?    ah 'cause I'm
                          0 (reduced)                             2
      (ɔʊ) (t)                    (Ciii)
  .  totally confused    anyway it's equally suitable for men and women of all
          1                         0

20.  ages as well as children    even the kids can join in with this    and er
                    (ɔʊ)    (ɔʊ)                 (t)                    (ri)
  .  the muscular control and coordination make it an excellent preparation
                     1       1             0             0
      (ri)      (ng)                                         (a:)
  .  for all sporting and athletic activities    now all sessions today are
          1        0                                              (reduced)
                    (ɔʊ)
  .  absolutely free    so ıf the weather's a little bit gone against you and
          1
                    (rii)  (ng)(rii) (aʊ)    (rii)     (t)                (ng)
  .  you fancy    well not running round in the rain    but er you fancy doing
                          0      1   0 2        0        0                  1
      (t)       (ai) (Ciii)
25.  a bit of excercise it's all on at the National Sports Centre for Wales
          1      2    1
      (Ciii)            (ri-intrusive)    (a:)        (ri) (ɔʊ)      (ɔʊ)    (ai)
  .  that's at Pontcanna of course    started an hour ago you can go any time
          0                 0              3         1    1          1       2
              (au) (ai)                     (ng) (ɔʊ)       (a:)     (ai)
  .  up until about five o'clock this evening    so there we are    as I said
              2    2                                1    1            4       2
      (a:) (ri) (a:)              (a:)                                    (ri)
  .  Bananarama    here they are    with a little touch of (cues record) Rough
          0  0  4                  4                             N/A (Americanized)
          (ai)(h)          (rii)(ai) (a:)        (ng)       (ɔʊ)
  .  Justice    I'll have to get me right arm in training you know    the
      (reduced) 1          1 2   4            1           1
      (ai) (a:)  (t)(ng)(h)                (ɔʊ)            (ri)           (t) (ng)
30.  pints are getting heavier ((have)) you noticed that    or is it me getting
      2 (reduced) 1   1 0                    1              1            1 1
              (h)             (h) (a:)
  .  weaker?    have to drink six halfs instead of me three usual darkies
          1               1  4                        4
```

  . ah (record)

The sequence of variant-values shown here is the usual mixed stylistic array (cf. Labov 1972a) of more standard and less standard forms, though the predominance of less standard forms (values higher than zero) is striking. At this stage in the analysis, studies in the quantitative paradigm typically produce averaged frequency scores for variants across the block of text to isolate a stylistic 'level' for the speaking-context. This procedure with the radio-show data produces the high index-scores shown in table 5–4, calculated across five randomly chosen extracts (including extract 5–5, total time 8mins.) to allow an adequate number of tokens for each variable. As the table shows, almost all variables produce very high index-scores, particularly the three diphthongal variables which (in the extracts examined) are categorically non-standard or very nearly so. The word-initial context of the (r) variable (rii) is an exception, but this variable has been shown by previous studies to have poor diagnostic value.

As they stand, these findings can be interpreted only to a limited extent. They are descriptive sociolinguistic support for the contention that FH marks local identity and affiliation through his speech in respect of a wide range of phonological features. This is significant if we see relatively standard speech as normative for radio broadcasting and broad Cardiff speech as definitely *non*-normative for public consumption in the media.

Table 5–4: % indices for nine sociolinguistic variables in FH's speech over five randomly chosen extracts (bracketed figures are numbers of tokens).

Variable	% Index	Variable	% Index
(ng)	83.3 (36)	(ri)	65.1 (43)
(h)	68.0 (50)	(rii)	17.9 (28)
		All (r)	41.5
(C cluster (i) (ii) (iii)	73.3 (15) 87.5 (8) 50.0 (14)	(ɔu) (ai)	100 (43) 99.4 (54)
All (C cluster	70.3	(ai) (au)	99.4 (54) 95.6 (15)
		(aː)	82.0 (43)
(intervoc.t)	63.6 (22)		

But it is most profitable to use the frequency data in table 5–4 only as a background against which to chart stylistic variation at the micro-level under the influence of social psychological motivations. Rather than taking the averaged index-values in the table as quantitative indices of a stylistic level, we can attempt to explain the selection of individual variants in the realization of particular discourse functions. This qualitative approach requires more faith than Labov felt appropriate when he claimed that 'the irregular fluctuations' (1972a : 101) that we find in the use of a particular sociolinguistic variable are unanalysable and that 'the basic unit of stylistic contrast is a frequency set up by as few as ten occurrences of a particular variable' (:109, and section 3.5 above).

The qualitative approach lets us conceive apparent heresies. Notably, (segmental phonological) stylistic variation seems not to be simply linear; speakers are not constrained to shifting up and down a scale of standardness (whether defined quantitatively *or* qualitatively). The clearest instances in the radio-show data are when FH transcends his 'normal' phonological repertoire, shifting with varying degrees of success in the direction of other dialects. The occasion for this sort of imitative metaphorical shift is often when introducing or commenting on a record. The most frequent category here is the adoption of American or mock-American English phonology in naming certain songs or their singers. For example:

(A008)	*'Late in the Evening'* (Paul Simon)
(A061)	*George Jones 'Shine On'*
(A066, after the record)	*mm George Jones*
(A291)	*Tania Tucker*
(B013)	*Fats Domino ooh man*
(B022)	*'Laurie don't go'* (Al Stewart)

FH's 'Americanization' of these sequences is marked by the use of many General American (Wells 1982) features: heavy velarization of /l/–[ɫ] *(late, Laurie)*; tapping of /t/ – [ɾ] *(late in)*; post vocalic /r/ *(George, Tucker)*; [a] for RP /ɒ/ *(on, Domino)*; short [ɔ] for /ɔ:/ *(George)*; and [æ] for /ɑ:/ *Tania)*. It is interesting that FH occasionally introduces non-American singers' records with the Americanized voice (e.g. A177 *with a little touch of Rough Justice* (Bananarama – see extract 5–5), reflecting the continuing normative association of British pop-music with American phonology (cf. Trudgill 1983, chapter 8). Drawing on this association, FH is able to mark his awareness of 'acting the pop-music DJ' (disc-jockey) by encoding occasional stretches of DJ register in the Americanized voice – e.g. (B112) *with the song of the same name*. The force of this brief phonological shift is not to subscribe to the norms of DJ 'patter' but rather to parody them and the presenter himself, to emphasize the divide between the slick transatlantic manner and the pervasive parochialism of FH's broadcasting style. There are also metaphorical shifts in the direction of other dialects. For example, the mention of *Dorsetshire* (in association with a quiz-question – A193) is enough to condition a shift toward South-West English dialect in the pronunciation of the word, marked by rhoticity and the quality of the final diphthong – [ɒɪ]. A record by Joe Brown and His Brovvers is introduced in an attempted cockney realization of *Brovvers* (A227), with the first syllable's vowel pronounced as cardinal 4 – [a]. Shifts like these are, of course, deliberate and intended to entertain, and inaccurate renderings can be more entertaining than accurate ones. After an attempt to imitate Michael Caine (A253), FH comments: (laughs) *you didn't know he was from* Cardiff *did you?*

These 'external' transfers (transfers from outside the 'normal' repertoire) are a very small subset of the instances of style-shifting detectable in the data. The remainder of the section attempts to chart FH's phonological shifts in relation to their dynamic function in marking identity. As we saw in chapter 4, phonological selection can mark many different dimensions of identity so that there may be complementary or competing interpretations for the choice of any feature or co-occurring set of features. What is needed is a model of sociolinguistic identity-marking which predicts specific phonological tendencies in defined social-psychological contexts. Figure 5–8 shows such a model, derived from the social psychological literature on situation-types (Giles and Ryan 1982: 220). It is important to point out that the source model was conceived for very different purposes from those of this study. It was an attempt to formalize the principal dimensions along which situations for language-attitudes studies may vary. Nevertheless, it is particularly valuable in bringing together the social-group and personality dimensions of identity-marking and encourages us to see style-shifting, once again, as *multidimensional.* The vertical dimension in the figure is primary in that it captures the principal associations between phonological selection and perceived personality on the one hand *and* power/solidarity on the other hand. According to both criteria, the model predicts (on the basis of research referred to in sections 4.2 and 4.3) that generally more standard phonological forms will be associated with situation-types towards the 'status-stressing' pole, and less standard forms with those towards the 'solidarity-stressing' pole. The horizontal dimension, however, captures the essential relationship between the criteria and invites us to look for phonological shifts *beyond* those which may simply be categorized as more standard/less standard.

The general ethos of FH's radio show is well characterized by describing it as 'located' towards the lower right quadrant of figure 5–8. We have seen

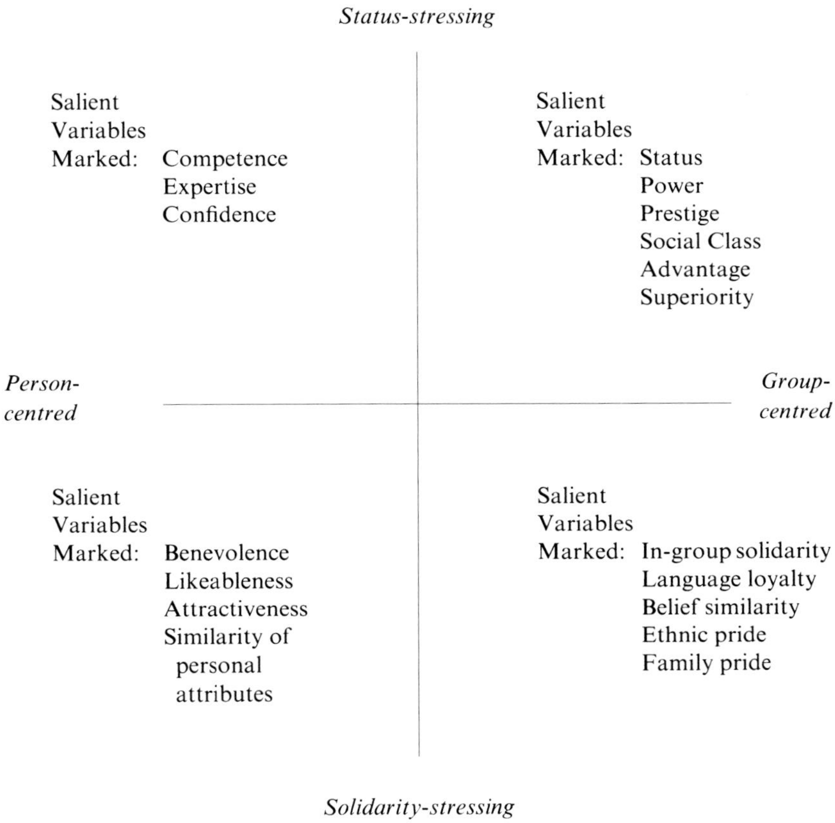

Status-stressing

Salient Variables Marked: Competence Expertise Confidence	Salient Variables Marked: Status Power Prestige Social Class Advantage Superiority

Person-   *Group-*
centred   *centred*

Salient Variables Marked: Benevolence Likeableness Attractiveness Similarity of personal attributes	Salient Variables Marked: In-group solidarity Language loyalty Belief similarity Ethnic pride Family pride

Solidarity-stressing

Figure 5–8: A model of situation-types predicting phonological selection (derived and adapted from Giles and Ryan 1982 :220).

how non-standard phonological features as well as non-linguistic aspects of the speech-event convey in-group solidarity and belief similarity. This is community radio which, particularly in its 'light entertainment' mode, reflects local rather than national values and interests. And *Hark Hark the Lark* is community radio at its most solidary. During the show, however, there are occasions where solidarity with the Cardiff community is marked particularly strongly (labelled the *High Ethnicity condition*), as in the following fragments:

                                                                       (a:)   (a:)
(A 107 – referring to a Cardiff-born singer) *there you* are *good old* Cardiff
                                                                        ⎯   ⎯
                                                                        4   4

(a:)   (ng)   *(ai)(ng)(h)
TV star Shakin' Stevens driving himself crazy
4   N/A   2   1   1

(A 131 – addressed to a young lady representing the city in a national quiz)

(rii)   (a:)   (rii)(ai)(ng)   (ri)
remember Cardiff is relying   on you to crack it for us
1   4   1 2   1   1

(A 276 – referring to FH's successor on the show) *and o'course Phil is a*

(ng)   (ai)   (Cii)   *(ai)
cracking feller ((I'm)) I couldn't think of anyone nicer to take
1   reduced 1   2
(ɔʊ)   *(a:)   (h)
over from me Cardiff born and bred he is . . .
1   4   1
    *(a:)   *(a:)   (ɔʊ)
you can't knock a good Cardiff bloke
    4   4   1
                              (h)
(B 177 – referring to Tom Jones, the Welsh singer) *he('ll)) be on the*
                              1
    (ɔʊ)   (h)   (ɔʊ)   (t) (h)   (a:) *(ai)
'phone in a minute from his Ponty telephone box out his backyard by
    1   1   1   1 1   4   2
(h)   (ng)   (h)   (h)*(a:) *(ai)
his swimming pool   . . . fair dos [du:z] he was half tidy
1   1   1   1 4   2
                         (ai)   (a:)(h)(a:)(h)*(a:)   *(a:)
(B 305 – near the end of the show) *stand by for the last Hark Hark   the Lark*
                         2   4 1 4   1 4   4

(jingle)

The referential expressions of solidarity here are reinforced partly by some non-standard lexical and grammatical forms and partly through the selection of phonological variants. Every variant of every variable marked in these fragments (which were chosen by their content not their phonological characteristics) is maximally non-standard according to the definitions given for the variables earlier. In fact, some of the vocalic Cardiff variants produced here are qualitatively *more* non-standard than allowed for by those definitions. So, occurrences of (ai) marked with an asterisk are realized as [ɔ̈ɪ], showing rounding and retraction of the glide's first element beyond the degrees of centralization required to score the variable as 1 or 2. Occurrences of (a:) similarly marked are even closer than [æ:], in the area of [ɛ̈] and even [ɛ]. This extreme non-standard style is of course not limited to supporting referential meanings and can function productively as a communicative resource, adding a homely, solidary key to referential meanings that might not otherwise convey these associations. For example:

            (ai) (t) (h)   *(ai)   (ai)

(B009)   *why not have a little lie in the day after your birthday*
           2   1 1   2   4

                              (ɔʊ) (Ci)   (ri)

(B043   – discussing a record) *you could almost smell the beer on the floor*
                                   1 1   1

           (Cii)
           couldn't you   ah
             1

Within the data there are two classes of situation-type which the model predicts will be associated with *more standard* phonological usage. The first is that set of speech acts a DJ necessarily produces in connection with the structuring and publicizing of the show. For example:

           (ai)   (ɔʊ)

(A020)   *I'll do the first of them in just a couple of moments*
        1   1

                          (ng)   (au)

(A029)   *and er you can contact us during the week in normal office hours*
                                  0   1

                      (ai)
         on three seven four seven five seven and Action Desk will take it
                           2

        from there

                  (ɔʊ)

(A147)   *back in just a moment*
                  0

              (Ci)   (au) (ɔʊ)

A213)   *we've got for the next two hours so stay with me until two o'clock*
                         0   1   1

          (h)   (h) (ri)

(A214)   *Frank Hennessy here on CBC two two one metres in the medium*
            0   0 0

              (ai)   (ri) (ɔʊ)
        wave and ninety-six VHF in stereo
             2   1 1

               (ɔʊ) (Cii)

(B047)   *stay with me won't you on CBC two two one metres medium wave*
                  1 0

            (ai)
        and ninety-six VHF
         1

The focus of these acts is more public than parochial. The need to mark in-group solidarity is temporarily attenuated and the general norms for public broadcasting come more to the fore. This is still local radio, and there is no question of FH breaking off his symbolic association with the target audience. We might characterize the situational shift as a slight upward movement from the lower right quadrant of figure 5–8. But this shift is arguably accompanied by a more significant one in the person-centred vertical dimension (the left of the figure). As presenter, FH's role changes quite dramatically from a genial 'conversationalist' to a public announcer, and competence and expertise become more salient personal characteristics *(the High Competence condition)*. Both these socio-psychological shifts (the more modest in group-identity-marking, the more significant in personal identity-marking) are likely to be marked phonologically. The literature suggests that both may be accompanied by phonological shifts in the direction of more standard pronunciation, and indeed, examination of the variants selected to encode the above utterances (and others in this category elsewhere in the data) shows that FH produces many standard (or less non-standard) forms in this context. But interestingly, it is particularly the more overtly stigmatized features that are regularly 'corrected' here (variables (ng), (h) and (C) in the above and similar fragments). These features are not only Cardiff English dialect features but social dialect markers of British speech as a whole. (ng), (h) and (C) are of course also consonantal variables with discrete, phonetic variants (analysable as present/absent) which lend themselves to full 'correction' during style-shifting. FH continues to produce many non-standard variants of the diphthongal Cardiff variables in the more public context, though some are noticeably less 'broad' – e.g. index scores of 1 with variables (au) and (ai). It seems then, that the two socio-psychological dimensions are being marked by two separable sets of phonological variables, one more closely tied to group-identity-marking, the other to the marking of personal characteristics. General social dialect features popularly associated with 'uneducated' 'sloppy' or 'vulgar' speech – many of which have popular labels like 'aitch-dropping', 'G-dropping' and 'T-dropping' – seem, on this evidence, to play a significant role in marking a speaker's competence or social attractiveness. Less easily 'corrected', regionally delimited dialect-features – including (ǝʊ), (ai), (au) and of course (a:) in Cardiff – have a primary role, as we might expect, in marking group-identity.[10]

The second situation-type we would expect to be associated with more standard speech relates to those occasions when FH makes public announcements of various sorts, sometimes based on information sent in by listeners. As we have seen, readers' letters are generally an integral part of the expression of community solidarity and are often read out (by FH) in a broad Cardiff voice. 'Announcement' letters, though, are read very differently. An example can be found in the central section of extract 5–5 (above), relating to the 'Margaret Morris Movement Special'. Although a local event is being publicized, it is certainly not within the bounds of Cardiff popular culture as promulgated by FH. This discourse sequence affords less opportunity than any other in the data to express in-group solidarity. In fact, referentially, we find FH expressing his own alienation from the event – *(are you <u>with</u> me? ah 'cause I'm <u>totally</u> con<u>fused</u>; so if . . . you fancy well not <u>running</u> around in the <u>rain</u> . . .)*. At the same time, the public announcing function demands an increased level of perceived competence/expertise. On this occasion the level of competence/ expertise arguably relates *not* to FH himself but, through him, to the writer of the letter; FH has the responsibility of protecting his correspondent from negative personality attributions. In this way, group- and individual-focused situational dimensions coincide *(the High Competence/Low Ethnicity condition)*, and our model predicts more standard variants of all the listed variants in this context. Leaving aside FH's interpretative and somewhat derisive 'ad lib' comments, we find many standard or almost standard variants here: for example, frequent preservation of /t/ in *it's, that's* and in the word *Movement;* avoidance of flapped realizations of intervocalic /t/ *(but it's, it's exceptional);* some velar realizations of (ng) *training, sporting;* also, the most standard realization of (a:) in the data as a whole occur here – (a:)–1 in *Margaret* on two occasions and even (a:)–0 on one–contrasting sharply with (a:)–4 in the 'catch-phrase' which rounds off the announcement *so there we are.*

The claim that phonological shifting is multi-dimensional can only be adequately tested when individual and group dimensions *fail* to coincide. One situation in the data where this conflict occurs is in the reading of another letter. It is from a group of canteen- and office-workers who are regular correspondents to the show and who, in a typically familiar letter, have asked for the words of their favourite song to be read out over the air. The group-solidarity function is strongly operative, but the verses need to be read with a reasonable degree of (perceived) competence since they are valued by and have been transcribed by the correspondents *(the High Competence/High Ethnicity condition)*. Once again, levels of competence may be attributed to the correspondents through FH. If this is an accurate analysis of social psychological dimensions of the situation, the model predicts relatively high index-values (non-standard) for the group-identity-marking variables like (a:) and the diphthongal variables, and low index-values (more standard) for the overtly stigmatized personality-marking variables like (h), (ng), (C) and (t). Extract 5–6, showing the variables and

Extract 5–6
(A 279–289)

line

```
        (ai)       (ng) (h) (ai)                        (rii) (ai) (ai)     (ng)
1. (reads) I'm walking behind you    this is the words right    I'm walking
            2        1    0 2                       1   2  reduced    1
   (h)(ai)                        (ng)     (ai) (h)                        (ɔʊ)
 . behind you   on your wedding day    I'll hear you promise   to love and obey
    0 2                            1        2  1                            reduced
   (ɔʊ)                                 (ai) (ai)          (ɔʊ)
 . though you may forget    you're still on my mind    look over your
    1                                 2   2              1
   (ɔʊ)       (ai)    (ng) (h) (ai)       (ai)
 . shoulder    I'm walking behind    maybe I'll kiss again    with a love
    1       reduced    1    0 2            2
   (Ciii)          (t) (ai)            (ai)      (ng)    (ai)(ɔʊ)
5. that's new    but I shall wish again    I was kissing you    I oh   this
    0            0 2                        reduced    0        2 1
   (ng)              (ɔʊ)    (ai)                    (ri)        (ɔʊ)
 . is breaking me up you know    I'll always love you    wherever you go    we
    1              1  reduced                   1            1
   (h)          (h)          (ai)   (a)     (ɔʊ) (ɔʊ)          (ɔʊ) (rii)
 . could have been happy    like Derby and Joan    so when things go wrong
    1          0           2   3        1   1              1  0
          (t)      (ai)    (Ci)    (ɔʊ)        (ɔʊ)      (ai)     (ng)
 . dear    and fate is unkind    just look over your shoulder    I'm walking
             0      2      0   1                  1         2         1
   (h)(ai)            (Ciii) (rii)(a) (ai)  (Cii)
 . behind    (sniffs) that's rather nice isn't it (clears throat)
    0 2               1 1 4     2     1
```

their index-scores, generally supports these predictions. All sixteen (non-reduced) instances of variable (ai) show maximally non-standard scores, as do all nine (non-reduced) instances in the read verses of (ɔʊ); (au) does not occur and the one instance of (aː) (*Derby*) scores 3 (relatively non-standard). In contrast, five of the seven occurrences of (h) are realized with standard variants (score 0); the alveolar stop is preserved in both occurrences of (C) during the reading and in neither of the two occurrences in FH's final quip *that's rather nice isn't it;* intervocalic /t/ (variable (t)) is not voiced or flapped on either of its two occurrences. Although the scores for (h), (C) and (t) derive from only eleven occurrences in all, they must be seen as significantly low against the background of the high overall scores for these variables in table 5–4 (above). In the light of these findings, FH's repeated 'G-dropping' in this situation is at first surprising. But if we remember that extract 5–6 is the text of a song, but it may be that FH is following a prevalent norm of pronunciation for many styles of popular songs.

Finally, we should consider some of the many instances of shifting in the data conditioned by situations emphasizing low competence/expertise/ confidence *(the Low Expertise condition)*. This socio-psychological context only occurs through FH's use of humour, and one humourous strategy in particular – self-denigration. An important component of FH's media image is humility and unpretentiousness which, for the purposes of humour, is extended to the portrayal of incompetence/lack of expertise. The sequence to do with the weight of pints of beer (at the end of extract 5–5) and the quip *this is breaking me up you know* (in extract 5–6) come into this category. Some of the many other examples are:

```
              (au) (ai)            (ai)                     (ng)(h)(au)(ai)
(A098)   now I've said that    I mean    (ironically) seeing how I've
              2 reduced           reduced                 1   1 2 reduced
                (ri) (ɔʊ)            (ai)        (ɔʊ)
         got carry so much influence like you know they probably all
              1    1               2            1
                (au)
         petrified now
              2
                (ai) (ɔʊ)(Cii)(t)(ri) (au)
(A198)   me    I don't get    around    much any more
              2  1  1       1   1    2
            *(ai) (ɔʊ)            *(ai)   (a:)      (ɔʊ)      *(ai)
(A329)   I know that Johnny    I'm not daft you know    well I am
            2   1               2      4          1         2
            *(ai)            (ng) (t)  (ɔʊ)              (h) (ɔʊ)
(A408)   I get sick looking at a bowl of milk    me    hopeless
            2               1    1    1                  1 1
            *(ai)   (ɔʊ)                  (ng) (au)           (rii)
         I'll be down below decks    swabbing out the engine-rooms
            2       1                       1  2               1

         probably (laughs)

              (Ciii) *(ai)  (ai) (Cii) (a:)           (ai)   (t)
(B222)   that's   why I didn't pass me eleven plus    I resat it
              1   2 reduced 1    4                    reduced 1
                      (ai)     (ai) (h) (ng)       (ɔʊ)
         seventy-three times    I'm having another go next year
                      2 reduced 1    1              1
            (Ciii)                              (ɔʊ)
         it's the fractions that get me stumped you know
              1                                         1
```

(ɔʊ)	(Ciii)	(h) (a:)	(t)
you know	*what's the biggest?*	*half?*	*three quarters?*
1	1	1 4	1

(t)	(t)
or thirty-two	*thirty-thirds?*
1	1

The primary focus of all these utterances is personal. They seek to convey the speaker's lack of experience, influence, academic prowess, physical strength and resiliance. At the same time, though, it could be argued that 'downward' shifts along the person-centred scale (in figure 2) necessarily imply strengthening of (group-centred) in-group solidarity. If an individual renders himself/herself more socially attractive and likeable to listeners, this is an indirect means of aligning him/herself with the group they constitute or identify with. Clearly, the model firmly predicts non-standard phonological selections in respect of both the general social dialect markers and the more regionally delimited features. As shown in the fragments above, this prediction is again supported by the data. As was the case in the High Ethnicity condition, FH produces maximally non-standard variants of all listed variables in all utterances (including the above) that can be assigned with confidence on non-phonological grounds to the Low Competence situation-type. However, on a small number of occasions, FH does produce phonetic/phonological features *unique* to this situation-type, though beyond the scope of the listed sociolinguistic variables, which were selected to show variation over a wide range of styles. Low competence, then, is occasionally uniquely marked by FH by the temporary use of a more lax vocal set (e.g.) in B291:

LAX	(t)	(ng)			(au)	(ai)		(ai)		(ai)				(h)
(h)	*getting*	*a*	*bit*	*sad*	*now*	*I*	*am*	*aye*		*feel*	*like*	*Buddy*	*Holly)*
1	1			2	2	2		2					1

and more often by certain extreme forms of phonological elision and assimilation, as shown in extract 5–7. These processes are not un common in rapid, informal speech generally and have been said to be particularly frequent and extreme in Cardiff speech, so that they can be considered a dialect feature (cf. chapter 2, above). But they are rare in FH's radio-speech, and, of course, in media-broadcasting as a whole.

The patterns of phonological shifting associated with the five socio-psychological conditions show the dynamic potential of style-shifting in marking personality and group-identity. It is necessarily the case that the charted shifts have involved small amounts of data and often quite minor phonetic variation, and that the various conditions identified have only

Extract 5–7
(A055–058)

line

   (ai)   (ai)   (ai)
1. I used to [ˈəɪstə] do things like that [ləɪˈkaʔ] I used to [ˈəɪstə]
   2̄   2   ―   2
 (rii)   (ɔʊ)   (ai) (ai)   (Cii)
. ring people up   in those days because I   I couldn't believe [əˈkʌmp
   1   1   2 reduced 1
                  (ng)   (ai)   (rii)
. bəˈliv] anyone was listening to me   I used to ring them [ˈrɪŋm̩]
                      1   2   1
                        (ɔʊ)   (ai)
. up and tell them [ˈtɛləm] to put the radio on and things like that
                           1   2
            (ri)   (t) (ng)
5. [ləˈkaʔ] (laughs)   desperation was setting in
                  1̄   1 1

been informally validated through discussion with FH. Still, the two-dimensional model (figure 5–8) relates to quite gross social psychological processes for which there is often explicit corroborative evidence at the level of referential meaning. The general trends emerging from the radio-show analyses are summarized in table 5–5, where 'S' represents more standard speech, 'NS' more non-standard speech and 'I' an intermediate level.

The category 'Social Dialect' relates to those variables which are heavily stigmatized in many non-standard British varieties (in this case, (h), (ng), (C cluster) and possibly (intervoc.t)); 'Regional Dialect' relates to more specifically Cardiff English variables (particularly (a:), (au), (ɔʊ) and (ai)). Consistent patterns of phonological selection across all variables are found in the High Competence/Low Ethnicity condition (more standard pronunciation) and in the High Ethnicity and Low Expertise conditions (more non-standard pronunciation). Shifting in these contexts is broadly as predicted in the literature – the speaker shifts up and down what appears to be a linear scale of dialectal standardness in response to variable needs or wishes to mark individual and group-identity. Either personal factors (low expertise) or group-related factors (high ethnicity) or both categories of factors operating in concert (high competence/low ethnicity) can trigger consistent patterns of shifting. What is most significant in these instances is that a particular set of phonological behaviours – a broad shift to more non-standard speech – can be produced as a result of and in the fulfilment of quite *different* socio-psychological functions, as in marking high in-group ethnicity and marking low personal expertise.

Table 5–5: Major trends in phonological shifting by FH across five socio-psychological conditions.

Socio-psychological conditions	Social Dialect	Regional Dialect
High Ethnicity	NS	NS
High Competence	S	I
High Competence/ Low Ethnicity	S	S
High Competence/ High Ethnicity	S	NS
Low Expertise	NS	NS

The High Competence condition suggests that personal and group-factors may, on occasions, independently trigger specific phonological shifts. FH marks competence primarily by general social dialect features in this condition and is able to standardize stigmatized social dialect variables without shifting to the same extent in respect of regionally delimited variables. Moreover, in a context where high competence at a personal level needs to be marked but where in-group solidarity marking is simultaneously appropriate (the High Competence/High Ethnicity condition), the two categories of variables show quite different trends. Although we might generally expect 'social dialect' and 'regional dialect' features to covary, just as personal and group-identity marking processes typically covary to form a single dimension of status-stressing - to - solidarity-stressing conditions (cf. figure 5–8), this *need* not be the case. Dialectal style-shifting, therefore, even when it occurs within the bounds of a speaker's normal repertoire, is not necessarily uni-dimensional.[11]

5.3 *Overview*

The two case-studies in this chapter have exemplified some of the motivational processes underlying stylistic variation in two quite different contexts. Since the studies have selectively examined micro-level socio-linguistic behaviours in tightly specified contexts, it is necessarily difficult to support generalized conclusions. But the impetus for a case-study approach to stylistic variation, and particularly for the more qualitative method adopted in the radio-show study, is the view that research aimed at generalizing about stylistic phonological processes can easily *over-regularize* complex behaviour and dehumanize individualistic responses to and influences on spoken discourse. Case-studies in this area may have to live with criticisms of particularism and untidiness as a consequence of their commitment to be true to the social and psychological dimensions of day-to-day talk.

Despite these limitations, the travel agency and radio-show findings in this chapter allow us to draw general inferences about the nature of stylistic dialectal variation and about how it may profitably be investigated. The studies show how both personal and interpersonal social psychological factors lie at the heart of dialectal style-shifting and can help us explain rather than merely describe stylistic variation in speech. Since the two corpora of data were consciously chosen to focus separately on accommodative and identity-marking processes, little has been said about the overlap between the interpersonal and personal dimensions, and this remains an area in need of clarification through further research.[12] But it is clear that both sets of processes can operate in an essentially dynamic manner, serving to guide shifts from moment to moment during spontaneous naturally situated discourse. As many previous studies have shown, phonological variables in particular are extremely sensitive to a wide range of contextual factors. The studies in this chapter have, moreover, shown that these variables are a significant communicative resource for speakers operating within their normal phonological repertoires rather than merely the automatic consequence of situational characteristics. The radio-show data demonstrate how a speaker may also occasionally be motivated to transfer symbolic associations from dialects outside his/her usual repertoire into the current speech situation. It follows from this, and from the finding that particular sets of phonological variables are differentially responsive to different socio-psychological factors, that phonological style-shifting is not restricted to a single dimension of 'accent standardness/non-standardness'. The illusion of unidimensional shifting up and down a simple standardness scale seems to have been created and sustained by a quantitative and deterministic methodology which is insensitive to the more qualitative shifts that realize speakers' momentary attitudes, intentions and communicative strategies. It is more appropriate and more revealing to take the basic unit of stylistic contrast to be a speaker's selection of an individual phonetic variant in a specified linguistic and socio-psychological context.

The commitment to explaining dialect-variation in use in day-to-day talk implies above all a willingness to cross the traditional boundaries between academic disciplines. The studies in this volume have drawn heavily on established paradigms in dialectology, sociolinguistics and social psychology while recognizing certain limitations of each of these: for example, the lack of synchronic relevance of traditional dialectology, the explanatory weakness of Labovian sociolinguistics and the dialectal and linguistic imprecision of the social psychology of language. There is enough evidence in the reported case-studies to show that the interfaces between these disciplines create a rich seam of possibilities. For instance, testing the predictions of accommodation theory pushes sociolinguistics to reconsider its methods and the assumptions that underlie them: is the quantitative paradigm appropriate for studying stylistic variation?; is the notion of phonological style tenable?; what features may be manipulated and to what extent during accent convergence? The application of sociolinguistic methods to theories of accommodation and identity-marking throws out challenges to social psychologists: does the heterogeneity that characterizes inter- and intra-personal linguistic variation follow from complex motivational factors?; can situational norms and/or self-presentational motives override accommodative strategies involving accent variation? The dialectological perspective presses us to question the geographical and socio-historical delimitation of these sociolinguistic and socio-psychological processes we are investigating: are patterns of dialect in use in Cardiff likely to be representative of Wales (or south Wales, or south-east Wales) as a whole?; is the claimed ethnic revitalization of Wales a factor influencing dialect use in the Welsh capital today?

None of these issues can be resolved by research within a single, self-contained discipline, which would risk failing even to ask relevant questions. It is most appropriate to take Hymes' view on the triviality of rigidly parcelling out the study of man (Hymes 1977) and to both accept and promote interdisciplinary co-operation. The investigations of variation in Cardiff English in this volume are intended as justification for and as a contribution to this sort of integrated explanatory research into dialect in use.

Notes

Notes to Chapter 1

1 Published works from the Survey of English Dialects are:
Orton (1960, 1962), Orton and Halliday (1962–3), Orton and Barry (1961-71), Orton and Tilling (1969–71), Orton and Wakelin (1967–8), Kolb (1964), Orton and Wright (1975) and Orton, Sanderson and Widdowson (1967). Useful overviews of traditional dialect geography can be found in Chambers and Trudgill (1980, Chapter 2), Wakelin (1977), Petyt (1980, 1982) and Trudgill (1983, chapter 2).

2 In his Introduction to *Sociolinguistic Patterns* (1972a: xix), Labov points out that he resisted the term sociolinguistics for many years because of its implication – unacceptable for him and for many – that linguistics could be studied in isolation from the social contexts of language use. For just this reason, Hymes (1972b:324) observes that the final goal of sociolinguistics must be 'to preside over its own liquidation'. Nevertheless, the term was required to point to the fact that Labov did not accept the dominant assumption of linguistics as autonomous, and would not tolerate what Sapir saw as linguists' 'failure to look beyond the pretty patterns of their subject matter' (Sapir 1929).

3 See Lavandera (1978) and Coupland (1983) for a full discussion of the boundaries of sociolinguistic variation.

4 cf. Bellin (1984) for a recent review of the sociolinguistics of Welsh and English in Wales; also Pryce (1978) and Thomas and Williams (1978).

5 cf. Coupland 1983: 464ff. for a more detailed discussion of the term 'service encounter', where it is argued that the travel agency encounters are communicatively more open than the 'commodity' encounters analysed by Merritt.

Notes to Chapter 2

1 Stylistic variation in Frank Hennessy's speech is the subject of a detailed case-study, in section 5.2, below.

2 There is, however, one interesting likely exception here: that the close fronted variants of Cardiff /a:/ do indeed derive substratally from a south-eastern regional dialect-variety of Welsh which regularly showed [ɛ:] variants of standard Welsh /a:/, as in /tɛ:d/ for orthographic *tad* ('father'); /tɛ:n/ for *tan* ('fire'); /glɛ:n/ for *glan* ('clean'); etc. (Awbery, pers. comm.).

3 Similarly, few of the grammatical features listed by Trudgill and Hannah deserve to be considered standard in Wales. Use of the 'invariant' tag *isn't it?* (cf. section 2.2 above) and the use of adjective/adverb reduplication for emphasis – *It was high high* relating to Standard English English *It was very high* – are stigmatized and not at all typical of 'educated speech'. To make these observations is in any case only to contradict one set of subjective views with another. What is needed is a detailed empirical study of standard Welsh English based on an adequate linguistic and social psychological definition of 'standard'.

Notes to Chapter 3

1   See Coupland (1981:66ff) for a more detailed objection to the use of composite indices of social class in sociolinguistic research.
2   Of the variables defined and discussed in this section, Mees analysed (ng), (h), (ai), (au) and (ɔʊ); the last of these is labelled (o:) by Mees. The discussion of these variables draws (sometimes directly) on Mees 1977 (:33ff.) and 1983.
3   It is difficult to appreciate the full significance of this point since, unfortunately, Mees does not quote the number of tokens on which the score for each individual speaker for each variable is based.
4   In fact, this refinement adds weight to the earlier interpretation of table 3–4 – that only two broad educational groups are distinguishable linguistically in the travel agency data.
5   In particular, cf. the pattern of 'hypercorrection' found with lower-middle class speakers by Labov 1972a and Trudgill 1974a.
6   The general view that 'it is important not to over-quantify sociolinguistic data' is shared by Thelander (1982:66).

Notes to Chapter 4

1   This comment was first brought to my attention by Sue Bates, whose work is referred to in sections 4.2 and 4.3. The use of Cardiff English in a local radio show is the subject of one of the studies reported in chapter 5.
2   The terms 'to mark' and 'marker' are suitably ambiguous in respect of intention. A full discussion of intention and marking can be found in Laver and Trudgill (1979).

Notes to Chapter 5

1   More polemical arguments against the appropriateness of positivist approaches to language in use are voiced by ethnomethodologists (e.g. Garfinkel 1967, Cicourel 1973, Speier 1973).
2   Variable (ng) was not included in the earlier study of stylistic stratification in Sue's speech (section 3.3) because, in the more informal speaking contexts included in that study, its standard variant /ŋ/ was very rare; that is, informal contexts were below the threshold level of regular variation for (ng) in Sue's speech.
3   In section 3.3 it was noted that scores for occupation-group IIIN, 'skilled non-manual', were weighted toward the female, more standard, norm. Therefore, the comparison drawn in table 5–2 is an appropriate one, even though the population of clients there consists of males and females.
4   In addition to the 4 quantified variables, variants of variable (r) are marked in extracts 5–3 and 5–4. This is firstly to assist the impressionistic assessment of levels of standardness here and secondly to exemplify accommodative processes discussed later in this section.
5   When the population of addressees is split by educational background (as it was in table 3–9) we find a comparable though somewhat less clear pattern of differentiation. For example, individuals who stayed in the education system to take public examinations are addressed by Sue with relatively standard levels of variables (h) and (C cluster) and are clearly distinguished in these respects from the 'no public examination' group.

6   Giles has pointed out (in a personal communication) that the present study treats the clients' speech as a static given, and not as *itself* accommodated, as is likely to be the case.

7   This is an approach suggested and adopted by Bell (1984). Figure 5–7 is derived from Bell's re-working of my data.

8   The literature on accommodation theory has sometimes discussed the interpretive procedures referred to here. Giles and Powesland (1975:158) say that ' . . . accommodation through speech can be regarded as an attempt on the part of a speaker to modify or disguise his persona in order to make it more acceptable to the person addressed'. These authors' subsequent schematic representation of accommodation talks of speaker A drawing inferences as to the personality characteristics of B, although this component of the 1975 statement is not included in the later propositional summary.

9   Frank Hennessy's role in promoting Cardiff English and Cardiff culture was referred to earlier (in section 2.1). I am very grateful to him for giving permission to use data from his radio-show for this study and particularly for his co-operation in discussing with me issues relating to Cardiff English, his experience of popular reactions to his own speech-style and his use of dialect on radio. Many aspects of the following analysis are an attempt to formalise pressures and tendencies that FH is aware of at a personal level. FH has recently left the Cardiff local radio-station and hosts weekly shows on national (Welsh) radio and television. This is a significant step in further exposing Cardiff English via the media.

10 We should note that this distinction between 'social dialect' and 'regional dialect' variables in FH's speech is not the distinction Labov (1972a) makes between 'indicators' and 'markers'. In Labov's terms, indicators show *no* stylistic variation, whereas social dialect variables in FH's speech clearly do.

11 Although evidence in the present study is too sparse to support the following view, we might hypothesize for future research that certain implicational relationships obtain in table 5–5. The table suggests that non-standard social dialect features are necessarily accompanied by (that is, imply the use of) non-standard regional dialect features, but not *vice versa;* and that standard regional dialect features are necessarily accompanied by standard social dialect features, but not *vice versa.*

12 For instance, Giles (pers. comm.) suggests that there is scope for interpreting aspects of FH's phonological shifting *within* the framework of speech accommodation theory. Certainly, it is entirely plausible to view what may be generally labelled 'monologue' in this instance as subject to *inter*personally motivated speech-strategies. FH's non-standard speech in the High Ethnicity condition, for instance, may be analysed as phonological convergence to (the speaker's stereotypical perception of) the dialect norm among his assumed audience. Given the highly personalized nature of some modes of FH's radio-show (as outlined at the beginning of section 5.2), it may even be possible to make more particular assumptions about individual addressees (or groups of addressees) to whom FH accommodates at different times.

References

Awbery, G. M. (1982) A bibliography of research on Welsh dialects since 1934. *Papurau Gwaith Ieithyddol Cymraeg Caerdydd* 2: 103–120 *(Cardiff Working Papers in Welsh Linguistics)* National Museum of Wales.

—— (1984) 'Welsh'. In Trudgill (ed.) (1984): 259–77.

Babbie, E. R. (1973) *Survey research methods.* Wadsworth Publishing Co.

Baetens-Beardsmore, H. (1982) *Bilingualism: Basic Principles.* Clevedon: Tieto.

Ball, P., Giles, H. Byrne, J. L. and Berechree, P. (1984) Situational constraints on the evaluative significance of speech accommodation: some Australian data. In H. Giles (ed.) 1984:115–130.

Bates, S. (1983) Attitudes towards Cardiff-accented speech: some social and educational implications. Unpublished Master's dissertation, University of Wales.

Beebe, L. M. and Giles, H. (1984) Speech-accommodation theories: a discussion in terms of second-language acquisition. In H. Giles (ed.) 1984:5–32.

Bell, A. (1984) Language style as audience design. *Language in Society* 13,2:145–204.

Bellin, W. (1984) Welsh and English in Wales. In P. Trudgill (ed) 1984:449–79.

Berdan, R. H. (1975) On the nature of linguistic variation. Unpublished Ph.D. dissertation. University of Texas at Austin.

Berger, C. R. and Bradac, J. J. (1982) *Language and Social Knowledge: Uncertainty in Interpersonal Relations.* London: Edward Arnold.

Bickerton, D. (1975) Review of P. Trudgill, Social Differentiation of English in Norwich. *Journal of Linguistics* 11:299–307.

Blom J-P. and Gumperz, J. J. (1972) Social meaning in linguistic structure: code switching in Norway. In J. J. Gumperz and D. Hymes (ed.) 1972.

Bodine, A. (1975) Sex differences in language. In B. Thorne and N. Henley (eds.) *Language and Sex: Difference and Dominance.* Rowley, Mass.

Bottomore, T. B. (1965) *Classes in Modern Society.* London: Allen and Unwin.

Bourhis, R. Y. and Giles, H. (1976) The language of co-operation in Wales: A field study. *Language Sciences* 42:13–16.

—— (1977) The language of intergroup distinctiveness. In H. Giles (ed.) (1977):119–136.

Bourhis, R. Y., Giles, H. and Tajfel, H. (1973) Language as a determinant of ethnic identity. *European Journal of Social Psychology* 3:447–460.

Bourhis, R. Y., Giles, H., and Lambert, W. E. (1975) Social consequences of accommodating one's style of speech: A cross-national investigation. *International Journal of the Sociology of Language* 6:55–72.

Bright, W. (1975) *Sociolinguistics*. Mouton.

Brown, R. and Gilman, A. (1972) The pronouns of power and solidarity. In Giglioli (ed.) (1972) *Language and Social Context*. Pelican.

Candlin, C. N., Leather, J. H. and Bruton, C. J. (1976) Doctors in casualty: applying communicative competence to components of specialist course design. *I.R.A.L.* 14, 3:245–272.

Chambers, J. K. and Trudgill, P. (1980) *Dialectology*. Cambridge: Cambridge University Press.

Chapman, A. J., Smith, J. R. and Foot, H. C. (1977) Language, humour and intergroup relations. In H. Giles (ed.) 1977:137–170.

Chen, M. and Wang, W. S-Y. (1975). Sound change: actuation and implementation. *Language* 51:255–81.

Cheshire, J. (1978) Present tense verbs in Reading English. In P. Trudgill (ed) 1978:52–68.

—— (1982) *Variation in an English Dialect: A Sociolinguistic Study*. Cambridge: Cambridge University Press.

Cheyne, W. (1970) Stereotyped reactions to speakers with Scottish and Regional accents. *British Journal of Social and Clinical Psychology* 9:77–9.

Cicourel, A. (1968) *The Social Organization of Juvenile Justice*. Wiley.

—— (1973) *Cognitive Sociology*. Harmondsworth: Penquin.

Connolly, J. H. (1982) On the segmental phonology of a South Welsh accent of English. Journal of the International Phonetic Association 11:51–61.

Coupland, N. (1980) Style-shifting in a Cardiff work-setting.*Language in Society*
—— (1981) The Social Differentiation of Functional Language Use: a sociolinguistic investigation of travel agency talk. Unpublished Doctoral dissertation, University of Wales.

—— (1983) Patterns of encounter management: further arguments for discourse variables. *Language in Society* 12, 4:459–476.

—— (1984a) Accommodation at work: some phonological data and their implications. *International Journal of the Sociology of Language* 46:49–70.

—— (1984b) Social and linguistic characteristics in the pronunciation of Welsh place-names in Cardiff. *Cardiff Working Papers in Welsh Linguistics* 3:31–44.

—— (1985a) Sociolinguistic aspects of place-names: ethnic affiliation and the pronunciation of Welsh in the Welsh capital. In W. Viereck (ed.) *Focus on: England and Wales Varieties of English Around the World, G5*. Amsterdam: Benjamins.

—— (1985b) Hark, hark the lark: social motivations for phonological style-shifting. *Language and Communication* 5,3: 153–171.

Crystal, D., and Davy, D. (1969) *Investigating English Style*. London: Longman.

Dines, E. R. (1980) Variation in discourse – 'and stuff like that'. *Language in Society* 9,1:13–33.

Douglas-Cowie, E. (1978) Linguistic code-switching in a Northern Irish village: social interaction and social ambition. In P. Trudgill (ed.) (1978):37–51.

Edwards, A. D. (1976) *Language in culture and class*. Heinemann.

Edwards, J. R. (1979) *Language and disadvantage*. London: Edward Arnold.

—— (1982) Language attitudes and their implications among English speakers. In E. B. Ryan and H. Giles (eds.) (1982): 20–33.

Elyan, O., Smith, P., Giles, H., and Bourhis, R. (1978) RP-accented female speech: the voice of perceived androgyny? In P. Trudgill (ed.) (1978): 122–31.

Ervin-Tripp, S. (1964) An analysis of the interaction of language, topic and listener. Supplement to *American Anthropologist* 66 (6), part 2.

Federer, W. T. (1973) *Statistics and Society: Data Collection and Interpretation*. Marcel Dekker Inc.

Firth, J. R. (1957) *Papers in Linguistics 1934–1951*. London: OUP.

Fishman, J. A. (1977) Language and ethnicity. In H. Giles (ed.) (1977a):15–57.

—— (1978) *Advances in the Study of Societal Multilingualism*. The Hague: Mouton.

Garfinkel, H. (1967) *Studies in Ethnomethodology*. Prentice Hall.

Giles, H. (1970) Evaluative reactions to accents. *Educational Review* 22:211–27.

—— (1971a) Patterns of evaluation interactions to RP, South Welsh and Somerset-accented speech. *British Journal of Social and Clinical Psychology* 10:280–1.

—— (1971b) Speech patterns in social interaction: accent evaluation and accent change. Unpublished doctoral dissertation, University of Bristol.

—— (1972) The effects of stimulus mildness-broadness in the evaluation of accents. *Language and Speech* 15:262–9.

—— (1973) Accent mobility: a model and some data. *Anthropological linguistics* 15:87–105.

—— (1977a) (ed.) *Language, Ethnicity and Intergroup Relations* London: Academic Press.

—— (1977b) Social psychology and applied linguistics: toward an intergrative approach. ITL. *Review of Applied Linguistics* 35:27–42.

—— (1979) Sociolinguistics and social psychology: an introductory essay. In H. Giles and R. St Clair 1979.

—— (1980) Accommodation theory: some new directions. In S. da Silva (ed.) *Aspects of linguistic behaviour.* York: University of York Press.

—— (1984) (ed.) *The Dynamics of Speech Accommodation. (International Journal of the Sociology of Language:* 46) Amsterdam: Mouton.

Giles, H. and Powesland, P. F. (1975) *Speech style and social evaluation.* London: Academic Press.

Giles, H. and Ryan, E. B. (1982) Prolegomena for developing a social psychological theory of language attitudes. In E. B. Ryan and H. Giles (eds.) 1982:203–23.

Giles, H. and St Clair, R. (eds.) (1979) *Language and social psychology.* Oxford: Basil Blackwell.

Giles, H. and Smith, P. M. (1979) Accommodation theory: optimal levels of convergence. In H. Giles and R. St Clair (eds.) (1979):45–65.

Giles, H., Taylor, D. M. and Bourhis, R. Y. (1973) Towards a theory of interpersonal accommodation through language: some Canadian data. *Language in Society* 2:177–192.

Gimson, A. C. (1972) *An introduction to the pronunciation of English* London: Edward Arnold.

Goffman, E. (1959) *The Presentation of Self in Everyday Life.* New York: Garden City.

—— (1961) *Encounters.* Indianapolis: Bobbs-Merrill.

—— (1964) The neglected situation. *American Anthropologist* 66, 6, part 2:133–6.

—— (1971) *Relations in Public.* New York: Harper.

Gregory, M. and Carroll, S. (1978) *Language and Situation: Language Varieties and their Social Contexts.* London: Routledge and Kegan Paul.

Gumperz, J. J. (1975) On the ethnology of linguistic change. In W. Bright (ed.) *Sociolinguistics: Proceedings of the UCLA Sociolinguistics Conference, 1964.* The Hague: Mouton:27–38.

—— (1982) (ed.) *Language and Social Identity.* Cambridge: Cambridge University Press.

Gumperz, J. J. and Hymes, D. (1972) (eds.) *Directions in Sociolinguistics: the Ethnography of Communication.* Holt, Rinehart and Winston, Inc.

Halliday, M. A. K. (1978) *Language as Social Semiotic*. Edward Arnold.

Hebdige, R. (1979) *Subculture: the Meaning of Style*. Methuen.

Helfrich, H. (1979) Age markers in speech. In K. R. Scherer and H. Giles (eds.) (1979):63–108.

Hudson, R. A. (1980) *Sociolinguistics*. Cambridge University Press.

Hughes, A. and Trudgill, P. (1979) *English accents and dialects*. Edward Arnold.

Hymes, D. (1972a) Models of the interaction of language and social life. In J. J. Gumperz and D. Hymes (eds.) 1972.

—— (1972b) The scope of sociolinguistics. In R. W. Shuy (ed) 1972:313–33.

—— (1977) *Foundations in sociolinguistics: an ethnographic approach*. London: Tavistock.

Jenkins, W. L. (1854) *A History of the Town and Castle of Cardiff*. Charles Wakeford.

Joos, M. (1961) *The five clocks*. Harbinger.

Khleif, B. (1978) Ethnic awakening in the First World: the case of Wales. In G. Williams (ed.) (1978):102–19.

Knowles, G. O. (1978) The nature of phonological variables in Scouse. In P. Trudgill (ed.) (1978):80–90.

Kolb, E. (1964) *Phonological Atlas of the Northern Region*. Franke Verlas, Berne.

Kramer, C. (1977) Perceptions of female and male speech. *Language and Speech* 20:151–161.

Kramarae, C. (1982) Gender: How she speaks. In E. B. Ryan and H. Giles (eds.) (1982):84–98.

Labov, W. (1966) *The social stratification of English in New York City*. Washington D. C.: Center for Applied Linguistics.

—— (1972a) *Sociolinguistic Patterns*. Philadelphia: University of Pennsylvania Press.

—— (1972b) Some principles of linguistic methodology. *Language in Society* 1:97–120.

Lambert, W. E. (1967) A social psychology of bilingualism. *Journal of Social Issues* 23:91–109.

Lavandera, B. R. (1978) Where does the sociolinguistic variable stop? *Language in Society* 7.2:171–182.

Laver, J. and Trudgill, P. (1979) Phonetic and linguistic markers in speech. In K. R. Scherer and H. Giles (eds.) (1979):1–32.

Lediard, J. (1977) The sounds of the dialect of Canton, a suburb of Cardiff. In D. Parry (ed.) *The Survey of Anglo-Welsh Dialects*. University College, Swansea: University of Wales Press.

Le Page, R. B. (1972) Preliminary Report on the sociolinguistic survey of Cayo District, British Honduras. *Language in Society* 1, 1:155–72.

—— (1977) Processes of pidginization and creolization. In A. Valdman (ed.). *Pidgin and Creole Linguistics*. Bloomington: Indiana University Press:222–55.

—— (1980) Projection, focussing, diffusion, or steps towards a sociolinguistic theory of language, illustrated from the Sociolinguistic Survey of Multi-lingual communities, stages I: Cayo District, Belize (formerly British Honduras) and II: St. Lucia. *York Papers in Linguistics*. University of York:9–31.

Le Page, R. B., Christie, P., Jurdan, B., Weekes, A. J. and Tabouret-Keller, A. (1977) Further report on the sociolinguistic survey of multilingual communities. *Language in Society* 3:1–32.

Lewis, J. Parry (1960) The Anglicisation of Glamorgan. *Morgannwg* iv:28–49.

Lewis, J. Windsor (1964) Specimen of Cardiff English. *Le Maitre Phonetique* 121:6–7.

—— (unpublished m.s. 1964) Description of Cardiff and Cymric in the County of Glamorgan.

Littlejohn, J. (1972) *Social Stratification*. Allen and Unwin.

Macaulay, R. K. S. (1975) Negative prestige, linguistic insecurity and linguistic self-hatred. *Lingua* 36:147–161.

—— (1976) Social class and language in Glasgow. *Language in Society* 5:173–88.

—— (1977) *Language, social class and education: a Glasgow study*. Edinburgh University Press.

—— (1978) Variation and consistency in Glaswegian English. In P. Trudgill (ed.) (1978).

Mees, I. (1977) Language and social class in Cardiff: a survey of the speech habits of schoolchildren. Unpublished Master's dissertation, University of Leiden.

—— (1983) The speech of Cardiff Schoolchildren: a Real Time Study. Unpublished Doctoral Dissertation: University of Leiden.

Merritt, M. (1976) Resources for saying in service encounters. Unpublished doctoral dissertation. Department of Linguistics, University of Pennsylvania.

Milroy, J. (1982) Probing under the tip of the iceberg: phonological 'normalization' and the shape of speech communities. In S. Romaine (ed.) (1982):35–48.

Milroy, J. and Milroy, L. (1978) Belfast: Change and variation in an urban vernacular. In P. Trudgill (ed.) (1978), 19–37.

Milroy, L. (1980) *Language and social networks*. Oxford: Basil Blackwell.

Morgan, K. O. (1981) *Rebirth of a Nation: Wales 1880–1980*. Oxford University Press.

O'Connor, J. D. and Arnold, G. F. (1961) *Intonation of Colloquial English*. Longman.

Office of Population Censuses and surveys classification of occupations (1970) HMSO.

Orton, H. (1960) An English dialect survey: linguistic atlas of England. *Orbis* 11.

Orton, H. (1962) *Survey of English Dialects: Introduction*. Leeds: E. J. Arnold.

Orton, H. and Halliday, W. J. (1962–3)

Orton, H. and Barry, N. V. (1969–71)   *Survey of English Dialects:*

Orton, H. and Tilling, P. M. (1969–71)   *Basic Material*. Leeds: E. J. Arnold

Orton, H. and Wakelin, M. F. (1967–8)

Orton, H. Sanderson, S. and Widdowson, J. (1978) *Linguistic Atlas of England*. London: Croom Helm.

Orton, H. and Wright, N. (1975) *Word Geography of England*. London: Seminar Press.

Parry, D. (1971) Newport English. *Anglo-Welsh Review* 19, 44:228–

—— (1972) Anglo-Welsh dialects in South-East Wales. In M. F. Wakelin (ed.) *Patterns in the Folk Speech of the British Isles*. London: Athlone Press: 140–163.

—— (1977) (Ed.) *The Survey of Anglo-Welsh Dialects. Vol. 1 (The South East)*. University College, Swansea.

—— (1979a) *The Survey of Anglo-Welsh Dialects, Vol. 2 (The South West)*. University College, Swansea.

—— (1979b) *Notes on Glamorgan Dialects*. University College, Swansea.

Pellowe, J. and Jones, V. (1978) On intonational variability in Tyneside speech. In P. Trudgill (1978) (ed.):101–21.

Petyt, M. (1980) *The Study of dialect: an introduction to dialectology*. Andre Deutsch.

—— (1982) Who is really doing dialectology? In D. Crystal (ed.) *Linguistic Controversies*. Edward Arnold:192–208.

Pride, J. B. (1974) *The Social meaning of language*. Oxford University Press.

Pride, J. B. and Holmes, J. (eds.) (1972) *Sociolinguistics*. Penguin.

Pryce, W. T. R. (1978) Welsh and English in Wales, 1750–1971: A spatial analysis based on the linguistc affiliation of parochial communities. *The Bulletin of the Board of Celtic Studies* Vol. XXV, 1:1–36.

Putnam, W. B. and Street, R. L. Jr. (1984) The conception and perception of noncontent speech performance: implications for speech-accommodation theory. In H. Giles (ed.) (1984):97–114.

Quirk, R. and Greenbaum, S. (1973) *A University Grammar*. London: Longman.

Reid, E. (1978) Social and stylistic variation in the speech of children: some evidence from Edinburgh. In P. Trudgill (ed.) (1978).

Robinson, W. P. (1979) Speech markers and social class. In Scherer and Giles (eds.) (1979):211–50.

Romaine, S. (ed.) (1982) *Sociolinguistic variation in speech communities*. Edward Arnold.

Rubin, A. M., and Rubin, R. B. (1982) Contextual age and television use. *Human Communication Research* 8:228–44.

Runciman, W. G. (1966) *Relative Deprivation and Social Justice*. Routledge and Kegan Paul.

Ryan, E. B. (1979) Why do low-prestige language varieties persist? In H. Giles and R. St Clair (eds.) (1979):145–157.

Ryan, E. B. and Giles, H. (1982) *Attitudes towards Language Variation*. London: Edward Arnold.

Ryan, E. B., Giles, H. and Sebastian, R. J. (1982) An integrative perspective for the study of attitudes toward language variation. In E. B. Ryan, and H. Giles (eds.) (1982):1–19.

Sankoff, G. (1972) Language use in multilingual societies: some alternative approaches. In J. B. Pride and J. Holmes (eds.) (1972) *Sociolinguistics*. Penguin Education.

Sankoff, G. and Thibault, P. (1977) L'alternance entre les auxiliaires *avoir* et *être* en français parlé à Montréal. *Langue Française* 34:81–108.

Sapir, E. (1929) Male and female forms of speech in Yana. In S. W. J. Teeuwen (ed.) *Donum Natalicum Schrijnen*. Nijmegen: Dekker & Van de Vegt: 79–85.

Schegloff, E. A. (1968) Sequencing in conversational openings. *American Anthropologist* 70. 6:1079–1095.

Scherer, K. R. (1979) Personality markers in speech. In K. R. Scherer and H. Giles (eds.) 1979:147–210.

Scherer, K. R. and Giles, H. (eds.) (1979) *Social markers in speech*. Cambridge University Press.

Selinker, L. (1972) Interlanguage. *IRAL* 10, 3:219–31.

Shockey, L. (1984) All in a flap: long-term accommodation in phonology. In H. Giles (ed.) (1984):87–96.

Shuy, R. W. (1970) Sociolinguistic research at the Center for Applied Linguistics: the correlation of language and sex. In *International Days of Sociolinguistics*. Rome.

—— (1972) (ed.) *Sociolinguistics: current trends and prospects.* Report on the 23rd Annual Round Table (Monograph Series on Languages and Linguistics) 25. Washington D.C. Georgetown University Press.

—— (1973) *Some New Directions in Linguistics.* Georgetown University Press.

Shuy, R. W., Baratz, J. C., and Wolfram, W. A. (1969) Sociolinguistic factors in speech identification. NIMHR Project MH–15048–01. Center for Applied Linguistics, Washington, D.C.

Smith, P. M. (1979) Sex markers in speech. In K. R. Scherer and H. Giles (eds.):109–146.

Smith, P. M., Giles, H., and Hewstone, M. (1980) Sociolinguistics: a social psychological perspective. In R. St Clair and H. Giles (eds.) *The social and psychological contexts of language.* New Jersey: Erlbaum. 273–298.

Speier, M. (1973) *How to observe face-to-face communication: a sociological introduction.* Goodyear.

Street, R. L. Jr. and Giles, H. (1982) Speech accommodation theory: a social cognitive approach to language and speech behaviour. In M. Roloff and C. Berger (eds.) *Social Cognition and Communication.* Beverly Hills, Calif.: Sage.

Street, R. L. Jr., and Hopper, R. (1982) A model of speech style evaluation. In E. B. Ryan and H. Giles (eds.) (1982):175–188.

Strongman, K. T. and Woosely, J. (1967) Stereotyped reactions to regional accents. *British Journal of Social and Clinical Psychology* 6:164–7.

Stubbs, M. (1980) *Language and literacy: the sociolinguistics of reading and writing.* London: Routledge and Kegan Paul.

Sudnow, D. (1965) Normal crimes: sociological features of the penal code in a public defender office. *Social Problems* 12:255–276.

Thakerar, J. N., Giles, H. and Cheshire, J. (1982) Psychological and linguistic parameters of speech accommodation theory. In C. Fraser and K. R. Scherer (eds.) *Advances in the Social Psychology of Language.* Cambridge: Cambridge University Press:205–55.

Thelander, M. (1982) A qualitative approach to quantitative data of speech variation. In S. Romaine (ed.) (1982):65–84.

Thomas, A. R. (1980) Some aspects of the bilingual situation in Wales. In W. Hüllen (ed.) *Understanding Bilingualism.* Frankfurt: Peter D. Lang.

—— (1982) Change and decay in language. In D. Crystal (ed.) *Linguistic Controversies*. Edward Arnold:209–20.

—— (1983) The English Language in Wales. In Y. Matsumura (ed.) *English Around the World*, Tokyo: Kenkyusha.

—— (1984) Welsh English. In P. Trudgill (ed.) (1984).

—— (1985) Welsh English: a grammatical conspectus. In W. Viereck (ed.) Focus on: *England and Wales Varieties of English Around the World, G5*. Amsterdam: Benjamins.

Thomas, B. (1960) The Growth of Population. In J. F. Rees (ed.) *The Cardiff Region: A Survey*. Cardiff: University of Wales Press.

Thomas, C. and Williams, C. (1978) Linguistic decline and nationalist resurgence in Wales: a case study of the attitudes of sixth-form pupils. In G. Williams (ed.) (1978):166–92.

Trudgill, P. (1974a) *The social differentiation of English in Norwich*. London: Edward Arnold.

—— (1974b) *Sociolinguistics: an introduction*. Harmondsworth: Penguin.

—— (1975) Sex, covert prestige, and linguistic change in the urban British English of Norwich. In B. Thorne and N. Henley (eds.) *Language and Sex: difference and dominance*. Rowley, Mass.

—— (1978) (ed.) *Sociolinguistic patterns in British English*. London: Edward Arnold.

—— (1981) Linguistic accommodation: sociolinguistic observations on sociopsychological theory. In C. Masek *et al.* (eds.) *Papers from the parasession on Language and Behaviour, Chicago Linguistic Society*. Chicago: University of Chicago Press.

—— (1983) *On Dialect: Social and Geographical Perspectives*. Oxford: Basil Blackwell.

—— (1984) (ed.) *Language in the British Isles*. Cambridge: Cambridge University Press.

Trudgill, P. and Hannah, J. (1982) *International English: a Guide to Varieties of Standard English*. London: Edward Arnold.

Wakelin, M. F. (1977) *English Dialects: an Introduction* (Revised Edition). London: Athlone Press.

Watkins, T. A. (1962) Background to the Welsh Dialect Survey. *Lochlann:* 2 38–49.

Weinreich, U. (1954) Is a structural dialectology possible? *Word* 10:388–400. Reprinted in J. Fishman (ed.) (1968) *Readings in the Sociology of Language*. Mouton.

Weinreich, U., Labov, W. and Herzog, M. (1968) Empirical foundations for a theory of language change. In W. P. Lehmann and Y. Malkiel (eds.) (1968) *Directions for historical linguistics*. Austin: Texas University Press.

Wells, J. C. (1970) Local accents in England and Wales. *Journal of Linguistics* 6:231–252.

—— (1982) *Accents of English*. Volumes 1, 2 and 3. Cambridge University Press.

Welsh Office (1983) *Crynhoad o Ystadegau Cymru (Digest of Welsh Statistics)* No. 28, 1982.

Westergard, J. H. and Resler, H. (1975) *Class in a Capitalist Society: a Study of Contemporary Britain*. Penguin.

Williams, G. (ed.) (1978) *Social and Cultural Change in Contemporary Wales*. London: Routledge and Kegan Paul.

Wolfson, N. (1976) Speech events and natural speech: some implicatons for sociolinguistic methodology. *Language in Society* 5:189–209.

Worsely, P. (1978) *Introducing sociology*. Harmondsworth: Penguin.

Index